Greek to GCSE: Part 1

# Greek to GCSE

## PART 1

John Taylor

Bristol Classical Press

This impression 2008
First published in 2003 by
Bristol Classical Press
an imprint of
Gerald Duckworth & Co. Ltd.
90-93 Cowcross Street, London EC1M 6BF
Tel: 020 7490 7300
Fax: 020 7490 0080
inquiries@duckworth-publishers.co.uk
www.ducknet.co.uk

A catalogue record for this book is available
from the British Library

ISBN 978 1 85399 656 6

Typeset by John Taylor
Printed in Great Britain by the
MPG Books Group, Bodmin and King's Lynn

# Contents

## Chapter 4

## Chapter 5

## Chapter 6

# Reference Grammar for Part 1

# Vocabulary for Part 1

# Preface

This two-volume course has a simple aim: to provide a fast track to GCSE without compromise in the understanding of grammar, enabling students to read Greek with the confidence which is essential to enjoyment. It was written in response to a survey of about 100 schools undertaken by the Greek Committee of JACT (Joint Association of Classical Teachers) in 1999. It is designed especially for those with limited time (where Greek is an extra-curricular activity, or is taught within periods allocated to Latin). It concentrates on the essentials, the grammar and vocabulary required for GCSE Greek. It assumes that most readers will know some Latin, and does not eschew comparisons; but it aims to be usable without. It does not have any grand theory or linguistic dogma, but is simply based on experience of what pupils find difficult. It tries to remember that Greek is only one of nine or ten subjects being studied, yet at the same time to give a solid foundation to those who will carry on to A-level and beyond. The approach is fairly traditional: there is a mildly inductive element in that constructions which translate naturally (indirect commands, some forms of indirect statement) are introduced before they are discussed, but no apology is made for the fact that new grammar begins each chapter. Every year examiners' reports comment that candidates muddle through unseen passages with too little attention to grammar: endings are ignored, and common constructions not recognised. *Greek to GCSE* aims to address this. But it also aims to be user-friendly. It concentrates on the understanding of principles, in both accidence and syntax: minor irregularities are subordinated, so that the need for rote learning is reduced, and beginners are not distracted by archaic conventions. The book does not have a continuous narrative, but after the preliminaries each section concentrates on stories with one source or subject: in Part 1 Aesop, the *Odyssey*, Alexander the Great; in Part 2 Socrates and the Sophists, the world of myth, and in the final chapters (as the target of the whole course) extended passages of lightly adapted Herodotus, who has some of the best stories in Greek (or any) literature.

The course was first published in 2003. It aimed to cover the requirements of the two examination boards then offering GCSE Greek, AQA (more streamlined overall, but with greater demands in grammar) and OCR (specifying considerably more vocabulary, and also with longer set texts). A year later AQA announced plans to discontinue examinations in Latin and Greek after 2006. Initial dismay at the demise of a syllabus particularly suited to students doing Greek in a hurry was allayed by the appearance (speedily, and to general satisfaction) of a revised OCR specification which provides a realistic target for all candidates. Meanwhile *Greek to GCSE* received a generally favourable reaction. Part 1 was however liked more than Part 2, which was justifiably criticised as overwhelming in scale, thus losing sight of its original aim (and only partly excused by the need to cater for two different examinations). Part 1 is unchanged, but the course now appears with a revised Part 2, considerably slimmed down and simplified.

The new second volume is physically shorter, but it can be shortened further in use: the GCSE vocabulary has all been covered by the end of Chapter 10, and the grammar by halfway through Chapter 11, with the rest of Part 2 providing practice and consolidation. Part 1 includes about 50 common words not strictly needed for GCSE: these continue to be used in the early chapters of Part 2 (otherwise exercises would be unduly constricted), and a few more are added (to illustrate particular grammatical points), providing a total vocabulary of about 480 words; but in the revision exercises which make up Chapter 12, and in the *Reference Grammar and Revision Guide* at the end of Part 2, the focus is entirely on GCSE requirements (hence a non-GCSE word is glossed there even if it has frequently been used earlier).

Together with the revised Part 2 appears a new book, *Greek Beyond GCSE*. This include: sections displaced from the original second volume, together with a wide range of new ma is designed as a continuation of *Greek to GCSE* but can be used independently. It covers (a: a bit beyond) all the linguistic requirements for OCR AS-level Greek, aiming to bring studen point where they can tackle original Greek texts with confidence. *Greek Beyond GCSE* includ: unadapted passages from prose authors, a summary of all constructions, a comprehensive refer: grammar, and a vocabulary of about 830 words. But despite its title, pre-GCSE students in the fortunate position of having time to spare can usefully make a start on it, and will benefit from the fuller explanation of some things which inevitably receive summary treatment in a GCSE course.

General linguistic features in *Greek to GCSE* remain as before. English-to-Greek exercises are included throughout (even though few candidates attempt them at GCSE), in the belief that they are an invaluable means of clarifying and reinforcing students' understanding of the language. They can of course simply be omitted; but I hope that they may have some use even for those without time to do them in full (the teacher could for example translate most of a sentence orally, asking students to supply the word or words relevant to the grammatical point being tested). Accents are introduced in Part 1 from Chapter 5, and in the Greek-English vocabulary; Part 2 has full accentuation throughout. The policy adopted (on an issue which divided respondents to the JACT survey more than any other) is inevitably a compromise: many felt that accents were an unnecessary complication in the earliest stages, when the priority is to recognise and write the letters and breathings correctly; yet the vocabulary and grammar required for unseen translation include words and forms where the accent materially affects the meaning, and GCSE candidates will of course study set texts printed with accents by universal convention. It is suggested that those wishing to make accents integral to the learning of vocabulary from the outset should insert them by hand in the checklists for the first few chapters. The rules of accentuation (even in outline) are beyond the scope of an accelerated GCSE course, and it is not expected that beginners should include accents in writing Greek sentences. Those seeking further information on this subject should consult Philomen Probert *A New Short Guide to the Accentuation of Ancient Greek* (Bristol Classical Press 2003).

I incurred many debts in writing *Greek to GCSE*, and I have incurred more since it was first published. Chris Burnand tried out the earliest drafts in the classroom, and improved the wording of the explanations of grammar in numerous places. Subsequent versions were tested by teachers in fifteen schools (to whom I hope a generalised acknowledgement may now serve), the trial copies subsidised by a grant from the Society for the Promotion of Hellenic Studies, kindly negotiated by Russell Shone. Stephen Anderson, Chris Wilson and the late Malcolm Willcock gave generous help with accentuation and proof-reading. Since 2003 I have been contacted by numerous people using the book in school or for private study: their encouraging feedback is much appreciated. Deborah Blake and Ray Davies at Duckworth have continued to provide extremely supportive guidance. Readers may obtain keys to the exercises and other back-up materials by contacting me via the publishers, and I am grateful to them for handling this as well as for facilitating the revised edition. Mark Farmer has managed to keep my ancient Acorn computer on the road. In the original preface I thanked the boys of Tonbridge School for pointing out mistakes in earlier versions with good-natured glee, but said they were bound to have missed some: they had, but I hope there are not too many more.

John Taylor
Tonbridge School

## Abbreviations

| | |
|---|---|
| *cc* | accusative |
| *idj* | adjective |
| *adv* | adverb |
| *aor* | aorist |
| *dat* | dative |
| *f* | feminine |
| *gen* | genitive |
| *irreg* | irregular |
| *m* | masculine |
| *n* | neuter |
| *nom* | nominative |
| *pl* | plural |
| *sg* | singular |
| *voc* | vocative |

## Vocabulary and glossing

The vocabulary checklists at the end of each chapter should be learned thoroughly. The sum of these equates to the vocabulary at the back of the book. Additional words required for translation passages are glossed as they occur. Underlining is not repeated within a passage when a word occurs again on the same page. Where a passage extends to a new page, glossing (except of proper names) is usually repeated. This inevitably means that words are sometimes glossed twice in quick succession.

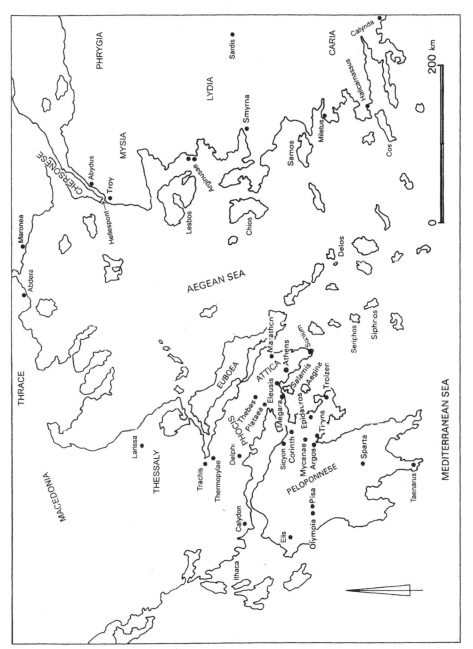

Map 1: Greece and the Aegean

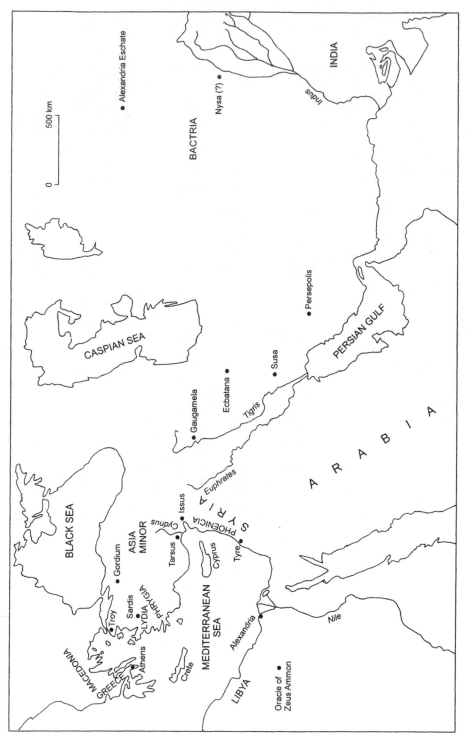

Map 2: The Empire of Alexander

# Chapter 1

## The Greek Alphabet

The Greek alphabet has twenty-four letters:

| symbol | name | English equivalent | pronunciation |
|---|---|---|---|
| α | alpha | a | short as in *bat* / long as in *father* |
| β | beta | b | b |
| γ | gamma | g | as in *get* ** |
| δ | delta | d | d |
| ε | epsilon | e (short) | as in *get* |
| ζ | zeta | z, sd | as in *wisdom* |
| η | eta | e (long) | as in *hair* |
| θ | theta | th | as in *ant-hill*, or as in *third* † |
| ι | iota | i | short as in *bit* / long as in *police* |
| κ | kappa | c, k | k |
| λ | lambda | l | l |
| μ | mu | m | m |
| ν | nu | n | n |
| ξ | xi | x | x, ks |
| o | omicron | o (short) | as in *got* |
| π | pi | p | p |
| ρ | rho | r | r |
| σ/ς* | sigma | s | s |
| τ | tau | t | t |
| υ | upsilon | u, y | short as in French *tu* / long as in *sur* |
| φ | phi | ph | as in *uphold*, or as in *phrase* † |
| χ | chi | ch | as in *packhorse*, or as in *loch* † |
| ψ | psi | ps | as in *lapse* |
| ω | omega | o (long) | between the sounds in *oar* and in *raw* |

* σ normally, ς at the end of a word: e.g. στασις

** gamma is pronounced as *n* rather than *g* when it comes before another gamma or before a *k* sound (kappa, xi or chi)

† with the *aspirated* ('breathed-on') consonants theta, phi and chi, the first pronunciation given (like *t*, *p* and *k* with emphatic breathing) represents more accurately the sound in classical times; but the second (with stronger *h* element), standard in later Greek, may be found more convenient in practice (to avoid confusion with the unaspirated tau, pi and kappa)

No recommendations about pronunciation command universal agreement. Our knowledge of ancient pronunciation is imperfect. Regional and other variations in the pronunciation of

English complicate the attempt to provide equivalents. You should of course aim to be as accurate as possible; but being consistent, confident and clear is very important too.

## Writing the letters

Most of the letters can be made with one stroke of the pen. But each letter is written separately: they are not joined in a cursive script. You should write them all several times, until you are familiar with them. Notice which go below the line. And be careful to differentiate between ones which can be confused if carelessly written: e.g. zeta and xi, nu and upsilon.

## Vowels

There are seven vowels (α ε η ι ο υ ω) rather than English five, because Greek uses different symbols for short and long *e* (epsilon and eta) and for short and long *o* (omicron and omega). The other vowels too can be short or long, but without separate symbols.

## Breathings

Any word starting with a vowel must have a *breathing* over the vowel: either a *rough* breathing (ʽ) to indicate an *h* sound before the vowel, or a *smooth* breathing (ʼ) simply to indicate the absence of an *h*. The breathing is important and counts as part of the spelling.

## Diphthongs

Greek (like English) can combine vowels into *diphthongs*, pronounced as one sound. Common ones are:

| | | |
|---|---|---|
| αι | pronounced as in | *high* |
| αυ | | *how* |
| ει | | *weigh* |
| ευ | | *feud* |
| οι | | *boy* |
| ου | | *pool* |

When a diphthong starts a word, the breathing is put over the second of the two vowels.

## Iota subscript

When iota comes after long alpha, eta or omega, it is written in miniature form underneath: ᾳ ῃ ῳ. It is not certain how far it was pronounced in classical times, but it is convenient to sound it slightly (to differentiate ᾳ from ordinary long alpha on the one hand, and from the diphthong αι on the other).

# Background: History of the Greek alphabet

• The Greek language is a lot older than the use of this alphabet. This alphabet was first used to write Greek about 750 BC.

• Long before that, there had been a completely different way of writing Greek, called 'Linear B'. This is found on clay tablets dating from about 1300 BC, found in various parts of Greece.

• The name Linear B naturally implies the existence of a Linear A. The names were given to two different scripts found by archaeologists in the late nineteenth century. Linear A was used in Crete from about 1700 BC. It has never been deciphered. It is probably a pre-Greek language.

• Linear B was deciphered (after many people had tried), and shown to be an early form of Greek, by Michael Ventris in 1952. The Linear B tablets listed goods stored in the fortresses of Bronze Age or Mycenean Greece - named after the great fortress at Mycenae, traditionally the headquarters of Agamemnon, which had been excavated by the German archaeologist Heinrich Schliemann in the 1870s. Ventris was helped by the fact that many of the tablets had diagrams as well as words indicating the items (e.g. chariot-wheels) listed.

• Mycenean civilisation declined after about 1200 BC: Greece entered a Dark Age, and the art of writing was forgotten.

• In the eighth century Greece emerged into a new period of prosperity and success. Travel, exploration and trade flourished. The Greeks seem to have borrowed the alphabet from the Phoenicians, with whom they traded. But it was simply a set of symbols. In Phoenician the symbols had had quite different meanings, standing for syllables or whole words (e.g. Phoenician *alph* meant *ox*, and *bet* meant *house* - and perhaps in origin the symbols were simplified diagrams of those things).

• Whoever allocated the symbols to the various sounds needed to pronounce Greek made a far-reaching decision. Apart from having one or two extra or variant letters in different parts of the Greek world in early times, the Greek alphabet has remained essentially the same. And it underlies, of course, our own alphabet.

• Linear B had, as far as we know, been used only for records, not literature. But the introduction of the Greek alphabet in the eighth century seems to have coincided with the lifetime of Homer, author of the *Iliad* and *Odyssey*. The stories had been transmitted orally for perhaps 400 years. It may be a lucky chance that writing became available to record permanently the works of a master poet - or it may be that he was stimulated by the new medium to compose poems of unprecedented length and sophistication.

• Not only the alphabet, but the language itself has remained remarkably constant. Most of the ancient Greek texts we commonly read come from the fifth century BC (when Homer was already a 'classic'). Greek has changed less in the 2500 years since then than English has in the 700 years since Chaucer. Pronunciation has changed a bit, but speakers of modern Greek can read ancient texts reasonably well without special training - and people who have studied ancient Greek can usually make sense of notices when they go to Greece.

# Transliteration

This means not translating but simply writing the same word in a different script. Because a lot of Greek words have come directly into English, there are many examples to practise with.

Before you start, remember:
• kappa can be either *c* or *k*
• both epsilon and eta come out as *e*, and both omicron and omega come out as *o*

Exercise 1.1

*Transliterate:*
1      ἰδεα
2      κινημα
3      χαρακτηρ
4      ἠλεκτρον
5      κομμα
6      χαος
7      διαγνωσις
8      κρατηρ
9      κριτηριον
10     πανθηρ

This can also be done the other way round, putting English words which are originally Greek back into Greek. Remember the breathing on words starting with a vowel. And beware of the places where two English letters are represented by one Greek one (e.g. *th*).

Exercise 1.2

*Transliterate:*
1      drama
2      basis
3      asthma
4      dogma (*short* o)
5      crisis
6      plasma
7      asbestos (*short* e *and short* o)
8      climax
9      nectar (*short* e)
10     parenthesis (*short* e *both times*)

Exercise 1.3 (Revision)

*Transliterate:*
1   διπλωμα
2   ὁριζων
3   ἰσοσκελης
4   ἐμφασις
5   κωλον
6   ἀμβροσια
7   καταστροφη
8   ἀντιθεσις
9   βακτηρια
10  μητροπολις

# Capital letters

Many of the capital letters can be deduced if you have learned the lower case ones. To prove this, here are the names of some Greek gods and heroes. Notice that where the name starts with a vowel, the breathing is written just in front of it.

Exercise 1.4

*Transliterate:*
1   Ζευς
2   Θησευς
3   Ποσειδων
4   ᾿Αγαμεμνων
5   ᾿Οδυσσευς
6   ῾Ερμης
7   ᾿Αφροδιτη
8   Προμηθευς
9   ῾Εκτωρ
10  ᾿Αρτεμις

Here are the capital letters for the whole alphabet:

| A | α | alpha |
|---|---|-------|
| B | β | beta |
| Γ | γ | gamma |
| Δ | δ | delta |
| E | ε | epsilon |
| Z | ζ | zeta |
| H | η | eta |
| Θ | θ | theta |
| I | ι | iota |
| K | κ | kappa |
| Λ | λ | lambda |
| M | μ | mu |
| N | ν | nu |
| Ξ | ξ | xi |
| O | o | omicron |
| Π | π | pi |
| P | ρ | rho |
| Σ | σ/ς | sigma |
| T | τ | tau |
| Y | υ | upsilon |
| Φ | φ | phi |
| X | χ | chi |
| Ψ | ψ | psi |
| Ω | ω | omega |

• The capital letters are used only for proper names (not to begin a sentence, as in English).

• Many of them are similar to the lower case letters. (In the fifth century BC, when many of the major Greek authors were writing, there was no distinction: everything was written in capitals. The lower case letters are in origin hastily written/simplified versions of the capitals.)

• Since you see the capital letters much less often, they take a bit longer to get used to. Some are actually easier (or more like English) than the lower case form: e.g. zeta. Others have misleading similarities to other English letters, and should be noted carefully: e.g. eta, rho. The similarity of capital upsilon to English *y* however is a reminder that upsilon is often transliterated as *y*. Gamma and lambda, or delta and lambda, in their capital forms are often confused by beginners.

• Capital delta can be remembered by thinking how *delta* is used in English (e.g. of the Nile), from its shape. How many other Greek letters are used in English, and how do their English meanings come about? How many were familiar to you already? (*Beta* particles, *gamma* rays, an *iota* of difference, *pi* as about 3.14159 - *the Alpha and the Omega*? Why is an American student association called *Phi Beta Kappa*?)

Exercise 1.5 (Revision)

Some more gods and figures from myth.
*Transliterate:*
1         Δημητηρ
2         Μιδας
3         ’Αρης
4         ‘Ηρακλης
5         ’Ανδρομαχη
6         ’Αθηνη
7         ‘Ηρα
8         Περσεφονη
9         Κυκλωψ
10        Διονυσος*

* the Greek ending -ος corresponds to the Latin -*us*, which is normally used when transliterating familiar names (which came to us via Latin) into English

Exercise 1.6 (Revision)

Both ways round. Remember upsilon usually transliterates as *y*, and that breathing goes on second letter if Greek word starts with a diphthong.

*Transliterate:*
1         ὀρχηστρα
2         mania
3         ἠχω
4         aroma (*long* o)
5         ἀναλυσις
6         automaton (*short o both times*)
7         σκηνη
8         iris
9         παραλυσις
10        genesis (*short* e *both times*)

# The verb: present tense

As in other languages, we use the terms *first*, *second* and *third person* for *I* (plural *we*), *you* (plural also *you*), and *he/she/it* (plural *they*).

παυω I stop (compare English *pause*)

| | |
|---|---|
| παυ-ω | I stop |
| παυ-εις | you (*singular*) stop |
| παυ-ει | he/she/it stops |
| | |
| παυ-ομεν | we stop |
| παυ-ετε | you (*plural*) stop |
| παυ-ουσι(ν)* | they stop |

* the nu - often called 'movable nu' - is added (to make pronunciation easier) if the next word starts with a vowel, or if this is the last word in the sentence

• The part of the verb that stays the same is called the *stem*. Hyphens will be used initially to show the division between stem and ending.

• Note the similarities to basic Latin endings (*-o, -s, -t, -mus, -tis, -nt*): only the third persons seem unrelated to them (and even here the plural -ουσι seems to have replaced an original form -οντι [compare Latin *-nt*], which has changed first to -ονσι and eventually to -ουσι).

• The vast majority of Greek verbs go like this. There is just one main conjugation.

Here are ten common verbs, which should be learned:

| | | |
|---|---|---|
| 1 | ἀγω | I lead |
| 2 | ἀκουω | I hear |
| 3 | βαινω | I go |
| 4 | γραφω | I write |
| 5 | διδασκω | I teach |
| 6 | διωκω | I chase |
| 7 | ἐχω | I have |
| 8 | τρεχω | I run |
| 9 | φερω | I carry, I bring |
| 10 | φυλασσω* | I guard |

* Greek words containing σσ can also be written with ττ, so this verb could also be φυλαττω (some places and some authors used one, some the other): σσ will be used in this book.

8

Exercise 1.7
Pay careful attention to the person endings. With second persons, indicate e.g. 'you (*sg*)' - *sg* and *pl* are the usual abbreviations for *singular* and *plural*.

*Translate into English:*
1       φερ-ομεν
2       γραφ-ει
3       διωκ-εις
4       ἀγ-ετε
5       φυλασσ-ουσι(ν)
6       ἐχ-ομεν
7       τρεχ-ει
8       ἀκου-εις
9       βαιν-ετε
10      διδασκ-ομεν


Exercise 1.8

*Translate into Greek:*
1       He carries.
2       We write.
3       You (*sg*) guard.
4       He teaches.
5       You (*pl*) have.
6       I hear.
7       You (*sg*) run.
8       They lead.
9       We chase.
10      You (*pl*) stop.


Exercise 1.9 (Revision)

*Translate into English:*
1       τρεχ-ουσι(ν)
2       διδασκ-ετε
3       βαιν-ει
4       παυ-ομεν
5       φυλασσ-ετε
6       παυ-εις
7       γραφ-ουσι(ν)
8       ἀγ-ω
9       διωκ-ει
10      φερ-ετε

# Revision checkpoint

*Make sure you know:*
• the alphabet
• how breathings are used
• the person endings for the present tense:

| | |
|---|---|
| -ω | I |
| -εις | you (*sg*) |
| -ει | he/she/it |
| | |
| -ομεν | we |
| -ετε | you (*pl*) |
| -ουσι(ν) | they |

# Nouns (first and second declension): nominative and accusative

*first declension feminine:*  τιμη = honour

| sg | nominative | τιμ-η |
|---|---|---|
| | accusative | τιμ-ην |

*second declension masculine:*  λογος = word (*also* reason, story)

| sg | nominative | λογ-ος |
|---|---|---|
| | accusative | λογ-ον |

• As with verbs, it is important to distinguish the stem (which stays the same) from the ending (which changes). Again hyphens are used initially.

• 'Declension' refers to the group a noun belongs to and the way its endings change. As in Latin, the nominative case is used for the subject of a verb and the accusative for the object. These nouns roughly correspond to ones like *puella* and *servus*. Notice that -ν is the characteristic ending for the accusative singular, as -*m* is in Latin.

Ten common nouns like τιμη:

| 1 | βοη | shout |
|---|---|---|
| 2 | βουλη | plan, *also* council |
| 3 | γη | earth |
| 4 | δικαιοσυνη | justice |
| 5 | εἰρηνη | peace |
| 6 | ἐπιστολη | letter |
| 7 | κωμη | village |
| 8 | νικη | victory |
| 9 | πυλη | gate |
| 10 | φωνη | voice |

Ten common nouns like λογος:

| 1  | ἀγγελος     | messenger             |
|----|-------------|-----------------------|
| 2  | διδασκαλος  | teacher               |
| 3  | δουλος      | slave                 |
| 4  | θεος        | god                   |
| 5  | ἱππος       | horse                 |
| 6  | ξενος       | stranger, foreigner   |
| 7  | ποταμος     | river                 |
| 8  | στρατηγος*  | general, commander    |
| 9  | στρατος     | army                  |
| 10 | συμμαχος    | ally                  |

* made up of στρατος + ἀγω, hence literally *army leader*


## The definite article

This is the word for *the*. Latin has no equivalent, but in Greek it is very important. If there is no article, translate *a*: e.g. ὁ δουλος = *the slave*, δουλος = *a slave*.

| *masculine* | *nominative* | ὁ   |
|-------------|--------------|-----|
|             | *accusative* | τον |
| *feminine*  | *nominative* | ἡ   |
|             | *accusative* | την |

• Notice the similarity to the noun endings. Again -ν marks the accusative.


## Word order

This is much more flexible than in Latin. The verb need not come at the end, though it can.

Exercise 1.10

*Translate into English:*

| 1  | ἀκου-ω την βο-ην.                    |
|----|--------------------------------------|
| 2  | ὁ ἀγγελ-ος διωκ-ει τον δουλ-ον.      |
| 3  | ὁ στρατ-ος φυλασσ-ει τον ποταμ-ον.   |
| 4  | ὁ ξεν-ος ἐπιστολ-ην γραφ-ει.         |
| 5  | ὁ ἱππ-ος φερ-ει τον δουλ-ον.         |
| 6  | φυλασσ-ομεν την κωμ-ην.              |
| 7  | τον ἱππ-ον διδασκ-ετε.               |
| 8  | ὁ δουλ-ος φυλασσ-ει την πυλ-ην.      |
| 9  | ὁ δουλ-ος διωκ-ει τον ἱππ-ον.        |
| 10 | ὁ διδασκαλ-ος διδασκ-ει τον δουλ-ον. |

# Negative

The normal negative is οὐ. This changes (to help pronunciation) to οὐκ if the next word starts with a vowel with a smooth breathing, and to οὐχ if the next word starts with a vowel with a rough breathing (the aspiration or 'breathed on' quality here spreading from the rough breathing to the preceding consonant). The negative normally comes just before the verb.

Exercise 1.11

*Translate into English:*
1       ὁ στρατηγ-ος βουλ-ην οὐκ ἐχ-ει.
2       ὁ θε-ος την τιμ-ην* ἐχ-ει.
3       ὁ δουλ-ος οὐκ ἀκου-ει την φων-ην.
4       ὁ ἀγγελ-ος διωκ-ει τον ἱππ-ον.
5       ὁ ξεν-ος φερ-ει την ἐπιστολ-ην.
6       την πυλ-ην οὐ φυλασσ-εις.
7       ἡ γ-η την εἰρην-ην* οὐκ ἐχ-ει.
8       συμμαχ-ον οὐκ ἐχ-ετε.
9       ὁ διδασκαλ-ος λογ-ον οὐ λεγ-ει.
10      ὁ θε-ος την νικ-ην* φερ-ει.

      λεγω    I speak, I say

* Greek often uses the definite article for general or abstract qualities, where English would not use *the*. In (2) and (7) here, *the* would be wrong with *honour* and *peace*; in (10), it would be correct to say either *victory* (in general) or *the* (particular) *victory*.

# Prepositions

• Prepositions indicating motion towards take the accusative, as in Latin. Two common ones are:
      προς            towards
      εἰς              into

Exercise 1.12

*Translate into English:*
1      ὁ στρατ-ος προς τον ποταμ-ον βαιν-ει.
2      ὁ θε-ος φων-ην οὐκ ἐχ-ει.
3      τον ἱππ-ον εἰς την κωμ-ην ἀγ-ω.
4      ὁ στρατ-ος την πυλ-ην οὐ φυλασσ-ει.
5      ὁ στρατηγ-ος τον στρατ-ον προς την κωμ-ην ἀγ-ει.
6      τον δουλ-ον προς τον ποταμ-ον διωκ-ω.
7      ὁ δουλ-ος εἰς τον ποταμ-ον τρεχ-ει.
8      ὁ διδασκαλ-ος τον δουλ-ον διδασκ-ει.
9      την ἐπιστολ-ην προς την κωμ-ην φερ-ω.
10    ὁ θε-ος προς την γ-ην βαιν-ει.

Exercise 1.13

*Give one English derivative from:*
1      γραφω
2      φωνη
3      ἀκουω
4      γη
5      στρατηγος

Exercise 1.14

*Translate into English:*
1      ὁ ἀγγελ-ος προς την κωμ-ην τρεχ-ει. ἐπιστολ-ην φερ-ει. ἡ βουλ-η
        τον λογ-ον ἀκου-ει. ὁ στρατ-ος νικ-ην ἐχ-ει.
2      ὁ ξεν-ος τον δουλ-ον διωκ-ει. ὁ δουλ-ος προς τον ποταμ-ον
        τρεχ-ει. ὁ ποταμ-ος τον δουλ-ον παυ-ει. ὁ ξεν-ος τον δουλ-ον
        φυλασσ-ει.
3      ὁ στρατηγ-ος τον στρατ-ον ἀγ-ει. ὁ στρατ-ος προς την κωμ-ην
        βαιν-ει. ὁ στρατηγ-ος φων-ην ἀκου-ει. ὁ θε-ος λογ-ον λεγ-ει.
        ὁ θε-ος την εἰρην-ην φερ-ει. ἡ κωμ-η εἰρην-ην ἐχ-ει. ὁ θε-ος
        τιμ-ην ἐχ-ει.

# Revision checkpoint

*Make sure you know:*
• the present tense
• the nominative and accusative of nouns like τιμη and λογος

# Vocabulary checklist for Chapter 1

*The words in the checklists for each chapter should be learned. Nouns are given with the appropriate form of the definite article as it is important to learn their gender.*

| | | |
|---|---|---|
| ἀγγελος | ὁ | messenger |
| ἀγω | | I lead |
| ἀκουω | | I hear |
| βαινω | | I go |
| βοη | ἡ | shout |
| βουλη | ἡ | plan, council |
| γη | ἡ | earth |
| γραφω | | I write |
| διδασκαλος | ὁ | teacher |
| διδασκω | | I teach |
| δικαιοσυνη | ἡ | justice |
| διωκω | | I chase |
| δουλος | ὁ | slave |
| εἰρηνη | ἡ | peace |
| εἰς | | into (+ *acc*) |
| ἐπιστολη | ἡ | letter |
| ἐχω | | I have |
| ἡ | | the (*feminine nom*) |
| θεος | ὁ | god |
| ἱππος | ὁ | horse |
| κωμη | ἡ | village |
| λεγω | | I speak, I say |
| λογος | ὁ | word, reason, story |
| νικη | ἡ | victory |
| ξενος | ὁ | stranger, foreigner |
| ὁ | | the (*masculine nom*) |
| οὐ (οὐκ, οὐχ) | | not |
| παυω | | I stop |
| ποταμος | ὁ | river |
| προς | | towards (+ *acc*) |
| πυλη | ἡ | gate |
| στρατηγος | ὁ | general |
| στρατος | ὁ | army |
| συμμαχος | ὁ | ally |
| την | | the (*feminine acc*) |
| τιμη | ἡ | honour |
| τον | | the (*masculine acc*) |
| τρεχω | | I run |
| φερω | | I carry, I bring |
| φυλασσω | | I guard |
| φωνη | ἡ | voice |

(41 words)

# Chapter 2

## Nouns (first and second declension): nominative and accusative plural

*first declension feminine:*          τιμη  honour

| | | |
|---|---|---|
| sg | nom | τιμ-η |
| | acc | τιμ-ην |
| | | |
| pl | nom | τιμ-αι |
| | acc | τιμ-ας |

*second declension masculine:*          λογος  word (*also* reason, story)

| | | |
|---|---|---|
| sg | nom | λογ-ος |
| | acc | λογ-ον |
| | | |
| pl | nom | λογ-οι |
| | acc | λογ-ους |

• Notice the similarities to Latin (*puellae, puellas; domini, dominos*).
The definite article forms its plurals in a similar way:

| | | *masculine* | *feminine* |
|---|---|---|---|
| sg | nom | ὁ | ἡ |
| | acc | τον | την |
| | | | |
| pl | nom | οἱ | αἱ |
| | acc | τους | τας |

Ten more verbs:

| | | |
|---|---|---|
| 1 | ἀποκτεινω | I kill |
| 2 | εὑρισκω | I find |
| 3 | λαμβανω | I take |
| 4 | λειπω | I leave |
| 5 | λυω | I release |
| 6 | μανθανω | I learn |
| 7 | μενω | I stay, I remain |
| 8 | πεμπω | I send |
| 9 | τασσω | I draw up, I arrange |
| 10 | φευγω | I flee, I run away |

Exercise 2.1

*Translate into English:*
1          ὁ ἀγγελ-ος οὐκ ἀκου-ει τας βο-ας.
2          οἱ δουλ-οι φευγ-ουσιν.

3        ὁ ξεν-ος ἐπιστολ-ας προς την κωμ-ην πεμπ-ει.
4        τους λογ-ους μανθαν-ετε.
5        ὁ ποταμ-ος οὐ παυ-ει τον στρατ-ον.
6        τους ἱππ-ους προς τον ποταμ-ον διωκ-ομεν
7        ἀποκτειν-εις τους δουλ-ους.
8        ὁ ἱππ-ος εὑρισκ-ει τον ποταμ-ον.
9        ὁ στρατηγ-ος τον στρατ-ον τασσ-ει .
10       οἱ συμμαχ-οι τους ἱππ-ους οὐ λειπ-ουσιν.

Exercise 2.2

*Translate into English:*
1        ὁ δουλ-ος την ἐπιστολ-ην λαμβαν-ει.
2        τον ἱππ-ον προς τον ποταμ-ον διωκ-ετε.
3        οἱ συμμαχ-οι τον ξεν-ον ἀποκτειν-ουσιν.
4        τον στρατ-ον τασσ-ετε.
5        οἱ δουλ-οι προς την κωμ-ην φευγ-ουσιν.
6        ὁ διδασκαλ-ος τους λογ-ους διδασκ-ει.
7        ὁ στρατ-ος την εἰρην-ην φυλασσ-ει.
8        την νικ-ην ἐχ-ομεν.
9        οἱ θε-οι την δικαιοσυν-ην φυλασσ-ουσιν.
10       τον ἱππ-ον λυ-εις.


# Revision checkpoint

*Make sure you know:*
• the nominative and accusative (*sg and pl*) of τιμη
• the nominative and accusative (*sg and pl*) of λογος
• the nominative and accusative (*sg and pl*) masculine and feminine of the definite article


Exercise 2.3 (Revision)

*Translate into English:*
1        βαιν-ετε
2        λειπ-ομεν
3        φυλασσ-ει
4        ἀγ-ουσι(ν)
5        παυ-ετε
6        πεμπ-ω
7        εὑρισκ-ει
8        τρεχ-ομεν
9        ἐχ-εις
10       τασσ-ουσι(ν)

## Exercise 2.4 (Revision)

*Translate into Greek:*
1        We carry.
2        They find.
3        He takes.
4        I remain.
5        You (*sg*) teach.
6        You (*pl*) learn.
7        They send.
8        I lead.
9        You (*sg*) write.
10       He goes.

## Exercise 2.5 (Revision)

*Change these combinations of noun + article into the plural, keeping the same case:*
1        ὁ ἱππ-ος
2        ἡ πυλ-η
3        τον δουλ-ον
4        την κωμ-ην
5        ὁ ποταμ-ος
6        την νικ-ην
7        τον θε-ον
8        ὁ στρατηγ-ος
9        τον συμμαχ-ον
10       ἡ ἐπιστολ-η

## Exercise 2.6 (Revision)

*Change these combinations of noun + article into the singular, keeping the same case:*
1        οἱ θε-οι
2        τας ἐπιστολ-ας
3        τους ἀγγελ-ους
4        αἱ κωμ-αι
5        τους ἱππ-ους

## Exercise 2.7

*Translate into English:*
ὁ στρατηγ-ος τον στρατ-ον τασσ-ει. ὁ στρατ-ος προς τον ποταμ-ον
βαιν-ει. ὁ στρατ-ος μεν-ει. τους ἱππ-ους λυ-ουσιν. οἱ συμμαχ-οι τους
ἱππ-ους φυλασσ-ουσιν. οἱ δουλ-οι φων-ην ἀκου-ουσιν. κωμ-ην
εὑρισκ-ουσιν. ὁ στρατηγ-ος τον στρατ-ον προς την κωμ-ην ἀγ-ει. ὁ
5     στρατ-ος την κωμ-ην λαμβαν-ει. ὁ στρατ-ος νικ-ην ἐχ-ει.

17

# The verb *to be* (present tense)

As in most languages, this is irregular, but will quickly become familiar:

εἰμι      I am
εἰ         you (*sg*) are
ἐστι(ν)*   he/she/it is

ἐσμεν    we are
ἐστε      you (*pl*) are
εἰσι(ν)*   they are

\* again the 'movable nu' is added (to make pronunciation easier) if the next word starts with a vowel, or if this is the last word in the sentence: notice that here this applies to the third person singular as well as the third person plural

• Notice the slight similarity to the Latin equivalent (*sum, es, est, sumus, estis, sunt*). Notice also that the -μεν and -τε endings resemble the equivalent parts of παυω.

• The verb *to be* takes not an object (in the accusative) but a *complement* (another nominative): distinguish between
     ὁ ξεν-ος δουλ-ον διωκ-ει.
     The stranger chases a slave.
and
     ὁ ξεν-ος δουλ-ος ἐστιν.
     The stranger is a slave.
In the second sentence the stranger is not doing something *to* a slave; we are just being told that he *is* a slave.

Exercise 2.8

*Translate into English:*
1        συμμαχ-οι ἐσμεν.
2        ὁ ἀγγελ-ος δουλ-ος ἐστιν.*
3        διδασκαλ-ος εἰ.
4        οἱ ξεν-οι συμμαχ-οι εἰσιν.*
5        δουλ-ος οὐκ εἰμι.

\* The word-order helps you decide which noun is the subject and which is the complement. Also, the subject usually has the definite article and the complement usually does not.

Exercise 2.9

*Translate into Greek:*
1      I am an ally.
2      We are not slaves.
3      You (*sg*) are a general.
4      The stranger is a teacher.
5      You (*pl*) are messengers.


# Connecting words

The following are very common:
    και                    and
    τε* ... και            both ... and
    ἀλλα                   but

\* This comes *second word in a phrase*, after the first (or only) word referring to the first of
the two items being joined: e.g.
    ὁ τε δουλος και ὁ ξενος            both the slave and the stranger
If the first item consists of just one word, τε and και end up next to each other:
    δουλος τε και ξενος                both a slave and a stranger


Exercise 2.10

*Translate into English:*
1      ὁ τε ξεν-ος και ὁ ἀγγελ-ος συμμαχ-οι εἰσιν.
2      ὁ στρατ-υς οὐ μεν-ει ἀλλα φευγ-ει.
3      ἀποκτειν-ομεν τους τε δουλ-ους και τους ξεν-ους.
4      ὁ διδασκαλ-ος γραφ-ει τε και λεγ-ει.
5      ὁ ἀγγελ-ος ἀκου-ει και φευγ-ει.
6      ὁ θε-ος διδασκαλ-ος ἐστιν.
7      οἱ συμμαχ-οι οὐ τασσ-ουσι τον στρατ-ον.
8      οἱ δουλ-οι οὐ λυ-ουσι τους ἱππ-ους.
9      οἱ ξεν-οι συμμαχ-οι οὐκ εἰσιν, ἀλλα τας πυλ-ας
        φυλασσ-ουσιν.
10     διδασκ-ω τε και μανθαν-ω.

# First declension feminine nouns: variant pattern

If the stem ends in a vowel or in rho, the singular endings have alpha instead of eta (the plurals still have alpha):

χωρα   land, country

| sg | nom | χωρ-α |
|----|-----|-------|
|    | acc | χωρ-αν |

| pl | nom | χωρ-αι |
|----|-----|--------|
|    | acc | χωρ-ας |

• Notice that this is even closer to Latin (*puella, puellam; puellae, puellas*).

Ten nouns like χωρα:

| 1 | ἀγορα | agora, marketplace, public square |
|----|-------|-----------------------------------|
| 2 | ἐκκλησια | assembly |
| 3 | ἑσπερα | evening |
| 4 | ἡμερα | day |
| 5 | θεα | goddess |
| 6 | θυρα | door |
| 7 | ναυμαχια | sea-battle |
| 8 | οἰκια | house |
| 9 | σοφια | wisdom |
| 10 | ὡρα | hour |

Exercise 2.11

*Translate into English:*
1       προς την ἀγορ-αν βαιν-ομεν.
2       ἡ θε-α την σοφι-αν διδασκ-ει.
3       ἡ ναυμαχι-α την νικ-ην φερ-ει.
4       ἡ οἰκι-α θυρ-ας οὐκ ἐχ-ει.
5       ἡ ἑσπερ-α την ἐκκλησι-αν παυ-ει.

Exercise 2.12

*Change these combinations of noun + article into the singular, keeping the same case:*
1       αἱ ναυμαχι-αι
2       τας ὡρ-ας
3       αἱ ἐπιστολ-αι
4       τας ἡμερ-ας
5       αἱ οἰκι-αι

Ten more nouns like λογος:

| 1 | ἀνθρωπος | man, human being |
| 2 | βιος | life |
| 3 | δημος | people, community |
| 4 | θανατος | death |
| 5 | κινδυνος | danger |
| 6 | νομος | law, *also* custom |
| 7 | πολεμος | war |
| 8 | φιλος | friend |
| 9 | φοβος | fear |
| 10 | χρονος | time |

## Translation of the definite article

As already noted, the definite article in Greek is sometimes used where *the* would not sound natural in English. As well as *abstract qualities* (*justice*, *wisdom*), the article is used for *general classes* (so οἱ δουλοι could mean *slaves* as a category, rather than *the slaves* i.e. the particular ones mentioned). In these instances it should not be translated. (Sometimes it is difficult to decide, in which case it is correct either to include *the* or to leave it out.)

Exercise 2.13

*Translate into English:*
1  ὁ δημ-ος νομ-ους ἐχ-ει.
2  οἱ ἀνθρωπ-οι οὐ μανθαν-ουσι την σοφι-αν.
3  ὁ χρον-ος τους ἀνθρωπ-ους διδασκ-ει.
4  ἡ ἑσπερ-α παυ-ει την ναυμαχι-αν.
5  ἡ θυρ-α την οἰκι-αν φυλασσ-ει.
6  ἡ χωρ-α την δικαιοσυν-ην ἐχ-ει.
7  ὁ κινδυν-ος μεν-ει.
8  ὁ φοβ-ος τον στρατ-ον λαμβαν-ει.
9  ἡ ναυμαχι-α τον πολεμ-ον παυ-ει.
10  ὁ θε-ος την σοφι-αν φερ-ει.

Exercise 2.14

*Translate into Greek:*
1       Time brings victory.
2       We go to the marketplace.
3       The house has gates.
4       Life teaches wisdom.
5       The goddess has honour.

21

# Expressing time (1)

*Time how long* is expressed by the accusative, as in Latin (e.g. *for ten hours, for five days*: no word *for* is needed).

Exercise 2.15

*Translate into English:*

1   οἱ συμμαχ-οι τας πυλ-ας <u>πεντε</u> ὡρ-ας φυλασσ-ουσιν.
2   οἱ φιλ-οι ἐπιστολ-ας γραφ-ουσιν.
3   ὁ πολεμ-ος τον τε κινδυν-ον και τον θανατ-ον φερ-ει.
4   ὁ στρατ-ος <u>δεκα</u> ἡμερας μενει.
5   προς την τε κωμ-ην και την ἀγορ-αν τρεχ-ομεν.

πεντε   five
δεκα    ten

# Second declension neuter nouns

δωρον    gift

| sg | nom | δωρ-ον |
|----|-----|--------|
|    | acc | δωρ-ον |

| pl | nom | δωρ-α |
|----|-----|-------|
|    | acc | δωρ-α |

• Notice that, as in Latin, nominative and accusative are always the same with neuter nouns; both nominative and accusative singular of the neuter are like the masculine accusative (compare *bellum, bellum* with *dominus, dominum*); nominative and accusative plural end -α (Latin -*a*).

• To find out whether a neuter noun is nominative or accusative, you must look at the rest of the sentence (e.g. is another word nominative, making it likely the neuter one is accusative? or vice versa; and does the person ending of the verb give a clue?).

• Neuter plurals in Greek normally take a singular verb. (There is no obvious reason for this: a neuter plural was perhaps felt to be a kind of collective singular.)

Neuter of the definite article:

| sg | nom | το |
|----|-----|-----|
|    | acc | το |

| pl | nom | τα |
|----|-----|-----|
|    | acc | τα |

Note that there is no -ν ending on the singular. As with nouns, nominative and accusative are the same. The τ- stem (which the article in the masculine and feminine uses for the accusative) here is used for both nominative and accusative.

Ten nouns like δωρον:

| | | |
|---|---|---|
| 1 | ἀθλον | prize |
| 2 | δενδρον | tree |
| 3 | δεσμωτηριον | prison |
| 4 | ἐργον | work, deed |
| 5 | ἱερον | temple |
| 6 | ναυτικον | fleet |
| 7 | ὁπλα (*plural*) | arms, weapons |
| 8 | πλοιον | boat |
| 9 | στρατοπεδον | camp |
| 10 | τοξον | bow |

Exercise 2.16

*Translate into English:*
1    ὁ δουλ-ος προς το δεσμωτηρι-ον τρεχ-ει.
2    οἱ ξεν-οι τοξ-α ἐχ-ουσιν.
3    τα δενδρ-α την οἰκι-αν φυλασσ-ει.
4    τα πλοι-α τον στρατ-ον φερ-ει.
5    ὁ ξεν-ος δωρ-α και ἀθλ-α ἐχ-ει.
6    ὁ στρατηγ-ος τα ὁπλ-α προς το στρατοπεδ-ον πεμπ-ει.
7    ὁ ἀγγελ-ος το ἐργ-ον διδασκ-ει.
8    οἱ συμμαχ-οι εἰς το στρατοπεδ-ον τρεχ-ουσιν.
9    ὁ τε θε-ος και ἡ θε-α ἱερ-α ἐχ-ουσιν.
10   το ναυτικ-ον εἰς την ναυμαχι-αν βαιν-ει.

Exercise 2.17

*Translate into Greek:*
1    I have the prize.
2    The boats guard the river.
3    You (*sg*) carry the gifts.
4    The messengers run to the temple.
5    The camp has gates.

Exercise 2.18

*Give one English derivative from:*
1      τοξον
2      βιος
3      φιλος
4      ναυτικον
5      φοβος

# Revision checkpoint

*Make sure you know:*
• present tense of the verb *to be*
• common connecting words
• the nominative and accusative (*sg and pl*) of χωρα
• use of the accusative for *time how long*
• the nominative and accusative (*sg and pl*) of δωρον
• the neuter forms of the definite article

# Vocabulary checklist for Chapter 2

| | | |
|---|---|---|
| ἀγορα | ἡ | agora, marketplace, public square |
| ἀθλον | το | prize |
| ἀλλα | | but |
| ἀνθρωπος | ὁ | man, human being |
| ἀποκτεινω | | I kill |
| βιος | ὁ | life |
| δεκα | | ten |
| δενδρον | το | tree |
| δεσμωτηριον | το | prison |
| δημος | ὁ | people, community |
| δωρον | το | gift |
| εἰμι | | I am |
| ἐκκλησια | ἡ | assembly  *language* |
| ἐργον | το | work, deed |
| ἑσπερα | ἡ | evening |
| εὑρισκω | | I find |
| ἡμερα | ἡ | day |
| θανατος | ὁ | death |
| θεα | ἡ | goddess |
| θυρα | ἡ | door |
| ἱερον | το | temple |
| και | | and |
| κινδυνος | ὁ | danger  *danger, high voltage, when we touch, when we kiss* |
| λαμβανω | | I take |
| λειπω | | I leave |
| λυω | | I release |
| μανθανω | | I learn |
| μενω | | I stay, I remain |
| ναυμαχια | ἡ | sea-battle |
| ναυτικον | το | fleet |
| νομος | ὁ | law, custom |
| οἰκια | ἡ | house |
| ὁπλα | τα | arms, weapons |
| πεμπω | | I send |
| πεντε | | five |
| πλοιον | το | boat |
| πολεμος | ὁ | war |
| σοφια | ἡ | wisdom |
| στρατοπεδον | το | camp |
| τασσω | | I draw up, I arrange |
| τε* ... και | | both ... and |
| τοξον | το | bow |
| φευγω | | I flee, I run away |
| φιλος | ὁ | friend |

| | | |
|---|---|---|
| φοβος | ὁ | fear |
| χρονος | ὁ | time |
| χωρα | ἡ | land, country |
| ὡρα | ἡ | hour |

(48 words)

\* τε comes after the first (or only) word referring to the first of the two items being joined

# Chapter 3

## Nouns: all cases

The nouns you have learned so far with genitive and dative added:

|        |     | *first declension* | | *second declension* | |
|--------|-----|--------------------|----------|---------------------|----------|
|        |     | *feminine*         |          | *masculine*         | *neuter* |
| sg     | nom | τιμ-η              | χωρ-α    | λογ-ος*             | δωρ-ον   |
|        | acc | τιμ-ην             | χωρ-αν   | λογ-ον              | δωρ-ον   |
|        | gen | τιμ-ης             | χωρ-ας   | λογ-ου              | δωρ-ου   |
|        | dat | τιμ-η              | χωρ-ᾳ    | λογ-ῳ               | δωρ-ῳ    |
|        |     |                    |          | (*voc λογ-ε)        |          |
| pl     | nom | τιμ-αι             | χωρ-αι   | λογ-οι              | δωρ-α    |
|        | acc | τιμ-ας             | χωρ-ας   | λογ-ους             | δωρ-α    |
|        | gen | τιμ-ων             | χωρ-ων   | λογ-ων              | δωρ-ων   |
|        | dat | τιμ-αις            | χωρ-αις  | λογ-οις             | δωρ-οις  |

The definite article with genitive and dative added:
*(notice the conventional order here is masculine-feminine-neuter, whereas the nouns are given in declension order)*

|    |     | *masculine* | *feminine* | *neuter* |
|----|-----|-------------|------------|----------|
| sg | nom | ὁ           | ἡ          | το       |
|    | acc | τον         | την        | το       |
|    | gen | του         | της        | του      |
|    | dat | τῳ          | τη         | τῳ       |
| pl | nom | οἱ          | αἱ         | τα       |
|    | acc | τους        | τας        | τα       |
|    | gen | των         | των        | των      |
|    | dat | τοις        | ταις       | τοις     |

• Notice that τιμη and χωρα have the same pattern in the singular, but with different vowels; and are identical in the plural.

• Notice that the dative singulars have iota subscript.

• Notice again broad similarities to Latin, particularly of the datives (*puellae, servo, templo; puellis, servis, templis*).

• Notice that *all* Greek genitive plurals end -ων (Latin has -*um*, but often as part of a longer ending: -*arum*, -*orum*, -*ium*, etc).

• There is no ablative case. (The jobs the ablative does in Latin are divided up between the genitive and dative.)

• There is a vocative case (used to address someone or something). For second declension nouns like λογος in the singular it ends -ε (compare Latin *domine*). For most other singulars (exceptions will be noted later) and for all plurals it is the same as the nominative.

• The genitive is the case of possession and definition, often translated *of*: e.g. *the house of the general = the general's house*. It is also has the idea of *separation* (going away from), and is used with prepositions indicating this (which in Latin would take the ablative).

• The dative is the case of the indirect object, often translated *to* or *for*:

e.g. I give the money *(direct object)* to the slave *(indirect)*.

It is used with prepositions indicating rest *in* or *at* a place (which in Latin would also take the ablative: notice that although Greek has fewer cases available, it often makes more distinctions).

## Prepositions

• You have already met two prepositions with the accusative, indicating *motion towards*:
εἰς                        into
προς                      towards

• The following take the genitive, indicating *motion away from*:
ἀπο                      (away) from
ἐκ                        out of
(ἐξ if the next word starts with a vowel)
Notice that εἰς and ἐκ are more specific than προς and ἀπο (which just indicate general direction).

• The following takes the dative, indicating *rest*:
ἐν                        in

Exercise 3.1

*Change these article + noun combinations into the* genitive:
1        ὁ ἀνθρωπ-ος
2        ἡ σοφι-α
3        το δενδρ-ον
4        οἱ συμμαχ-οι
5        αἱ βο-αι

28

Exercise 3.2

*Change these article + noun combinations into the* dative*:*

1      ὁ ξεν-ος
2      το ἐργ-ον
3      τα ὁπλ-α
4      αἱ ἡμερ-αι
5      οἱ φιλ-οι

Exercise 3.3

*Translate into English:*

1      ὁ δουλ-ος ἀπο της οἰκι-ας προς την ἀγορ-αν τρεχ-ει.
2      ἐστι* δουλ-ος ἐν τῳ δεσμωτηρι-ῳ.
3      ὁ στρατ-ος εἰς κινδυν-ον βαιν-ει.
4      οἱ ξεν-οι ἐκ του δεσμωτηρι-ου τρεχ-ουσιν.
5      εἰσι* νομοι ἐν τῳ πολεμ-ῳ.
6      τους ἱππ-ους ἐκ του κινδυν-ου λυ-ομεν.
7      ὁ στρατ-ος ἐκ του στρατοπεδ-ου βαιν-ει.
8      τον ἀγγελ-ον προς την ἀγορ-αν πεμπ-ω.
9      τα ἀθλ-α ἐκ της οἰκι-ας εἰς το ἱερ-ον φερ-εις.
10    τα δενδρ-α ἐν τῃ κωμ-ῃ ἐστιν.

* note that, as in Latin, if the verb *to be* comes at the beginning of the sentence, it is usually translated *there is, there are* etc

# Sandwich construction

This is one of the most important and distinctive features of Greek grammar. A description, specifying which person or thing, is sandwiched inside the article-noun combination. The description is often a genitive phrase (with its own article):

             ┌─ possesed object ─┐

e.g.        │ ἡ │του στρατηγ-ου │οἰκι-α│
*literally*    the of-the-general house           *i.e.* the general's house
                            possesing

             το των συμμαχ-ων ναυτικ-ον
*literally*    the of-the-allies fleet             *i.e.* the allies' fleet

A 'genitive sandwich' can often be recognised by two forms of the definite article next to each other. It is important to get the sandwich the right way round: the outer part is the main thing being talked about (and can be in any case, depending on its job in the sentence); the inner part is telling you *which one* or *whose* (and is in the genitive). When translating into Greek it is helpful to do the outer part of the sandwich first, coming back to fill in the gap.

Exercise 3.4

*Translate into English:*

1  ὁ τοῦ στρατηγ-οῦ ἱππ-ος φευγ-ει.
2  τοὺς τοῦ διδασκαλ-ου λογ-ους μανθαν-ετε.
3  οἱ των θε-ων νομ-οι τοὺς ἀνθρωπ-ους διδασκ-ουσιν.
4  ἀκου-ομεν τοὺς τοῦ ἀγγελ-ου λογ-ους.
5  προς το της θε-ας ἱερ-ον βαιν-ομεν.

Exercise 3.5

*Translate into Greek:*

1  The teacher's slave runs away.
2  I hear the voice of the goddess.
3  You (*sg*) learn the words of the teacher.
4  The boats of the fleet guard the village.
5  We release the gates of the camp.


# Revision checkpoint

*Make sure you know:*
• the present tense of παυω (six bits)
• the present tense of εἰμι (six bits)
• the declensions of τιμη, χωρα, λογος and δωρον in the nominative, accusative, genitive and dative, singular and plural (eight bits of each, plus vocative for λογος)
• how the sandwich construction works
• the definite article in all three genders and four cases, singular and plural (twenty-four bits)

To help you, here again is the whole of the definite article (it is better to learn the columns downwards rather than across):

|     |     | *masculine* | *feminine* | *neuter* |
| --- | --- | --- | --- | --- |
| *sg* | *nom* | ὁ | ἡ | το |
|     | *acc* | τον | την | το |
|     | *gen* | του | της | του |
|     | *dat* | τῳ | τη | τῳ |
|     |     |     |     |     |
| *pl* | *nom* | οἱ | αἱ | τα |
|     | *acc* | τους | τας | τα |
|     | *gen* | των | των | των |
|     | *dat* | τοις | ταις | τοις |

• Notice that the article starts with a rough breathing instead of tau in the masculine and feminine nominative, singular and plural.

• Notice that the endings are very similar to those of the nouns τιμη, λογος and δωρον, except that there is no -ς on the masculine nominative singular, and no -ν on the neuter nominative and accusative singular.

Exercise 3.6 (Revision)

*Translate into English:*

1      τα δωρ-α ἐν τη οἰκι-ᾳ ἐστιν.
2      ὁ δουλ-ος το ἐργ-ον μανθαν-ει.
3      το των συμμαχ-ων ναυτικ-ον νικ-ην ἐχ-ει.
4      ὁ στρατηγ-ος τα ὁπλ-α φερ-ει.
5      ὁ στρατ-ος ἐν τῳ στρατοπεδ-ῳ ἐστιν.
6      ὁ ἀγγελ-ος το δωρ-ον πεμπ-ει.
7      οἱ συμμαχ-οι προς το στρατοπεδ-ον τρεχ-ουσιν.
8      οἱ φιλ-οι τα ἀθλ-α λαμβαν-ουσιν.
9      οἱ τε θε-οι και αἱ θε-αι δωρ-α ἐχ-ουσιν.
10      ἡ του ναυτικ-ου νικ-η φυλασσ-ει την χωρ-αν.


# Imperative

The imperative, used for giving an order, is:

*sg*      παυ-ε      stop!
*pl*      παυ-ετε

Notice that the plural is the same as the ordinary second person plural. Imperatives however are easy to recognise. They are very often accompanied by a noun in the vocative, preceded by ὦ (*O ...* ), though this is usually better left out in English.

Exercise 3.7

*Translate into English:*

1      φευγ-ε, ὦ δουλ-ε.
2      διωκ-ετε τον δουλ-ον, ὦ φιλ-οι.
3      ὦ συμμαχ-οι, εὑρισκ-ετε τα ὁπλ-α.
4      διδασκ-ε, ὦ διδασκαλ-ε.
5      φερ-ετε τα ἀθλ-α, ὦ στρατηγ-οι.

Exercise 3.8

*Translate into Greek:*

1      Release the horses, friends!
2      Write a letter, slave!
3      Stay, allies!
4      Draw up the army, general!
5      Teacher, listen to the words!

Ten more verbs:

| | | |
|---|---|---|
| 1 | ἀποθνησκω | I die |
| 2 | γιγνωσκω | I get to know |
| 3 | ἐλαυνω | I drive |
| 4 | θαυμαζω | I am amazed (at), I admire |
| 5 | κελευω | I order |
| 6 | παρεχω | I produce, I provide |
| 7 | πειθω | I persuade |
| 8 | πιπτω | I fall |
| 9 | πιστευω | I trust, I believe (+ *dative*) |
| 10 | φαινω | I show |

## Adverbs (1)

The following adverbs of time and place are common:

| | |
|---|---|
| νυν | now |
| πολλακις | often |
| ἀει | always |
| ἐνθαδε | here |
| ἐκει | there |

Adverbs do not change their ending. They typically come just before the verb.

## Cases taken by verbs

Most Greek verbs which are followed naturally by a noun have it in the accusative, as direct object. A few however are followed by other cases. As noted above, πιστευω is followed by the dative, because the underlying idea is of *giving trust to* another person. Of verbs you have met already, ἀκουω takes an accusative direct object for a *thing* (e.g. βοην ἀκουω = *I hear a shout*) but a *genitive* for a person (e.g. του δουλου ἀκουω = *I hear the slave*). Different again is διδασκω, which can take a double accusative (e.g. τον δουλον τους λογους διδασκομεν = *We teach the slave the words*).

Exercise 3.9

*Translate into English:*

1      οἱ του ἀγγελ-ου λογ-οι νυν πειθ-ουσι τον δημ-ον.
2      ὁ του στρατηγ-ου ἱππ-ος ἐκει ἐστιν.
3      ὁ ξεν-ος του στρατηγ-ου ἀκου-ει.
4      οἱ συμμαχ-οι ἐν ταις ναυμαχι-αις πολλακις ἀποθνησκ-ουσιν.
5      οἱ δουλ-οι τον ἱππ-ον προς τον ποταμ-ον ἐλαυν-ουσιν.
6      την της θε-ας σοφι-αν θαυμαζ-ομεν.
7      τους λογ-ους ἀει μανθαν-ετε, ὦ φιλ-οι.

8    ὁ διδασκαλ-ος τῃ ἐπιστολ-ῃ οὐ πιστευ-ει.
9    γιγνωσκ-ω τας των συμμαχ-ων φων-ας.
10   ὁ ξεν-ος βουλ-ην τῃ ναυμαχι-ᾳ παρεχ-ει.

## Infinitive

The present infinitive (*to* do something) is formed by adding -ειν to the verb stem:
    παυ-ειν            to stop

Exercise 3.10

*Translate into English:*
1    φερ-ειν
2    πιστευ-ειν
3    μεν-ειν
4    παρεχ-ειν
5    διωκ-ειν

Exercise 3.11

*Translate into Greek:*
1    To order
2    To get to know
3    To drive
4    To die
5    To provide

Exercise 3.12

*Translate into English:*
1    οἱ ἀγγελ-οι πειθ-ουσι τον στρατ-ον φευγ-ειν.
2    ὁ στρατηγ-ος κελευ-ει τους δουλ-ους τρεχ-ειν.
3    ὁ στρατ-ος οὐκ ἐθελ-ει ἐν κινδυν-ῳ μεν-ειν.
4    πειθ-ε τους συμμαχ-ους τῳ ἀγγελ-ῳ πιστευ-ειν, ὦ στρατηγ-ε.
5    ἐθελ-ομεν τους νομ-ους ἀει φυλασσ-ειν.

    ἐθελω   I wish, I am willing

33

# Adjectives

The commonest type of adjective is easy if you have learned the nouns:

σοφος   wise, clever

|    |     | masculine | feminine | neuter |
|----|-----|-----------|----------|--------|
| sg | nom | σοφ-ος    | σοφ-η    | σοφ-ον |
|    | acc | σοφ-ον    | σοφ-ην   | σοφ-ον |
|    | gen | σοφ-ου    | σοφ-ης   | σοφ-ου |
|    | dat | σοφ-ῳ     | σοφ-η    | σοφ-ῳ  |
| pl | nom | σοφ-οι    | σοφ-αι   | σοφ-α  |
|    | acc | σοφ-ους   | σοφ-ας   | σοφ-α  |
|    | gen | σοφ-ων    | σοφ-ων   | σοφ-ων |
|    | dat | σοφ-οις   | σοφ-αις  | σοφ-οις |

• This is exactly the same as τιμη, λογος and δωρον.

• As with the nouns, there is a variant form of the feminine singular if the stem ends with a vowel or rho:

φιλιος   friendly

| sg | nom | φιλι-α  |
|----|-----|---------|
|    | acc | φιλι-αν |
|    | gen | φιλι-ας |
|    | dat | φιλι-ᾳ  |

This is exactly the same as the singular of χωρα.

• As in Latin, adjectives agree with the nouns they refer to in number, gender and case.

• Adjectives commonly use the sandwich construction:

e.g.        ὁ σοφ-ος δουλ-ος
            the wise slave

Another way of achieving the same effect is to repeat the article*:

e.g.        ὁ δουλ-ος ὁ σοφ-ος
literally   the slave the wise (one), i.e.
            the wise slave

Both these expressions *specify which slave* - the wise one rather than (say) the stupid one. The position of an adjective used in either of these two ways is often called *bound* (fastened to the noun) or *attributive* (telling you an *attribute* or quality).

* The genitive sandwich can also do this:

            ἡ οἰκ-ια ἡ του στρατηγ-ου
literally   the house the (one) of the general, i.e.
            the general's house

34

• If on the other hand you want to tell us for the first time that the slave *is* wise, you say:

ὁ δουλ-ος σοφ-ος ἐστιν
The slave is wise

(or just: ὁ δουλ-ος σοφ-ος, with ἐστιν understood: this is called the *predicative* position, because it *predicates* or tells you something new)

Five adjectives like σοφος:

| | | |
|---|---|---|
| 1 | ἀγαθος | good |
| 2 | δεινος | strange, terrible |
| 3 | κακος | bad |
| 4 | καλος | fine, beautiful |
| 5 | χαλεπος | difficult, dangerous |

Five adjectives like φιλιος:

| | | |
|---|---|---|
| 1 | ἀνδρειος | brave |
| 2 | ἐλευθερος | free |
| 3 | ἐχθρος | hostile |
| 4 | μικρος | small |
| 5 | νεος | new |

Exercise 3.13

*Translate into English:*
1   το των συμμαχ-ων ἐργ-ον χαλεπ-ον ἐστιν.
2   ὁ ἀγγελ-ος τους ξεν-ους νε-ους λογ-ους διδασκ ει.
3   ἡ νικ-η ἐστι καλ-η.
4   ὁ νε-ος ἱππ-ος μικρ-ος ἐστιν.
5   ὁ ποταμ-ος οὐ χαλεπ-ος ἐστιν.
6   ἡ βουλ-η κακ-η.
7   ἡ χωρ-α ἐλευθερ-α μεν-ει.
8   οἱ ξεν-οι ἐχθρ-οι εἰσιν.
9   ὁ θε-ος καλ-α δωρ-α ἐχ-ει.
10  ὁ πολεμ-ος δειν-ος ἐστιν.

Exercise 3.14

*Translate into Greek:*
1       The teacher is wise.
2       The god is friendly.
3       The bad slave runs away.
4       The new camp is good.
5       The allies are brave.

# Adverbs (2)

Most ordinary adjectives can be changed into adverbs (usually used to describe *how* an action is done) simply by changing the -ων of the genitive plural to -ως: e.g. σοφ-ων becomes σοφ-ως (= *wisely*). As we saw with adverbs of time, the adverb itself does not change its ending.

## Exercise 3.15

*Translate into English:*

1      ὁ στρατ-ος την χωρ-αν ἀνδρει-ως φυλασσ-ει.
2      ὁ ἀγγελ-ος καλ-ως λεγ-ει.
3      ὁ διδασκαλ-ος σοφ-ος ἐστι και σοφ-ως διδασκ-ει.
4      ὁ δουλ-ος τους ἱππ-ους χαλεπ-ως ἐλαυν-ει.
5      ὁ ξεν-ος τα δωρ-α φιλι-ως παρεχ-ει.


# Particles

Words connecting sentences are called *particles*. Many of them come second word in the new sentence, but are translated at the beginning (compare e.g. *enim, tamen, igitur* in Latin). Very common are:

| | |
|---|---|
| γαρ | for |
| δε | but *or* and |
| μεντοι | however |
| οὐν | therefore |

Also very important are the paired
         μεν ... δε
These link two clauses, drawing a contrast between them: they can sometimes be translated on the *one hand ... on the other*, but often this sounds clumsy, and it is better to leave μεν untranslated and for δε to put e.g. *but* or *whilst*.

Exercise 3.16

# How the Locrians make laws (1)

*Words underlined are given below in basic form in the order they occur*

οἱ <u>Λοκρ-οι</u> τους <u>παλαι-ους</u> νομ-ους <u>ἐτι</u> ἐχ-ουσιν. τους γαρ των <u>προγον-ων</u>
νομ-ους ἀει φυλασσ-ουσιν. <u>ἐι</u> <u>τις</u> <u>ἐθελ-ει</u> νομ-ον νε-ον παρεχ-ειν, τον
<u>τραχηλ-ον</u> ἐν <u>βροχ-ῳ</u> ἐχ-ει. <u>ἐπειτα</u> δε <u>περι</u> του νομ-ου λεγ-ει. ἐι μεν
σοφ-ως λεγ-ει, και ὁ νομ-ος <u>χρησιμ-ος</u> ἐστι, και ἡ των Λοκρ-ων ἐκκλησι-α
5  ἐθελ-ει ἐχ-ειν τον νομ-ον τον νε-ον, ὁ ἀνθρωπ-ος <u>ἐπαιν-ον</u> ἐχ-ει και
<u>ἀποβαιν-ει</u>. ἐι δε ὁ νομ-ος κακ-ος τε και χαλεπ-ος ἐστιν, οἱ Λοκρ-οι τον
βροχ-ον <u>ἐλκ-ουσι</u> και τον ἀνθρωπ-ον ἀποκτειν-ουσιν. ὁ οὖν φοβ-ος
<u>κωλυ-ει</u> τους Λοκρ-ους. ὁ γαρ του θανατ-ου κινδυν-ος δειν-ος ἐστιν. οὐ
πολλακις περι νομ-ων νε-ων ἀκου-ουσιν. ἐν <u>διακοσι-οις</u> <u>ἐνιαυτ-οις</u>
10 <u>εἱς</u> νομ-ος νε-ος ἐστιν.

| | | |
|---|---|---|
| | Λοκρος | Locrian (*person from Locris, in central Greece*) |
| | παλαιος | ancient |
| | ἐτι | still |
| | προγονος | ancestor |
| | εἰ | if |
| | τις | someone |
| | ἐθελω | I wish |
| | τραχηλος | neck |
| | βροχος | noose |
| | ἐπειτα | then |
| | περι | (+ *gen*) about |
| | χρησιμος | useful |
| 5 | ἐπαινος | praise |
| | ἀποβαινω | I go away |
| | ἑλκω | (*here*) I pull on |
| | κωλυω | I hinder |
| | διακοσιοι | 200 |
| | ἐνιαυτος | year |
| 10 | εἱς | one (*note rough breathing; do not confuse with* εἰς = into) |

# Background: The rule of Law

The story about the Locrians is told in the course of a speech by the great orator (public speaker and politician) Demosthenes (384-322 BC). Each city-state in Greece had its own laws and customs, and the Greeks looked with interested curiosity at the laws of their neighbours. The conservatism of Locrian institutions stands in remarkable contrast to Demosthenes' own city of Athens, which (at an opposite extreme) changed its laws with excessive ease and frequency. But the Greeks were generally united in their belief in the centrality of the legal system in the running of a city: many myths told of a pre-legal society dominated by family vendetta (if someone killed your brother, you went and killed one of his relatives), and of the transition from this to a more ordered system where you could take him to court.

# How the Locrians make laws (2)

οἱ Λοκρ-οι, <u>εἰ</u> <u>τις</u> <u>ὀφθαλμ-ον</u> <u>ἐκκοπτ-ει</u>, <u>ἀναγκαζ-ουσι</u> τον ἀνθρωπ-ον
ὀφθαλμ-ον παρεχ-ειν <u>ἀντεκκοπτ-ειν</u>. Λοκρος τις <u>μονον</u> ὀφθαλμ-ον ἐχ-ει.
<u>ἐχθρ-ος</u> τις τον ὀφθαλμ-ον ἐκκοπτ-ει. <u>οὑτως</u> ὁ ἀνθρωπ-ος ὀφθαλμ-ον οὐκ
ἐχ-ει. νομ-ον οὖν νε-ον <u>ἐθελ-ει</u> παρεχ-ειν. φοβ-ον γαρ οὐκ ἐχ-ει, <u>διοτι</u> ὁ
5   βι-ος ἐστι νυν <u>ἀβιωτ-ος</u>. τον οὖν <u>τραχηλ-ον</u> ἐν τῳ <u>βροχ-ῳ</u> ἐχ-ει, και περι
του νομ-ου <u>λεγ-ει</u>.

|  |  |  |
|---|---|---|
|  | εἰ | if |
|  | τις | some one, (*as adjective*) a certain |
|  | ὀφθαλμος | eye |
|  | ἐκκοπτω | I knock out |
|  | ἀναγκαζω | I force |
|  | ἀντεκκοπτω | I knock out in return |
|  | μονος | single |
|  | ἐχθρος | (*as noun*) enemy |
|  | οὑτως | in this way |
|  | ἐθελω | I·wish |
|  | διοτι | because |
| 5 | ἀβιωτος | not worth living |
|  | τραχηλος | neck |
|  | βροχος | noose |
|  | λεγω | I speak |

*Read the rest of the passage and answer the questions which follow:*

7   "<u>εἰ</u> τις τον <u>ἑτεροφθαλμ-ου</u> ὀφθαλμ-ον ἐκκοπτ-ει, <u>δει</u> παρεχ-ειν
<u>ἀμφοτερ-ους</u> τους ὀφθαλμ-ους ἀντεκκοπτ-ειν. ἀμφοτερ-οι οὖν οἱ
ἀνθρωπ-οι <u>ὁμοιως</u> <u>πασχ-ουσιν</u>." ὁ ἀνθρωπ-ος σοφ-ως λεγ-ει, και ὁ νομ-ος
10  <u>χρησιμ-ος</u> ἐστιν. ἡ των Λοκρ-ων ἐκκλησι-α ἐθελ-ει ἐχ-ειν τον νομ-ον τον
νε-ον. ὁ μεν οὖν του ἑτεροφθαλμ-ου ἐχθρ-ος ἀμφοτερ-ους τους ὀφθαλμ-ους
παρεχ-ει ἀντεκκοπτ-ειν. ὁ δε ἑτεροφθαλμ-ος <u>ἐπαιν-ον</u> ἐχ-ει και <u>ἀποβαιν-ει</u>,
και οἱ Λοκρ-οι νε-ον νομ-ον νυν ἐχ-ουσιν.

|  |  |  |
|---|---|---|
|  | ἑτεροφθαλμος | one-eyed man |
|  | δει | it is necessary (*impersonal verb*, + *infinitive*) |
|  | ἀμφοτεροι | both |
|  | ὁμοιως | in the same way |
|  | πασχω | I suffer |
| 10 | χρησιμος | useful |
|  | ἐπαινος | praise |
|  | ἀποβαινω | I go away |

| | | |
|---|---|---|
| 1 | What does the proposed new law say should happen if anyone knocks out the eye of a one-eyed man (lines 7-8)? | (3) |
| 2 | What is the justification for this (lines 8-9)? | (3) |
| 3 | What is the assembly's verdict on the proposed new law, and why (lines 9-11)? | (4) |
| 4 | What happens to the enemy of the one-eyed man (lines 11-12)? | (3) |
| 5 | What happens to the proposer of the new law (line 12)? | (2) |

15 marks

## Future tense

For most verbs this is very easy. Add sigma to the stem, before adding the same endings as the present tense has:

| | |
|---|---|
| παυ-σ-ω | I shall stop |
| παυ-σ-εις | you (*sg*) will stop |
| παυ-σ-ει | he/she/it will stop |
| | |
| παυ-σ-ομεν | we shall stop |
| παυ-σ-ετε | you (*pl*) will stop |
| παυ-σ-υυσι(ν)* | they will stop |

\* again the movable nu is added if the next word starts with a vowel, or if this is the last word in the sentence

With some verbs where the stem ends in a consonant, adding the sigma requires some adjustment or alternative spelling.

• Because pi and sigma make psi, the future of πεμπω is πεμψω. And because phi and sigma sounds almost the same as pi and sigma, the future of γραφω is γραψω.

• Because kappa and sigma make xi, the future of διωκω is διωξω. Because gamma and sigma sounds almost the same as kappa and sigma, the future of ἀγω is ἀξω. Because sigma, kappa and sigma is awkward to pronounce, the future of διδασκω is διδαξω (the first sigma drops out). And because theta and sigma is awkward to pronounce, the future of πειθω is πεισω (the theta just drops out).

• Some verbs form their future in a different way: this will be explained later.

From this point onwards hyphens will no longer be inserted between stem and ending in exercises, but will continue to be used for new grammar.

Exercise 3.18

*Translate into English:*
1 παυσομεν
2 λυσετε
3 λειψω
4 πεισουσι(ν)
5 διωξει
6 πεμψεις
7 ἀξω
8 διδαξομεν
9 παυσεις
10 λυσει

Exercise 3.19

*Translate into English:*
1 ὁ ἀνδρειος ξενος λυσει τον ἱππον.
2 ἡ ἑσπερα οὐ παυσει την ἐκκλησιαν.
3 ὁ στρατηγος διωξει τους κακους δουλους./
4 ὁ διδασκαλος πεμψει την ἐπιστολην.
5 οἱ συμμαχοι ἀει πεισουσι τον δημον.
6 τῳ του στρατηγου ἱππῳ οὐ πιστευσω.
7 ὁ ἀγγελος τους του θεου λογους καλως λεξει.
8 τον στρατον προς τον ποταμον ἀξω.
9 λειψομεν το στρατοπεδον.
10 λυσεις την μικραν πυλην.

Exercise 3.20

*Translate into Greek:*
1 He will release.
2 We shall stop.
3 You (*pl*) will lead.
4 They will write.
5 You (*sg*) will chase.

# Revision checkpoint

*Make sure you know:*
• how the imperative and infinitive are formed
• adjective declensions (σοφος and φιλιος)
• how the 'bound' or 'attributive' position works (sandwich construction or repeated article)
• how adverbs are formed from adjectives
• what particles are
• how the future tense is formed (with adjustment to consonant stems in adding sigma)

# Imperfect tense

As well as a set of endings, this has a marker on the beginning of each bit to indicate that it is a past tense. This is epsilon with a smooth breathing (ἐ-) and is called the *augment*.

| | |
|---|---|
| ἐ-παυ-ον | I was stopping |
| ἐ-παυ-ες | you (*sg*) were stopping |
| ἐ-παυ-ε(ν)* | he/she/it was stopping |
| | |
| ἐ-παυ-ομεν | we were stopping |
| ἐ-παυ-ετε | you (*pl*) were stopping |
| ἐ-παυ-ον | they were stopping |

\* again the movable nu is added (to make pronunciation easier) if the next word starts with a vowel, or if this is the last word in the sentence

• The imperfect (literally *unfinished*) strictly refers to an action that is not completed. It has a similar range of meanings to the Latin imperfect: *was doing, used to, did (over a long period)*.

• Notice that the first person singular and third person plural are identical. The context in a sentence should enable you to tell which it is.

• Notice some similarities to the set of endings you have already seen used for the present and future tenses: not only the identical ones for first and second persons plural (where only the augment indicates the imperfect), but also the final sigma for second person singular.

• In order to look up in a dictionary or wordlist a verb in the imperfect, you must remove the augment to see the original stem.

Exercise 3.21

*Translate into Greek:*
1    I was releasing.
2    We were chasing.
3    You (*pl*) were running away.
4    They were leaving.
5    You (*sg*) were sending.

Excercise 3.22

*Translate into English:*
1    ὁ δουλος ἐλυε τον καλον ἱππον.
2    ὁ ἀγγελος νεους λογους σοφως ἐλεγεν.
3    τας ἐπιστολας ἐπεμπες.
4    ὁ στρατηγος τα ἀθλα ἐφερεν.

5    ὁ ξενος ἐπειθε τον δημον.
6    οἱ συμμαχοι το στρατοπεδον ἀνδρειως ἐφυλασσον.
7    το ἐργον ἐμανθανετε.
8    ὁ του στρατηγου δουλος ἐφευγεν.
9    οἱ ἱπποι προς τον ποταμον ἐτρεχον.
10   ἐφυλασσομεν την της οἰκιας θυραν.

Exercise 3.23

*Convert these present tense verbs to imperfect (keeping the same person and number), each time writing the Greek word, then translating it:*
1    παυω
2    πεμπομεν
3    διωκουσι(ν)
4    φυλασσεις
5    μανθανει


# Imperfect of the verb *to be*

| | |
|---|---|
| ἦ (*or* ἦν*) | I was |
| ἦσθα | you (*sg*) were |
| ἦν | he/she/it was |
| | |
| ἦμεν | we were |
| ἦτε | you (*pl*) were |
| ἦσαν | they were |

* ἦν is a common alternative form for the first person singular, but in this book ἦ will normally be used to avoid confusion with the third person

Exercise 3.24

*Translate into English:*
1    δεκα ὡρας ἐκει ἦμεν.
2    ὁ κινδυνος δεινος ἦν, ἀλλα νυν μικρος ἐστιν.
3    οἱ συμμαχοι το στρατοπεδον πεντε ἡμερας ἐφυλασσον.
4    οἱ ἀγγελοι ἀει ἀνδρειοι ἦσαν.
5    σοφος ἦσθα, ὠ φιλε.
6    ἐμανθανομεν τους λογους.
7    ὁ των συμμαχων ἀγγελος ξενος ἦν.
8    σοφοι ἦτε και σοφοι νυν ἐστε, ὠ φιλοι.
9    προς την μικραν κωμην πολλακις ἐβαινομεν.
10   ὁ του πολεμου κινδυνος δεινος ἦν.

Exercise 3.25

*Translate into Greek:*
1   We were slaves.
2   The general was wise.
3   The wise general was speaking for five hours.
4   You *(sg)* were always an ally.
5   The words of the messenger were new.

Exercise 3.26 (Revision)

*Translate into English:*
1   ὁ ἀγγελος εἰς την ἀγοραν ἐβαινεν.
2   καλα δενδρα ἐν τη κωμη ἦν.
3   τα δωρα εἰς την οἰκιαν πεμπε, ὦ φιλε.
4   οἱ ἀνδρειοι συμμαχοι πολλακις ἐν κινδυνῳ ἦσαν.
5   τα πλοια προς τον ποταμον πεμψω.
6   οἱ δουλοι ἐκ του δεσμωτηριου ἐτρεχον.
7   δεκα ἡμερας ἐν τῳ στρατοπεδῳ ἐμενομεν.
8   ὁ ξενος δουλος ἦν, ἀλλα νυν ἐλευθερος ἐστιν.
9   την του θεου φωνην ἐθαυμαζομεν.
10  τους λογους σοφως ἐγιγνωσκετε.

Exercise 3.27

*Give one English derivative from:*
1   ἀνθρωπος
2   σοφια
3   δημος
4   οἰκια
5   στρατηγος
6   φαινω
7   ἱερον
8   φωνη
9   ἀθλον
10  ἐργον

# Revision checkpoint:

*Make sure you know:*
• future tense of παυω (six bits), and how common verbs with consonant stems form the future
• imperfect tense of παυω (six bits)
• imperfect tense of εἰμι (six bits)

Exercise 3.28

*Translate into Greek:*
1      The new slave was carrying the gifts into the house.
2      The allies were brave but not wise.
3      We shall chase the horses towards the river.
4      You (*sg*) were guarding the door of the house.
5      The general was drawing up both the fleet and the allies.


# Punctuation

The comma and full stop are used as in English.
Greek also has a punctuation mark consisting of one dot above the line (·), marking a pause somewhere between a comma and a full stop, like the English semi-colon or colon.
The Greek question mark looks like the English semi-colon (;).
There is no exclamation mark.
Though not strictly authentic, quotation marks are conventionally used to indicate direct speech.


# Questions

Many sentences can be turned into questions simply by putting a question mark at the end. But an open question (e.g. *Is he stupid?* - to which the answer will be either *yes* or *no*) can be signalled at the start by putting ἀρα as first word (where Latin adds *-ne* to the end of the first word).

Questions asking for specific information are introduced by particular question words, many of which begin with π- (comparable to Latin *qu-* and English *wh-* : all are historically related). Common examples are:

πoυ;      where?
ποτε;     when?
πως;      how?


Exercise 3.29

*Translate into English:*
1      ἀρα οἱ λογοι σοφοι ἠσαν;
2      που ἐστιν ἡ θυρα;
3      ἀρα καλος ἠν ὁ ἱππος;
4      πως ἐγραφετε τας ἐπιστολας;
5      ἀρα φυλασσετε την κωμην;

| 6 | πολλακις κακος ἦ· νυν δε ἀει ἀγαθος εἰμι. |
|---|---|
| 7 | ἐμανθανες τους λογους; |
| 8 | πως ἐκ του δεσμωτηριου ἐπιστολην πεμψομεν; |
| 9 | ποτε ἦν ἡ ναυμαχια; |
| 10 | ἀρα ἀκουεις την του δουλου βοην; |

Exercise 3.30

*Translate into Greek:*
1    Where are we?
2    How were you (*pl*) learning the words?
3    Is the general wise?
4    When were you (*pl*) carrying the prizes?
5    Were you (*sg*) teaching the slaves?


Exercise 3.31

# Athenian Wit

ὁ* Στρατονικος ᾿Αθηναιος ἦν και γελοιος. προς την* Μαρωνειαν μετα
των φιλων ἐβαινεν. "ἐν τη Μαρωνεια προτερον οὐκ ἦ. ἀλλα, ὦ φιλοι,
καλυπτετε τους ἐμους ὀφθαλμους και ἀγετε με περι την κωμην, και λεξω
ἀκριβως που ἐσμεν." οἱ οὐν φιλοι τον Στρατονικον περι την κωμην
5   ἦγον**. "που ἐσμεν; ἀρα γιγνωσκεις;" "προ του καπηλειου." "προ του
καπηλειου ἐσμεν. ἀλλα πως γιγνωσκεις;" "διοτι οὐδεν ἐν τη Μαρωνεια
ἐστιν εἰ μη καπηλεια."

* note that proper names (of people and places, starting with a capital letter) normally have the
definite article (on the grounds that the name specifies *a particular one*), but this is not translated

** the augment added to a stem starting with alpha usually makes eta

| | |
|---|---|
| Στρατονικος | Stratonicus |
| ᾿Αθηναιος | Athenian |
| γελοιος | wit, witty person |
| Μαρωνεια | Maronea (*seaside place in the far north of Greece*) |
| μετα | (+ *genitive*) with |
| προτερον | previously, before |
| καλυπτω | I cover |
| ἐμος | my (*used with the article, though this is not translated*) |
| ὀφθαλμος | eye |
| με | me |
| περι | (+ *accusative*) around |
| ἀκριβως | exactly |
| προ | (+ *genitive*) in front of |
| καπηλειον | pub |
| διοτι | because |
| οὐδεν | nothing |
| εἰ μη | except |

# Vocabulary checklist for Chapter 3

*Nouns are given with nominative and genitive singular endings, and (as before) the article to show gender.*
*Adjectives are given with masculine, feminine, and neuter nominative singular endings.*

| | |
|---|---|
| ἀγαθος -η -ον | good |
| ἀει | always |
| ᾿Αθηναιος -α -ον | Athenian |
| ἀνδρειος -α -ον | brave |
| ἀπο | from (+ *gen*) |
| ἀποθνησκω | I die |
| ἀρα; | (*introduces a question, e.g.* Is it ... ?) |
| γαρ* | for |
| γιγνωσκω | I get to know |
| δε* | but, and |
| δεινος -η -ον | strange, terrible |
| διοτι | because |
| ἐθελω | I wish, I am willing |
| ἐκ (ἐξ) | out of (+ *gen*) |
| ἐκει | there |
| ἐλαυνω | I drive |
| ἐλευθερος -α -ον | free |
| ἐν | in (+ *dat*) |
| ἐνθαδε | here |
| ἐχθρος -α -ον | hostile |
| θαυμαζω | I am amazed (at), I admire |
| κακος -η -ον | bad |
| καλος -η -ον | fine, beautiful |
| κελευω | I order |
| μεν* ... δε* | (*expresses contrast, e.g.* on the one hand ... on the other, *or just* ... , but ... ) |
| μεντοι* | however |
| μικρος -α -ον | small |
| νεος -α -ον | new |
| νυν | now |
| οὐν* | therefore |
| ὀφθαλμος -ου ὁ | eye |
| παρεχω | I produce, I provide |
| πειθω | I persuade |
| πιστευω | I trust, I believe (+ *dat*) |
| πολλακις | often |
| ποτε; | when? |
| που; | where? |
| προτερον | before, previously |
| πως; | how? |
| σοφος -η -ον | wise, clever |

| φαινω | I show |
| φιλιος -α -ον | friendly |
| χαλεπος -η -ον | difficult, dangerous |
| ὦ | O (*or omit; used + voc, to address someone*) |

(44 words)

\* comes second word in its sentence, clause or phrase

# Chapter 4

## Aorist tense (1)

• The simple past tense, used for a single action in the past (e.g. *he arrived*) is in Greek called the *aorist*.

• This is what other languages call just *past*, or *simple past*, or *past historic*. In Latin the perfect (literally *finished*) tense is used both for the simple past (*he arrived*) and for the much less common 'true perfect' (*he has arrived*, implying *and is still here now*): only the context in a Latin sentence enables you to tell which it is. The perfect tense exists in Greek, but is used *only* for this 'true perfect' sense (almost equivalent to a present tense), is not very common, and will be learned later. The normal past tense in Greek is the aorist (literally *unlimited*: i.e. a past tense not limited by a suggestion that the action is *incomplete* or *repeated* - like the imperfect - or that that the action or its effect *still continues* - like the perfect).

• There are two different ways of forming the aorist, known as *first* and *second* aorist. Verbs have one or the other (in rare cases either is possible). They are differences just of form, not of meaning. First aorist is commoner and will be dealt with first.

• This situation is roughly comparable to English: most verbs add *-ed* to make a simple past tense (*arrived, walked, guarded*), and this can be thought of as equivalent to first aorist. But there exists also another broad category (*ran, sang*) - which roughly equates to second aorist - as well as some that are completely irregular (*went*), again with equivalents in Greek.

• To sum up: the *aorist* is the standard simple past tense, describing an action which happened once (*we walked, they ran*). The *first aorist* is the most common way of forming it, like English *-ed*.

• Like the imperfect, the aorist has the *augment* (epsilon with a smooth breathing) on the beginning of each bit to indicate that it is a past tense.

• The first aorist also normally adds sigma to the stem, like the future tense does.

• The first aorist is also often referred to as the *weak aorist*. This has nothing to do with emphasis or lack of it in its meaning, but simply refers to the fact that the stem needs to be 'strengthened' by the addition of sigma before the endings proper are added.

*first (= weak) aorist:*

 ἐ-παυ-σ-α      I stopped
 ἐ-παυ-σ-ας      you (*sg*) stopped
 ἐ-παυ-σ-ε(ν)*    he/she/it stopped

 ἐ-παυ-σ-αμεν    we stopped
 ἐ-παυ-σ-ατε    you (*pl*) stopped
 ἐ-παυ-σ-αν     they stopped

\* again the movable nu is added (to make pronunciation easier) if the next word starts with a vowel, or if this is the last word in the sentence

• The person endings (the last bit, after the added sigma) therefore are:

| | | |
|---|---|---|
| *singular* | 1 | -α |
| | 2 | -ας |
| | 3 | -ε(ν) |
| | | |
| *plural* | 1 | -αμεν |
| | 2 | -ατε |
| | 3 | -αν |

• The first aorist is easy to spot not only because of the combination of augment and sigma added to the stem, but by the characteristic vowel alpha which occurs in five of the six bits. The first aorist endings are also easy to learn, and to equate to person endings of other tenses:
- second person singular ends in sigma like other tenses you have met
- third person singular ends in epsilon (+ movable nu) like the imperfect
- first person plural ends -μεν like other tenses you have met
- second person plural ends in -τε like other tenses you have met
- third person plural ends in nu like the imperfect

• Adding the sigma to some verbs where the stem ends in a consonant requires an adjustment of spelling similar to the future. For example:

| *present* | *future* | *first (weak) aorist* |
|---|---|---|
| γραφω | γραψω | ἐγραψα |
| διδασκω | διδαξω | ἐδιδαξα |
| διωκω | διωξω | ἐδιωξα |
| λεγω | λεξω | ἐλεξα |
| πειθω | πεισω | ἐπεισα |
| πεμπω | πεμψω | ἐπεμψα |

• The aorist quickly becomes familiar because it is so common. It is the normal tense for telling a story in the past. It is also often contrasted with the imperfect (*we were in the middle of doing X* [imperfect] *when Y happened* [aorist]).

Exercise 4.1 (All first [weak] aorists)

*Translate into English:*
1      ἐλυσα
2      ἐπιστευσαμεν
3      ἐκελευσε(ν)
4      ἐπαυσατε
5      ἐλεξαν
6      ἠκουσα*
7      ἐπεμψας
8      ἐγραψαν
9      ἐδιωξαμεν
10    ἐδιδαξε(ν)

* remember that when the augment is added to a word starting with alpha, the two vowels combine to make eta

Exercise 4.2 (Mixed tenses)

*Translate into English:*
1      ἀγομεν
2      ἐφυλασσον (*two possible answers*)
3      ἐδιωξας
4      ἐφερομεν
5      φευγετε (*two possible answers*)
6      ἐπιστευσα
7      ἐπειθες
8      ἐπεισε(ν)
9      λυσομεν
10    ἐκελευσατε

Exercise 4.3

*Translate into Greek:*
1      You (*pl*) released.
2      He trusted.
3      We ordered.
4      You (*sg*) sent.
5      They wrote.

50

Exercise 4.4 (All verbs first [weak] aorist)

*Translate into English :*
1    ὁ φιλιος δουλος ἐλυσε τους ἱππους.
2    την ἐπιστολην οὐκ ἐγραψα.
3    ὁ ξενος ἐκελευσε τους ἀγγελους φευγειν.
4    τους του στρατηγου λογους ἐν τη ἀγορα ἠκουσαμεν.
5    οἱ δουλοι τους ἱππους προς το στρατοπεδον ἐδιωξαν.
6    οἱ του ἀγγελου λογοι ἐπαυσαν την ναυμαχιαν.
7    ὁ στρατηγος ἐπιστευσε τη του θεου φωνη.
8    ἐδιδαξα τους συμμαχους.
9    ὁ των ξενων ἀγγελος ἐλεξε νεους λογους.
10   οἱ του δημου συμμαχοι ἐπεμψαν τα δωρα.

Exercise 4.5

*Convert these present tense verbs to first (weak) aorist, keeping the same person and number, each time writing the Greek word then translating it:*
1    παυεις
2    κελευομεν
3    λυετε
4    πεμπουσι(ν)
5    γραφω


# Background: Aesop's Fables

Aesop was a Greek slave who lived on the island of Samos in the sixth century BC. We have little reliable information about his life. A fable is usually defined as an anecdote with a moral, in which the characters are animals behaving as men. Fables were very popular in Greece. The most famous ones were attributed to Aesop. He may well have written the original versions of many of them himself, but the collection which has come down to us probably includes many that have been altered, and some that have been added from other sources.

Exercise 4.6

# The Sun and the Frogs

θερος ἠν, και ὁ του Ἡλιου γαμος. ζωον οὐν ἑκαστον ἐχαιρε, και δωρον ἐπεμψεν. ὁ δε βατραχος τοις ἀλλοις ἐλεξε, "μωροι· δια τί χαιρετε; ὁ γαρ Ἡλιος ξηραινει την λιμνην. ἀει οὐν κακα πασχομεν. και νυν ὁ ἡλιος υἱον ἰσως ἑξει. τον κινδυνον οὐ γιγνωσκετε."

5    ὁ μυθος φαινει ὁτι πολλοι ἀνευ αἰτιας χαιρουσιν.

|   |   |   |
|---|---|---|
| | θερος | summer |
| | Ἡλιος | sun |
| | γαμος | wedding |
| | ζωον | animal |
| | ἑκαστος | each |
| | χαιρω | I am happy, I rejoice |
| | βατραχος | frog |
| | ἀλλοι | others |
| | μωρος | fool, foolish |
| | δια τί; | why? |
| | ξηραινω | I dry (something) up |
| | λιμνη | marsh |
| | πασχω | I suffer |
| | υἱος | son |
| | ἰσως | perhaps |
| | ἑξω | *future of* ἐχω |
| 5 | μυθος | story |
| | ὁτι | that |
| | πολλοι | many |
| | ἀνευ | without (+ *gen*) |
| | αἰτια | cause, reason |

Exercise 4.7 (Verbs in mixed tenses)

*Translate into English:*

1    δυο ὡρας ἐγραφον, ἀλλα την ἐπιστολην οὐκ ἐπεμψα.
2    αἱ νικαι ἐπαυσαν τον κινδυνον.
3    διδαξω τε και πεισω τους συμμαχους.
4    προς το δεσμωτηριον ἐβαινομεν.
5    ὁ ἀγγελος ἐδιδαξε τον δημον.
6    ἐπει ἐμενομεν, τους του στρατηγου λογους ἡκουσαμεν.
7    οἱ δουλοι προς τον ποταμον τρεχουσιν.
8    ὁ στρατηγος τον τε στρατον και τα πλοια ἐτασσεν.
9    τους δουλους ἐλυσαμεν.
10   ἡ ἑσπερα την ναυμαχιαν ἐπαυσεν.

        δυο  two
        ἐπει  when

52

Exercise 4.8

# The Frogs and their Ruler (1)

οἱ <u>βατραχοι</u> ἀγγελους προς τον <u>Δια</u> ἐπεμψαν <u>διοτι</u> <u>μοναρχον</u> οὐκ εἰχον*.
οἱ των βατραχων ἀγγελοι ἐλεξαν· "ὦ Ζευ, μοναρχος εἰ των θεων. ἀρα
ἐθελεις μοναρχον τοις βατραχοις παρεχειν;" ὁ Ζευς ἐθαυμαζε, και
<u>ἐρριψε</u> <u>ξυλον</u> εἰς τον ποταμον. οἱ βατραχοι <u>πρωτον</u> μεν φοβον του ξυλου
5   εἰχον, και ἐφευγον. <u>ἐπειτα</u> δε, <u>ἐπει</u> το ξυλον <u>ἀκινητον</u> ἐμενε, πολλακις <u>ἐπι</u>
τῳ ξυλῳ <u>ἐκαθιζον</u>. φοβον γαρ νυν οὐκ εἰχον. ἐλεξαν οὐν τῳ ξυλῳ· "ὦ
ξενε, ἀρα θεος εἰ <u>ἠ</u> ἀνθρωπος ἠ <u>ζῳον</u>;" ἀλλα το ξυλον οὐκ ἐλεξεν.

* the augment added to a stem starting with epsilon already here contracts to form the diphthong ει

|   |   |   |
|---|---|---|
| | βατραχος | frog |
| | Ζευς, *irreg acc* Δια | Zeus |
| | διοτι | because |
| | μοναρχος | ruler |
| | ῥιπτω, *aorist* ἐρριψα | I throw |
| | ξυλον | log of wood |
| | πρωτον | at first |
| 5 | ἐπειτα | then |
| | ἐπει | since, because |
| | ἀκινητος | motionless |
| | ἐπι | (+ *dative*) on |
| | καθιζω | I sit |
| | ἠ | or |
| | ζῳον | animal |

Exercise 4.9

*Give one English derivative from:*
1   μοναρχος
2   ξυλον
3   φοβος
4   ζῳον
5   ἀνθρωπος

Exercise 4.10

*Convert these singular phrases to plural, keeping the same case, then translate:*
1   το ἀκινητον ξυλον
2   του μικρου βατραχου
3   την καλην φωνην
4   τῳ νεῳ νομῳ
5   ὁ σοφος θεος

Exercise 4.11

*Convert these plural phrases to singular, keeping the same case, then translate:*

1    τα καλα δενδρα
2    οἱ κακοι βατραχοι
3    τας νεας οἰκιας
4    τοις ἀνδρειοις συμμαχοις
5    των καλων νικων

Exercise 4.12

# The Frogs and their Ruler (2)

οἱ βατραχοι οὐκ ἠθελον* το ξυλον ὡς μοναρχον ἐχειν, διοτι
ἀκινητον και οὐ χρησιμον ἠν. τους οὐν ἀγγελους προς τον Δια αὐθις
ἐπεμψαν, διοτι ἠθελον τον θεον ἀλλον μοναρχον παρεχειν. οἱ των
βατραχων ἀγγελοι ἐλεξαν· "ὠ Ζευ, οἱ βατραχοι ἐθελουσιν ἀλλον
5    μοναρχον ἐχειν διοτι ὁ πρωτος ἀκινητος και οὐ χρησιμος ἐστιν." ὁ οὐν
Ζευς ὀργῃ ἐπεμψεν ὑδραν τοις βατραχοις. ἡ οὐν ὑδρα μοναρχος των
βατραχων ἠν. ἡ ὑδρα τους βατραχους ἠσθιεν*.

οὐκ ἀει οὐν, ὡς ὁ μυθος φαινει, κακον ἐστι μοναρχον ἀργον ἐχειν.

* the augment added to a stem starting with epsilon already here lengthens the vowel to eta (this is
more common than the contraction to form the diphthong ει which we saw in the previous passage)

| | | |
|---|---|---|
| | βατραχος | frog |
| | ἐθελω | I wish |
| | ξυλον | log of wood |
| | ὡς | as |
| | μοναρχος | ruler |
| | διοτι | because |
| | ἀκινητος | motionless |
| | χρησιμος | useful |
| | Δια | *irregular accusative of* Ζευς |
| | αὐθις | again |
| | ἀλλος | another |
| 5 | πρωτος | first |
| | ὀργη | anger |
| | ὑδρα | hydra, monstrous water-snake |
| | ἐσθιω | I eat |
| | μυθος | story |
| | ἀργος | lazy, inactive |

• Note that Greek has two words for 'story': μυθος tends to be used for a myth (its English
derivative) or fable, λογος for a more factual or historical account.

# Aorist tense (2)

• The alternative way of forming the aorist tense is known as the *second aorist* (or *strong aorist*). This is less common than the first aorist, but a significant number of frequently used verbs form their aorist in this way.

• The difference between the two types of aorist is simply one of *form*, not meaning.

• Like the imperfect and first aorist, the second aorist has the augment (epsilon with a smooth breathing) on the beginning of each bit to indicate that it is a past tense.

• The second aorist uses *exactly the same endings as the imperfect* [-ον, -ες, -ε(ν), -ομεν, -ετε, -ον], but puts them onto a *different stem*.

• This aorist stem is often a *shortened* or *telescoped* version of the present stem:
    e.g.     λαμβανω : present stem λαμβαν- , aorist stem λαβ-
             μανθανω : present stem μανθαν- , aorist stem μαθ-
             φευγω :  present stem φευγ- , aorist stem φυγ-

The aorist stems need to be learned, though when you have seen a few you can often predict them.

• The alternative name *strong aorist* again has nothing to do with emphasis or meaning, but refers to the fact that with this type the stem does not need to be 'strengthened' by the addition of sigma before putting on the endings proper.

*second (= strong) aorist:*
    ἐ-λαβ-ον                I took
    ἐ-λαβ-ες                you (*sg*) took
    ἐ-λαβ-ε(ν)*            he/she/it took

    ἐ-λαβ-ομεν           we took
    ἐ-λαβ-ετε              you (*pl*) took
    ἐ-λαβ-ον               they took

\* again the movable nu is added (to make pronunciation easier) if the next word starts with a vowel, or if this is the last word in the sentence

• Notice that, although the augment and ending are the same, there is no confusion with the imperfect, because of the different stem:
e.g.     ἐ-λαμβαν-ομεν   we were taking           *imperfect*
         ἐ-λαβ-ομεν          we took                   *second (strong) aorist*

• With some verbs the stem is changed more:
e.g.      ἀγω : aorist ἠγαγον            (*aorist stem* ἀγαγ-)*
          πιπτω : aorist ἐπεσον          (*aorist stem* πεσ-)

* Notice here the *reduplication* or repetition of the consonant, comparable to Latin perfect tenses such as *cecidi* (from *cado* = I fall) and *tetigi* (from *tango* = I touch). Also notice again (as we saw with the first aorist of ἀκουω) how, when the augment is added to a word starting with alpha, the two vowels *contract* (i.e. combine) to make eta.

• With a few verbs the aorist stem appears totally unrelated to the present (being originally from a different root: compare English *go, went*). These of course have to be learned:
e.g.     τρεχω : aorist ἐδραμον (aorist stem δραμ-)

• Here are some verbs you have met already with second (strong) aorists:

| *present* | | *aorist* | *aorist stem* |
|---|---|---|---|
| ἀγω | I lead | ἠγαγον | ἀγαγ- |
| εὑρισκω | I find | ηὑρον* | εὑρ- |
| ἐχω | I have | ἐσχον | σχ- |
| λαμβανω | I take | ἐλαβον | λαβ- |
| λειπω | I leave | ἐλιπον | λιπ- |
| μανθανω | I learn | ἐμαθον | μαθ- |
| πιπτω | I fall | ἐπεσον | πεσ- |
| τρεχω | I run | ἐδραμον | δραμ- |
| φευγω | I run away | ἐφυγον | φυγ- |

* Note that when the augment is added to epsilon which is part of a diphthong, this too results in eta here; and that the syllable remains a diphthong (both vowels pronounced together), indicated by the breathing being on the second letter.

• Note also that λεγω (*I say*), in addition to a first (weak) aorist ἐλεξα, also has a second (strong) aorist εἰπον, from a different root but with the same meaning (and more commonly found). The aorist stem of this is εἰπ- (unusually not changing to remove the augment).

Exercise 4.13 (All second [strong] aorists)

*Translate into English:*
1     ἐλαβετε
2     ἐφυγομεν
3     ἐμαθον (*two possible answers*)
4     ἐλιπες
5     ἠγαγε(ν)
6     ἐδραμον (*two possible answers*)
7     ἐπεσετε
8     ηὑρομεν
9     ἐσχον (*two possible answers*)
10    ἐλαβες

Exercise 4.14 (Imperfect and second [strong] aorist)

*Each time, state whether the verb is imperfect or aorist, then translate into English:*
1        ἐλαμβανες
2        ἐλαβες
3        ἐμανθανομεν
4        ἐμαθε(ν)
5        ἠγετε
6        ἠγαγον  *(two possible answers)*
7        ἐφυγομεν
8        ἐφευγες
9        ἐλιπον  *(two possible answers)*
10      ἐλειπε(ν)

Exercise 4.15

*Translate into Greek:*
1        We left.
2        They took.
3        You (*sg*) learned.
4        You (*pl*) ran away.
5        I led.

Exercise 4.16 (Mixed tenses: imperfect, first [weak] and second [strong] aorist)

*Translate into English:*
1        ἐδραμε(ν)
2        ἐφυλασσομεν
3        ἐλαβετε
4        ἠκουσαν
5        ἐφερον  *(two possible answers)*
6        ηὑρετε
7        ἐγραψατε
8        ἐφευγον  *(two possible answers)*
9        ἐσχες
10      ἐπεσετε

Exercise 4.17 (All verbs second [strong] aorist)

*Translate into English:*
1        οἱ ἀνδρειοι συμμαχοι οὐκ ἐφυγον.
2        ἐμαθομεν τους των ξενων νομους.
3        ὁ δουλος εἰς τον ποταμον ἐπεσεν.
4        τα ὁπλα ἐν τῳ ἱερῳ ἐλιπον. (*two possible answers*)
5        ὁ στρατηγος εἰς το στρατοπεδον ἐδραμεν.

• Here are three new common verbs with second (strong) aorists, illustrating the various ways in which the aorist stem (always *different* from the present stem, in one way or another) can be formed:

1  (*stem shortened or telescoped*):
     βαλλω               I throw: *aorist* ἐβαλον (*aorist stem* βαλ-)

2  (*stem changed more, but still related*):
     πασχω               I suffer: *aorist* ἐπαθον (*aorist stem* παθ-)

3  (*stem completely different, from separate root*):
     ἐσθιω               I eat: *aorist* ἐφαγον (*aorist stem* φαγ-)

• English derivatives from verbs with second (strong) aorists quite often come from the aorist stem rather than the present: e.g. *mathematics, pathology.*

• The extent to which the stem changes for the second (strong) aorist of course affects how similar or otherwise it is to the imperfect. If the stem just shortens slightly, the forms for the two tenses may differ only by one letter (e.g. βαλλω : imperfect ἐβαλλον, second [strong] aorist ἐβαλον). If however the aorist stem is from a different root, the forms for the two tenses will be completely different (though with the same endings), because the imperfect uses the present stem (e.g. τρεχω : imperfect ἐτρεχον, second [strong] aorist ἐδραμον).

• To recap: alternative names for the two types of aorist are *weak* (for *first*) and *strong* (for *second*). The logic of these is that the *weak* aorist does not have a distinctive stem and so needs to have its identity as an aorist strengthened by distinctive endings; the *strong* aorist does have its own stem, and so does not need this reinforcement. These terms refer only to the *formation* of the aorist tense, and do not imply any difference of emphasis in the *meaning*. The terms *first* and *second* avoid any such impression, and are now more commonly used.

## Revision checkpoint

*Make sure you know*
• what the aorist tense is used for, and the two main ways of forming it:
     (1)   first (weak) aorist: augment, present stem, normally plus sigma, then the distinctive endings (mostly including alpha): -α, -ας, -ε(ν), -αμεν, -ατε, -αν
     (2)   second (strong) aorist: augment, distinctive aorist stem, then the same endings as the imperfect:  -ον, -ες, -ε(ν), -ομεν, -ετε, -ον

• Here are all the second (strong) aorists you have met so far. Notice the various ways in which the aorist stem differs from the present:

| present | present stem | meaning | aorist | aorist stem |
|---------|--------------|---------|--------|-------------|
| ἀγω | ἀγ- | I lead | ἠγαγον | ἀγαγ- |
| βαλλω | βαλλ- | I throw | ἐβαλον | βαλ- |
| ἐσθιω | ἐσθι- | I eat | ἐφαγον | φαγ- |
| εὑρισκω | εὑρισκ- | I find | ηὑρον | εὑρ- |
| ἐχω | ἐχ- | I have | ἐσχον | σχ- |
| λαμβανω | λαμβαν- | I take | ἐλαβον | λαβ- |
| λεγω | λεγ- | I speak, I say | εἰπον | εἰπ- |
| λειπω | λειπ- | I leave | ἐλιπον | λιπ- |
| μανθανω | μανθαν- | I learn | ἐμαθον | μαθ- |
| πασχω | πασχ- | I suffer | ἐπαθον | παθ- |
| πιπτω | πιπτ- | I fall | ἐπεσον | πεσ- |
| τρεχω | τρεχ- | I run | ἐδραμον | δραμ- |
| φευγω | φευγ- | I run away | ἐφυγον | φυγ- |

Exercise 4.18

*Convert these present tense verbs to second (strong) aorist, keeping the same person and number, each time writing the Greek word then translating it:*
1    βαλλετε
2    ἐσθιει
3    λαμβανεις
4    λειπουσι(ν)
5    πιπτει

Exercise 4.19

# Zeus and the Tortoise

ὁ <u>Ζευς</u> τοις <u>ζῳοις</u> <u>δειπνον</u> <u>παρεσχεν</u>. ἡ δε <u>χελωνη</u> <u>μονη</u> οὐ <u>παρην</u>. ὁ οὖν
Ζευς ἐθαυμασεν. <u>τη</u> δε <u>ὑστεραιᾳ</u> εἰπε τη χελωνη "<u>δια τί</u> <u>συ</u> μονη οὐ
παρησθα;" "οἰκια <u>φιλη</u>, οἰκια <u>ἀριστη</u>" εἰπεν ἡ χελωνη. <u>ἐπειτα</u> δε ὁ Ζευς
<u>δια</u> <u>ὀργην</u> ἐκελευσε την χελωνην την οἰκιαν ἀει φερειν.

| | |
|---|---|
| Ζευς Διος ὁ* | Zeus |
| ζῳον -ου το | animal |
| δειπνον -ου το | dinner |
| παρεχω παρεσχον | I provide |
| χελωνη -ης ἡ | tortoise |
| μονος -η -ον | alone, only |
| παρειμι imperfect παρην | I am present (formed like εἰμι) |
| τη ὑστεραιᾳ | on the next day |
| δια τί; | why? |
| συ | you (sg) |
| φιλος -η -ον | dear |
| ἀριστος -η -ον | best |
| ἐπειτα | then |
| δια | through, on account of (+ acc) |
| ὀργη -ης ἡ | anger |

*from this point onwards, vocabulary for passages will usually be given with the following grammar
details:

> nominative, genitive, and article (to show gender) for nouns
> present and aorist (first person singulars) for verbs
> masculine, feminine, and neuter (nominative singulars) for adjectives
> case taken by prepositions

# Gender and declension (1)

• As in Latin, there is a broad correlation in Greek between gender and declension: most
words in the first declension are feminine; and in the second declension most are masculine,
with a distinctive variant type that is neuter. But there are exceptions. In Latin, second
declension feminine words are very few indeed (they include names of trees, e.g. *fagus* =
beech). In Greek there are rather more, and they include some very common words. Here are
four:

| | |
|---|---|
| βιβλος | book |
| νησος | island |
| νοσος | disease |
| ὁδος | road, journey |

They decline exactly like masculine second declension nouns, but of course have the
feminine forms of the article and of adjectives with them. (Because these must *agree* in
number, gender, and case - not necessarily have identical endings or 'rhyme'.)

Hence e.g.              την καλην βιβλον
                        τας κακας νοσους
(Contrast more straightforward examples such as:
                        την καλην κωμην
                        τας κακας οἰκιας
                        τον καλον ἱππον
                        τους κακους νομους
where the nouns have the more typical gender for their declensions.)

Exercise 4.20

*Translate into English:*
1       ηὑρομεν τας νεας βιβλους.
2       ὁ δουλος κακην νοσον ἐχει.
3       ἐν τη ὁδῳ κινδυνος ἠν.
4       οἱ ξενοι ἐκ της νησου ἐφυγον.
5       ἐλιπομεν τας μικρας νησους.

# Gender and declension (2)

• Just as we saw that there are some feminine nouns in the second declension, there are also some masculine ones in the first declension. As in Latin, these arc mostly words denoting male occupations or roles (*sailor*, *poet* in both languages; in Greek also *judge, young man* and others).

• This time some small changes are made to the declension. Masculine nouns of the first declension in the nominative singular add sigma to what the ending would be for a feminine noun. So, corresponding to feminine nouns like τιμη are the masculine ones:

| | |
|---|---|
| κριτης | judge |
| ναυτης | sailor |
| ποιητης | poet |
| πολιτης | citizen |
| στρατιωτης | soldier |

Like τιμη, these have eta in the ending because the stem ends in a consonant. But there are also a few corresponding to χωρα (where the stem ends in a vowel or rho), with alpha in the ending:

νεανιας                  young man

• Probably because the nominative would with these nouns otherwise be the same as the genitive, the genitive changes to -ου: i.e. masculine nouns in the first declension *borrow* the genitive ending of the more naturally masculine second declension (like λογος).

61

Hence the singular declensions are:

| | | |
|------|------------|-------------|
| *nom* | κριτ-ης* | νεανι-ας* |
| *acc* | κριτ-ην | νεανι-αν |
| *gen* | κριτ-ου | νεανι-ου |
| *dat* | κριτ-η | νεανι-α |

\* the vocative for both types ends in alpha: κριτ-α (long alpha), νεανι-α (short alpha)

• In the plural they have the same endings as any first declension noun:
-αι, -ας, -ων, -αις

• These nouns must of course have the masculine forms of the article and of adjectives (because these must *agree* in number, gender, and case).

Exercise 4.21

*Change from singular to plural or vice versa, keeping the same case; write the new version of the Greek, then translate it into English:*
1       ὁ ἀγαθος ποιητης
2       οἱ ἀνδρειοι στρατιωται
3       του σοφου κριτου
4       τους κακους νεανιας*
5       τον φιλιον ναυτην
        \* note that the accusative plural here has the same ending as the nominative singular

Exercise 4.22

*Translate into English:*
1       ἐπιστευσαμεν τῳ κριτη.
2       ἀκουε τους του στρατηγου λογους, ὦ στρατιωτα.
3       ὁ νεανιας προς την οἰκιαν ἐδραμεν.
4       οἱ ἀνδρειοι ναυται οὐκ ἐφυγον.
5       οἱ πολιται ἐν τη ἐκκλησια ἠσαν.
6       ὁ ποιητης σοφος.
7       τους στρατιωτας τους ἀνδρειους θαυμαζομεν.
8       ὁ των νεανιων διδασκαλος οὐκ ἐστι πολιτης.
9       ὁ στρατηγος τους νεους στρατιωτας ἐτασσεν.
10      τους τε ναυτας και τους στρατιωτας πεμπετε, ὦ πολιται.

Exercise 4.23

*Translate into Greek:*
1       The brave young men ran to the village.
2       The judge's house is new.
3       The soldier fell into the river.
4       We sent the sailors to the prison.
5       You (*sg*) trusted the wise citizens.

Exercise 4.24 (Revision)

*Translate into English:*

1   ὁ σοφος κριτης ἐπιστολην ἐγραψεν.
2   οἱ ἱπποι οἱ του στρατηγου καλοι εἰσιν.
3   τους νεανιας προς την κωμην ἐπεμψα.
4   νεαν βουλην νυν ἐχω.
5   οἱ ναυται τα πλοια ἐλιπον.
6   οἱ στρατιωται τα ὁπλα ἐκ του στρατοπεδου ἐλαβον.
7   τασσε τον στρατον, ὠ στρατηγε.
8   οἱ πολιται τον σοφον κριτην ἐθαυμαζον.
9   οἱ στρατιωται τας πυλας ἐφυλασσον.
10  ὁ ναυτης ἐκ του πλοιου ἐπεσεν.

Exercise 4.25

*Give one English derivative from:*

1   κριτης
2   ἐμαθον
3   ναυτης
4   ἐφυγον
5   στρατηγος

# Gender and declension (3)

• You have now seen almost all forms of first and second declension nouns. There remain a couple of oddments in the first declension.

• Both the feminine and the masculine nouns in the first declension normally have eta or alpha in the singular endings, according to how the stem ends: eta after a consonant, alpha after a vowel or rho. Hence:

| | |
|---|---|
| *feminine* | τιμη, χωρα |
| *masculine* | κριτης, νεανιας |

But among feminine nouns there are a few exceptions:

(1) κορη = *girl* declines like τιμη, even though stem ends in rho.

(2) Some nouns are exceptions the other way round, i.e. they have alpha as the nominative ending even though the stem ends in a consonant (usually sigma). But in this case they revert after the accusative to the eta that would be more natural after a consonant:

| | | |
|---|---|---|
| *nom* | θαλασσ-α | sea |
| *acc* | θαλασσ-αν | |
| *gen* | θαλασσ-ης | |
| *dat* | θαλασσ-η | |

63

Another common noun that declines like this is μουσα = *Muse* (goddess of poetic inspiration).

• These various exceptions and minor changes may seem confusing, but the variants within first declension singulars (all plurals are the same, and straightforward) can easily be represented by a table of endings:

| | | | | |
|---|---|---|---|---|
| *nom* | -η | *or* | -α | (adds -ς if masculine) |
| *acc* | -ην | *or* | -αν | |
| *gen* | -ης | *or* | -ας | (changes to -ου if masculine) |
| *dat* | -η | *or* | -α | |

# Revision overview of first and second declension nouns:

*first declension:*

| | | feminine: | | | masculine: | |
|---|---|---|---|---|---|---|
| | | honour | country | sea | judge | young man |
| sg | nom | τιμ-η | χωρ-α | θαλασσ-α | κριτ-ης | νεανι-ας |
| | acc | τιμ-ην | χωρ-αν | θαλασσ-αν | κριτ-ην | νεανι-αν |
| | gen | τιμ-ης | χωρ-ας | θαλασσ-ης | κριτ-ου | νεανι-ου |
| | dat | τιμ-η | χωρ-α | θαλασσ-η | κριτ-η | νεανι-α |
| | | | | | (*voc* κριτ-α) | (*voc* νεανι-α) |
| pl | nom | τιμ-αι | χωρ-αι | θαλασσ-αι | κριτ-αι | νεανι-αι |
| | acc | τιμ-ας | χωρ-ας | θαλασσ-ας | κριτ-ας | νεανι-ας |
| | gen | τιμ-ων | χωρ-ων | θαλασσ-ων | κριτ-ων | νεανι-ων |
| | dat | τιμ-αις | χωρ-αις | θαλασσ-αις | κριτ-αις | νεανι-αις |

*second declension:*

| | | masculine:* | neuter: |
|---|---|---|---|
| | | word | gift |
| sg | nom | λογ-ος | δωρ-ον |
| | acc | λογ-ον | δωρ-ον |
| | gen | λογ-ου | δωρ-ου |
| | dat | λογ-ῳ | δωρ-ῳ |
| | | (*voc* λογ-ε) | |
| pl | nom | λογ-οι | δωρ-α |
| | acc | λογ-ους | δωρ-α |
| | gen | λογ-ων | δωρ-ων |
| | dat | λογ-οις | δωρ-οις |

\* feminine nouns such as βιβλος = *book* are identical in declension

Exercise 4.26

*Translate into English:*

1    ὁ καλος ἱππος ἐκ της θαλασσης ἐδραμεν.
2    ἡ κορη ἡ καλη ἐδιωξε τον δουλον.
3    την νεαν βιβλον νυν ἐχω.
4    ὁ ποιητης την της μουσης σοφιαν μανθανει.
5    τα τε δωρα και τας βιβλους ἐκ της οἰκιας ἐλαβομεν.


# Compound verbs

• Many of the common prepositions can also be used as prefixes to form compound verbs:

e.g.    προς = towards

| | |
|---|---|
| *as preposition* | προς την θαλασσαν<br>towards the sea |
| *as prefix* | προστρεχειν<br>to run towards |

|  |  |
|---|---|
| ἐκ = out of | |
| *as preposition* | ἐκ του στρατοπεδου<br>out of the camp |
| *as prefix* | ἐκβαινω<br>I go out |

It is usually easy to work out the meaning of a compound, and it is not necessary to learn them all individually.

• Greek often uses the same prefix/preposition twice, for slight extra emphasis:
    ἐκβαινει ἐκ του στρατοπεδου.
*literally*
    He goes out out of the camp.
but in fact just
    He goes out of the camp.

• It is also possible however to give two separate pieces of information, one by a prefix and another by a preposition:
    ἐκβαινει εἰς την ὁδον.
    He goes out (*implying from his house, or wherever he is*) into the road.

• Sometimes Greek uses compounds where they are not strictly necessary, and some verbs are normally found only in compound form. You have met two:
    ἀποθνησκω            I die
    ἀποκτεινω            I kill
You could explain the prefix as implying 'away from life', but in practice it is hardly noticed.

65

• When compound verbs form their past tenses, the augment goes after the prefix:
προστρεχω                                 I run towards
προσεδραμον                             I ran towards

• ἐκ either as a preposition or a prefix always changes to ἐξ before a vowel. Hence e.g.
ἐξαγω = *I lead out*. If the verb stem starts with a consonant, the prefix is ἐκ- in the present tense, but changes to ἐξ- in the imperfect and aorist, because the augment has introduced a vowel. Hence:

ἐκβαινεις                                you (*sg*) go out
ἐξεβαινες                               you (*sg*) were going out

• Similarly ἀπο- changes to ἀπ- before a vowel, whether because the verb stem starts with a vowel (e.g. ἀπαγω = I lead away) or because the augment is inserted: hence
ἀποτρεχομεν                           we run away
ἀπεδραμομεν                          we ran away

• The aorist of ἀποθνησκω is ἀπεθανον (second [strong] aorist), and the aorist of ἀποκτεινω is ἀπεκτεινα (first [weak] aorist; without the usual sigma, but otherwise with the normal endings).

Exercise 4.27

*Translate into English:*
1        ὁ νεανιας ἐξαγει τον ἱππον.
2        ὁ δουλος ἐκ της οἰκιας ἐξεδραμεν.
3        αἱ κοραι προς το της θεας ἱερον προσεβαινον.
4        ὁ ἀγγελος εἰς τον ποταμον εἰσεπεσεν.
5        ὁ διδασκαλος ἀποβαλλει τας βιβλους.
6        ὁ στρατηγος τους δουλους ἀπεκτεινεν.
7        την ἐπιστολην προς την ἐκκλησιαν προσεπεμψα.
8        οἱ πολιται εἰς την ἀγοραν ἐκτρεχουσιν.
9        ὁ ποιητης ὁ μεγιστος ἀπεθανεν.
10      οἱ συμμαχοι το ναυτικον προς την νησον προσηγαγον.

Exercise 4.28

*Translate into Greek:*
1        You (*pl*) go away.
2        We run towards the house.
3        They ran out.
4        He died.
5        We were throwing away the books.

# Revision checkpoint

*Make sure you know:*
- how gender and declension relate to each other
- first-declension masculine nouns like κριτης and νεανιας
- first-declension feminine nouns like θαλασσα
- how these less common forms fit into the overall pattern of the first and second declensions
- how compound verbs work
- the relation of prefixes and prepositions

Exercise 4.29

*✻ test day piece*

## The Stag and the Lion

A thirsty stag came to a spring. After drinking he noticed his own reflection in the water. He was proud of his magnificent antlers, but dissatisfied with his spindly legs. At that moment a lion appeared and ran towards him. The stag started to run away.

ὁ ἐλαφος, διοτι ταχιστα τρεχειν οἱος τ' ἠν, ῥαδιως ἐξεφυγεν. και μεχρι
οὐκ ἠν δενδρα ἐν τοις ἀγροις, ὁ λεων τον ἐλαφον οὐκ ἐλαβεν. ἀλλα ἐπει
εἰς την ὑλην εἰσεδραμον, ὁ ἐλαφος ἐν κινδυνῳ ἠν. οἱ γαρ των δενδρων
κλαδοι ἐνεποδισαν τα του ἐλαφου κερατα. ὁ οὐν ἐλαφος οὐκετι οἱος τ' ἠν
5   τρεχειν. ὁ δε λεων προσεδραμεν. ὁ οὐν ἐλαφος προ του θανατου εἰπε
"προτερον μεν ἐθαυμασα τα κερατα, οὐ τα κωλα. νυν δε τα κερατα ἐμε
ἀπεκτεινεν".

ὁ μυθος φαινει ὁτι ἐν κινδυνῳ ῥαδιον ἐστι φιλοις κακοις πιστευειν.

|  |  |  |
|---|---|---|
| | ἐλαφος -ου ὁ | stag |
| | ταχιστα | very fast |
| | οἱος τ' εἰμι | I am able (*formed as adjective* + εἰμι) |
| | ῥαδιος -α -ον | easy |
| | ἐκφευγω ἐξεφυγον | I escape |
| | μεχρι | as long as, while |
| | ἀγρος -ου ὁ | field |
| | λεων ὁ | lion |
| | ὑλη -ης ἡ | forest |
| | κλαδος -ου ὁ | branch |
| | ἐμποδιζω ἐνεποδισα | obstruct, get in the way of |
| | κερατα -ων τα | antlers |
| | οὐκετι | no longer |
| 5 | προ | before |
| | κωλον -ου το | leg |
| | ἐμε | me |

67

# Vocabulary checklist for Chapter 4

*Verbs you have met already are normally given here with their aorist. (Irregular aorists are also given alphabetically in the vocabulary in the back of the book.)*

| | |
|---|---|
| ἀγω ἠγαγον | I lead |
| ἀποβαλλω ἀπεβαλον | I throw away |
| βαλλω ἐβαλον | I throw |
| βιβλος -ου ἡ | book |
| γραφω ἐγραψα | I write |
| δειπνον -ου το | dinner, supper |
| διδασκω ἐδιδαξα | I teach |
| διωκω ἐδιωξα | I chase |
| δυο | two |
| εἰσπιπτω εἰσεπεσον | I fall into |
| ἐκβαινω | I go out |
| ἐκτρεχω ἐξεδραμον | I run out |
| ἐξαγω ἐξηγαγον | I lead out |
| ἐπει | when, since |
| ἐπειτα | then, next |
| ἐσθιω ἐφαγον | I eat |
| εὑρισκω ηὑρον | I find |
| ἐχω ἐσχον | I have |
| ζῳον -ου το | animal |
| θαλασσα -ης ἡ | sea |
| κελευω ἐκελευσα | I order |
| κορη -ης ἡ | girl |
| κριτης -ου ὁ | judge |
| λαμβανω ἐλαβον | I take |
| λεγω ἐλεξα *or* εἰπον | I say, I speak |
| λειπω ἐλιπον | I leave |
| λυω ἐλυσα | I release |
| μακρος -α -ον | long |
| μανθανω ἐμαθον | I learn |
| μεγιστος -η -ον | very big |
| μετα | (+ *acc*) after |
| μουσα -ης ἡ | Muse (*goddess of poetic inspiration*) |
| μυθος -ου ὁ | story (myth, fable) |
| ναυτης -ου ὁ | sailor |
| νεανιας -ου ὁ | young man |
| νησος -ου ἡ | island |
| νοσος -ου ἡ | disease, illness |
| ὁδος -ου ἡ | road, way |
| πασχω ἐπαθον | I suffer |
| πειθω ἐπεισα | I persuade |
| πεμπω ἐπεμψα | I send |

| | |
|---|---|
| πιπτω ἐπεσον | I fall |
| πιστευω ἐπιστευσα | I trust, I believe (+ *dat*) |
| ποιητης -ου ὁ | poet |
| πολιτης -ου ὁ | citizen |
| προσαγω προσηγαγον | I lead to(wards) |
| προσβαινω | I go to(wards) |
| προσπεμπω προσεπεμψα | I send to(wards) |
| προστρεχω προσεδραμον | I run to(wards) |
| πρωτον | first, at first |
| στρατιωτης -ου ὁ | soldier |
| τρεχω ἐδραμον | I run |
| φευγω ἐφυγον | I run away |
| φυλασσω ἐφυλαξα | I guard |
| χρησιμος -η -ον | useful |
| ὡς | as |

(56 words)

# Chapter 5

## Accents

Accents (acute ´, grave `, and circumflex ˆ) were not used in the period when most of the famous Greek authors lived but were a later development. They have not been used so far in this book. Greek texts are however by long tradition normally printed with accents, and they are introduced from this point onwards (you will already have noticed them in the Greek-to-English vocabulary at the back of the book).

Accents were devised about 200 BC as an aid to pronunciation, originally indicating pitch (acute high, grave low, circumflex falling from high to low). This is very difficult for English speakers to reproduce. Later they were (all) taken as *stress* accents. This *can* be reproduced easily enough, but the tradition in Britain since the seventeenth century has been to stress Greek words of several syllables on the same principle as Latin ones: on the next-to-last (penultimate) syllable if that is *long* or *heavy*, on the third from the end (antepenultimate) if the penultimate is *short* or *light*. Hence ἄνθρωπος would traditionally be stressed on the penultimate (*di-DUM-di*), ἀγαθός on the antepenultimate (here first) syllable (*DUM-di-di*). In both cases this is different from where the accent is written. Like many traditions, the British pronunciation has little logical justification. If you wish to be in the forefront of reform, you can pronounce Greek words with the stress on the accented syllable: ἄνθρωπος as *DUM-di-di*, ἀγαθός as *di-di-DUM*. This is done in many continental countries, and has the effect of making classical Greek sound more like the modern language which is its descendant. On the other hand, since stressing the accented syllable is still a compromise (a second-best representation of the original *pitch* accent), you may prefer to stick with tradition. The important thing as always is to be clear and consistent.

• Full knowledge of accents is not a high priority for beginners with limited time. The rules governing their use are beyond the scope of this book. You should not at this stage attempt to include accents when you translate English-to-Greek sentences.

• Accents sometimes differentiate otherwise identical words. In such cases, attention is drawn to them in this book. (These instances however are few, and ambiguity is usually avoided anyway by the context.)

## Third declension

• This is the only remaining category of nouns (there is no fourth or fifth declension). The third declension includes masculine, feminine and neuter nouns. There is no difference in declension between masculine and feminine ones. Neuter nouns in this declension resemble those in the second declension by having nominative and accusative the same, and by having nominative and accusative plural ending in alpha (this is also of course similar to Latin neuter nouns both of second declension - e.g. *bellum* - and of third - e.g. *nomen*).

• A list of third declension nouns in the nominative singular shows a wide variety of endings (the article is added to show gender, as it usually is in wordlists):

| | | |
|---|---|---|
| γέρων | ὁ | old man |
| γίγας | ὁ | giant |

70

| | | |
|---|---|---|
| νύξ | ἡ | night |
| ὄνομα | τό | name |
| σῶμα | τό | body |
| φύλαξ | ὁ | guard |

But the more important part is the *genitive stem* (which is not necessarily visible in the nominative: this stem needs to be learned, though - as for example with second [strong] aorist stems of verbs - there are recurrent patterns, and clues from English derivatives). You then just need to learn the endings and add them to the stem. The last noun listed above has φύλακ-ος as its genitive (-ος is the genitive sigular ending), i.e. its genitive stem is φυλακ-, and it would normally be listed as:

φύλαξ -ακος    ὁ    (*abbreviated form of* φύλαξ φύλακος)

Understanding the principle avoids the necessity to learn several different types of third declension noun separately. (It is usual to list nouns of any declension by giving the nominative and genitive, but this is particularly important for third declension).

• The pattern of endings for third declension is:

| sg | nom | (wide range of possibilities) | |
|---|---|---|---|
| | acc | stem + α | for masc and fem; same as nom if neuter |
| | gen | stem + ος | |
| | dat | stem + ι | |

| pl | nom | stem + ες | for masc and fem; stem + α if neuter |
|---|---|---|---|
| | acc | stem + ας | for masc and fem; stem + α if neuter |
| | gen | stem + ων | |
| | dat | stem + σι(ν)* | |

\* movable nu is added if the next word starts with a vowel, or if this is the last word in the sentence

• Notice some further broad similarities to Latin: the principle of using the genitive stem (compare e.g. *rex, regis*: stem *reg-*); a comparable ending in genitive singular (-ος where Latin has *-is*); similar endings in dative singular and in masculine/feminine nominative plural (though Greek has a different accusative).

• For a typical masculine noun this gives:

φύλαξ -ακος ὁ = guard (stem φυλακ-)

| sg | nom | φύλαξ |
|---|---|---|
| | acc | φύλακ-α |
| | gen | φύλακ-ος |
| | dat | φύλακ-ι |

| pl | nom | φύλακ-ες |
|---|---|---|
| | acc | φύλακ-ας |
| | gen | φυλάκ-ων |
| | dat | φύλαξι(ν)* |

\* the dative plural represents φυλακ-σι(ν), because as usual kappa followed by sigma produces xi

71

• And for a typical neuter noun:

σῶμα -ατος τό = body (stem σωματ-)

| sg | nom | σῶμα |
|----|-----|------|
| | acc | σῶμα |
| | gen | σώματ-ος |
| | dat | σώματ-ι |

| pl | nom | σώματ-α |
|----|-----|---------|
| | acc | σώματ-α |
| | gen | σωμάτ-ων |
| | dat | σώμασι* |

* here the dative plural represents σωματ-σι, with the tau dropped to aid pronunciation

• Here again is the list of nouns, showing genitive and stem:

| | | | | |
|---|---|---|---|---|
| γέρων -οντος | ὁ | old man | (stem γεροντ-) |
| γίγας -αντος | ὁ | giant | (stem γιγαντ-) |
| νύξ νυκτός | ἡ | night | (stem νυκτ-) |
| ὄνομα -ατος | τό | name | (stem ὀνοματ-) |
| σῶμα -ατος | τό | body | (stem σωματ-) |
| φύλαξ -ακος | ὁ | guard | (stem φυλακ-) |

• Notice the convention that monosyllabic nouns such as νύξ usually have their genitive written out in full in a wordlist.

Exercise 5.1

*Give the Greek for the following, with the appropriate form of the article (take care with the gender). Example:*

The guards (*nominative*)          *answer:* οἱ φύλακες

1        The giant (*accusative*)
2        Of the old men (*genitive*)
3        The nights (*accusative*)
4        For the name (*dative*)
5        The body (*accusative*)

• Here are two of the main types of third declension noun. Notice how they follow the pattern described above.

γέρων -οντος ὁ = old man (stem γεροντ-)

| sg | nom | γέρων | (voc γέρον) |
| | acc | γέροντ-α | |
| | gen | γέροντ-ος | |
| | dat | γέροντ-ι | |
| | | | |
| pl | nom | γέροντ-ες | |
| | acc | γέροντ-ας | |
| | gen | γερόντ-ων | |
| | dat | γέρουσι(ν)* | |

* Again there is an adjustment to the dative plural in the interests of pronunciation. This represents γεροντ-σι(ν). The contracted form resembles the third person plural ending of a verb e.g. παυ-ουσι(ν), and this is not just coincidence, because the verb form similarly represents an original παυ-οντι - compare e.g. *portant* in Latin - altered over time in pronunciation.

γίγας -αντος ὁ = giant (stem γιγαντ-)

| sg | nom | γίγας | |
| | acc | γίγαντ-α | |
| | gen | γίγαντ-ος | |
| | dat | γίγαντ-ι | |
| | | | |
| pl | nom | γίγαντ-ες | |
| | acc | γίγαντ-ας | |
| | gen | γιγάντ-ων | |
| | dat | γίγασι(ν)* | |

* A similar thing happens again. This represents γιγαντ-σι(ν), adjusted in the interests of pronunciation.

• The vocative singular is for many third-declension nouns the same as the nominative. Where it has a special form (as with γέρον), this is usually a shortened version of the nominative (or of the stem): a long vowel becomes short, or a final consonant is dropped.

• The dative plural is the only part of a third declension noun that cannot always be predicted exactly, given the stem and gender. But even the dative plural often can be predicted once you have seen a few. The nominative singular can give a clue to it:

| | φύλαξ | becomes | φύλαξι(ν) |
| | γίγας | becomes | γίγασι(ν) |
| Similarly: | | | |
| | νύξ | becomes | νύξι(ν) |

• The -κτσ- in the original νυκτ-σι(ν) ends up as xi, just as the -κσ- in the original φυλακ-σι(ν) does. Similarly, the -ντσ- in the original γιγαντ-σι(ν) ends up as sigma, just as the -τσ- in the original σωματ-σι(ν) does. Simply trying to pronounce the stem plus the dative plural ending will often help work out the contracted form.

• Third declension nouns, like any others, must of course agree with the article and with adjectives in number, gender, and case.

Exercise 5.2

*Translate into English:*

| | |
|---|---|
| 1 | οἱ ἀνδρεῖοι φύλακες τὸν ποταμὸν ἐφύλασσον. |
| 2 | διώκετε τὸν γίγαντα, ὦ ναῦται. |
| 3 | ἐμάθομεν τὰ τῶν θεῶν ὀνόματα. |
| 4 | ὁ γέρων ὁ σοφὸς ἐδίδαξε τοὺς νεανίας. |
| 5 | φόβον τῆς νυκτὸς οὐκ ἔχομεν. |
| 6 | δύο νύκτας ἐν κινδύνῳ ἦμεν. |
| 7 | οἱ γίγαντες πρὸς τὴν θάλασσαν προσέδραμον. |
| 8 | ἐκέλευσα τὸν δοῦλον δεῖπνον τοῖς γέρουσι παρέχειν. |
| 9 | τὸ τοῦ γίγαντος σῶμα μέγιστον ἦν. |
| 10 | ὁ ποιητὴς τοὺς τῶν γερόντων λόγους ἀκούει. |

# Revision checkpoint

*Make sure you know:*
• how the third declension works (use of the stem; neuter variants; adjustments in the dative plural)

# Background: Homer and the *Odyssey*

As we saw in Chapter 1, Homer probably lived in the eighth century BC, just after the Greek alphabet had been introduced. Drawing on a vast stock of stories that had been transmitted orally for perhaps 400 years, he was enabled - and no doubt inspired - by the newly available medium of writing to compose epics (long poems recounting heroic deeds) of a length and complexity unknown before.

The *Iliad* deals with part of the final year of the ten-year war fought by the Greeks against Troy. According to the story, the purpose was to win back Helen, wife of the Greek Menelaus (whose brother Agamemnon led the expedition). Helen had been seized by the Trojan prince Paris (after Aphrodite had promised him the most beautiful woman in the world, and by that bribe beaten Hera and Athene in a beauty contest judged by him). This is of course the stuff of myth. There may well have been a real Trojan War, but its cause is likely to have been access to the Black Sea for trade. (Troy was crucially sited on the route, and in a position to tax passing ships; and the multiple destructions of the city revealed by archaeology suggest it was unpopular.) Homer is not an historian, but he is a supreme storyteller. He deliberately limits himself to one part of the story, for concentrated effect; but he manages to give us a sense of the whole war.

Many stories also dealt with the homecomings of the victorious Greeks. Again Homer concentrates: Odysseus is made representative not only of his comrades, but in a sense also of everyone in their journey through life. (It cannot be proved that both epics are by the same author, but the *Odyssey* has many features in common with the *Iliad*, and certainly was written to follow it, assuming the audience's knowledge of it.) Much of the *Odyssey* consists of a flashback. Odysseus is near the end of adventures which lasted almost as long as the war itself. Just before his return to his home island of Ithaca, he is being entertained by the hospitable Phaeacians, at whose court he recounts his earlier experiences. This device enables Homer to use the supernatural with more freedom, because we can always take refuge in the conclusion that stories have been improved in the telling. The adventures of Odysseus and his men in the cave of the Cyclops form one of the most famous episodes in the *Odyssey*. Some 250 versions of this story (or uncannily similar stories of independent origin) have been found in different parts of the world.

Exercise 5.3

# The Cyclops (1)

ὁ πόλεμος μακρὸς ἦν, ἀλλὰ μετὰ δέκα ἐνιαυτοὺς οἱ Ἀχαιοὶ τὴν Τροίαν ἔλαβον. μετὰ δὲ τὸν πόλεμον ὁ τ'* Ὀδυσσεὺς καὶ οἱ ἑταῖροι μακρὰν ὁδὸν ἐν τοῖς πλοίοις ἔσχον. ἐν δὲ τῇ ὁδῷ κακὰ ἔπαθον· πολλάκις γὰρ εἰς κινδύνους ἔπιπτον. οἱ μὲν θεοὶ πολλάκις τοὺς κινδύνους ἔπεμπον·
5    ὁ δ' Ὀδυσσεὺς αὐτὸς τοὺς ἑταίρους εἰς μέγιστον κίνδυνόν ποτε ἤγαγεν. ἦν νῆσος καλὴ καὶ ἐρήμη. δένδρα καλὰ ἐν τῇ νήσῳ ἦν, ἀλλ'* οὔτ'* οἰκίαι οὔθ'* ἱερὰ οὔτ'* ἄνθρωποι. ἀντὶ τῆς νήσου ἦν ἡ χώρα ἡ τῶν Κυκλώπων.

* the final vowel is often *elided* (i.e. cut off) when the next word starts with a vowel: see below

|   |   |
|---|---|
| μακρός -ά -όν | long |
| μετά | (+ *acc*) after |
| δέκα | ten |
| ἐνιαυτός -οῦ ὁ | year |
| Ἀχαιοί -ῶν οἱ | Greeks |
| Τροία -ας ἡ | Troy |
| τ' | = τε (*elided*) |
| Ὀδυσσεύς ὁ | Odysseus |
| ἑταῖρος -ου ὁ | companion |
| 5    δ' | = δέ (*elided*) |
| αὐτός | himself |
| ποτε | once |
| ἐρῆμος -η -ον | deserted |
| ἀλλ' | = ἀλλά (*elided*) |
| οὔτε ... οὔτε ... οὔτε | neither ... nor ... nor |
| (here elided each time as οὔτ' or οὔθ') | |
| ἀντί | opposite, facing (+ *gen*) |
| Κύκλωψ -ωπος ὁ | Cyclops, *pl* Cyclopes |

# Elision

Elision (= *cutting off*) often occurs when a word ending with a vowel (typically a short vowel) comes before another word starting with a vowel. We saw several examples in the passage above: ἀλλ' οὔτ' for ἀλλὰ οὔτε. An apostrophe marks the place where the vowel

next word has a rough breathing, tau left ending the elided word changes to ⏤⏤ ἱερά), and similarly pi to phi: the *aspiration* ('breathed-on' quality) of the rough ⏤eathing spreads to the consonant. Elision simply reflects what would have happened in speech. It is usually easy to work out what letter has been elided. There are some restrictions on when elision can happen (and Greek authors themselves vary in how widely they use it), but it is frequently seen with words such as conjunctions and prepositions. In this book common examples of elision are included in passages, but some combinations of words where elision could have occurred are left unelided for clarity.

Exercise 5.4

# The Cyclops (2)

ὁ Ὀδυσσεύς, διότι ἤθελε <u>περὶ</u> τῶν Κυκλώπων μανθάνειν, <u>πολλοὺς</u> τῶν <u>ἑταίρων</u> ἐν τῇ νήσῳ ἔλιπεν. ἔπειτα <u>δ'</u> <u>ὀλίγους</u> ἐν πλοίῳ ἤγαγε καὶ πρὸς τὴν τῶν γιγάντων χώραν <u>προσῆλθεν</u>. <u>ἄντρον</u> ἦν <u>ἐγγὺς</u> τῆς θαλάσσης. τὸ ἄντρον οἰκία τοῦ Κύκλωπος τοῦ μεγίστου ἦν. ὁ γίγας πολλὰ <u>μῆλα</u>
5 εἶχεν. τὸ τοῦ γίγαντος ὄνομα ἦν <u>Πολύφημος</u>. ὁ Πολύφημος <u>ἑτερόφθαλμος</u> ἦν. <u>εἷς</u> ὀφθαλμός, <u>κύκλος</u> μέγιστος, ἐν <u>μέσῳ</u> τῷ <u>προσώπῳ</u> ἦν. ὁ Κύκλωψ ἀνθρώπους ἤσθιεν.

ὁ <u>τ'</u> Ὀδυσσεὺς καὶ οἱ ἑταῖροι τὸ πλοῖον ἐν τῇ <u>ἀκτῇ</u> ἔλιπον καὶ πρὸς τὸ ἄντρον προσῆλθον. τὸ ἄντρον <u>κενὸν</u> ἦν. ὁ γὰρ Κύκλωψ <u>ἀπῆν</u>. τὰ
10 μῆλα ἐν τοῖς <u>ἀγροῖς</u> <u>ἔνεμεν</u>. ὁ δ' Ὀδυσσεὺς καὶ οἱ ἑταῖροι ἐν τῷ ἄντρῳ ἐθαύμασαν. τὸ ἄντρον <u>θησαυρὸς</u> <u>τυροῦ</u> ἦν. οἱ μὲν ἑταῖροι τυρὸν

| | | |
|---|---|---|
| | περί | (+ *gen*) about |
| | πολλοί -αί -ά | many |
| | ἑταῖρος -ου ὁ | companion |
| | δ' | = δέ (*elided*) |
| | ὀλίγοι -αι -α | few |
| | προσῆλθον (*irregular second [strong] aorist*) | I went towards, I approached |
| | ἄντρον -ου τό | cave |
| | ἐγγύς | near (+ *gen*) |
| | μῆλα -ων τά | sheep |
| 5 | Πολύφημος -ου ὁ | Polyphemus |
| | ἑτερόφθαλμος | one-eyed |
| | εἷς | one |
| | κύκλος -ου ὁ | circle |
| | μέσος -η -ον | middle (part) of |
| | πρόσωπον -ου τό | forehead |
| | τ' | = τε (*elided*) |
| | ἀκτή -ῆς ἡ | shore |
| | κενός -ή -όν | empty |
| | ἄπειμι | I am away |
| 10 | ἀγρός -οῦ ὁ | field |
| | νέμω | I pasture |
| | θησαυρός -οῦ ὁ | treasure-house |
| | τυρός -οῦ ὁ | cheese |

λαμβάνειν καὶ ἀποτρέχειν ἤθελον· ὁ δ᾽ Ὀδυσσεὺς ἤθελεν εὑρίσκειν καὶ γιγνώσκειν τὸν Πολύφημον.

μετὰ <u>ὀλίγας</u> ὥρας ὁ Κύκλωψ <u>παρῆν</u>. τὰ <u>μῆλα</u> ἦγε καὶ <u>ξύλον</u> ἔφερεν.
15 ἡ τοῦ <u>ἄντρου</u> θύρα ἦν <u>λίθος</u> μέγιστος. ὁ Κύκλωψ <u>μόνος</u> <u>οἷός τ᾽ ἦν</u> <u>κυλίνδειν</u> τὸν λίθον. ἡ θύρα <u>κλειστὴ</u> ἦν. ὁ Κύκλωψ <u>πῦρ ἔκαυσε</u> καὶ <u>εἶδε</u> τοὺς ἀνθρώπους. βοὴ μεγίστη ἦν. "<u>τίνες</u> ἐστέ, ὦ ξένοι, καὶ <u>πόθεν</u>;" "<u>᾽Αχαιοὶ</u> ἐσμεν καὶ ἀπὸ τῆς <u>Τροίας</u> <u>ἐπλέομεν</u>," εἶπεν ὁ Ὀδυσσεύς, "δῶρα ἐθέλομεν ἔχειν. ὁ γὰρ Ζεὺς ξένους ἀεὶ φυλάσσει." "<u>μῶρος</u> εἶ, ὦ ἄνθρωπε,"
20 εἶπεν ὁ Κύκλωψ, "οἱ γὰρ Κύκλωπες φόβον τῶν θεῶν οὐκ ἔχουσιν." ἔπειτα δ᾽ ἔλαβε δύο τῶν <u>ἑταίρων</u> καὶ δεῖπνον ἔσχεν. μετὰ τὸ δεῖπνον εἰς <u>ὕπνον</u> <u>βαθύτατον</u> ἔπεσεν. ὁ Ὀδυσσεὺς ἤθελεν ἀποκτείνειν τὸν Πολύφημον, ἀλλ᾽ οἱ ἄνθρωποι οὐχ οἷοί τ᾽ ἦσαν κυλίνδειν τὸν λίθον καὶ φεύγειν. ἡ νὺξ μακρὰ ἦν. ἐπεὶ μέντοι ἡμέρα ἦν ὁ Πολύφημος τὰ μῆλα ἐξήγαγε, καὶ ὁ
25 Ὀδυσσεὺς νέαν βουλὴν ἔλαβεν. ἐν τῷ ἄντρῳ <u>ῥόπαλον</u> μέγιστον ηὗρον. <u>ὤξυναν</u> τὸ ῥόπαλον καὶ ἐν τῷ πυρὶ ἔλιπον <u>ὥστε σκληρὸν</u> ἦν. ἔπειτα δ᾽ ἔμενον τὸν Πολύφημον.

| | | |
|---|---|---|
| | μετά | (+ acc) after |
| | ὀλίγοι -αι -α | few |
| | πάρειμι *imperfect* παρῆν | I am here, I arrive |
| | μῆλα -ων τά | sheep |
| | ξύλον -ου τό | wood |
| 15 | ἄντρον -ου τό | cave |
| | λίθος -ου ὁ | stone |
| | μόνος -η -ον | alone, only |
| | οἷός τ᾽ εἰμί* | I am able |
| | κυλίνδω | I roll |
| | κλειστός -ή -όν | closed, shut |
| | πῦρ πυρός τό | fire |
| | καίω *aorist* ἔκαυσα | I kindle |
| | εἶδον (*irregular second [strong]* | |
| | *aorist*) | I saw |
| | τίνες; | who? (*pl*) |
| | πόθεν; | where from? |
| | ᾽Αχαιοί -ῶν οἱ | Greeks |
| | Τροία -ας ἡ | Troy |
| | πλέω | I sail |
| | μῶρος -α -ον | foolish |
| 20 | ἑταῖρος -ου ὁ | companion |
| | ὕπνος -ου ὁ | sleep |
| | βαθύτατος -η -ον | very deep |
| 25 | ῥόπαλον -ου τό | club |
| | ὀξύνω ὤξυνα | I sharpen |
| | ὥστε | with the result that |
| | σκληρός -ά -όν | hard |

\* note this common expression for *I am able*: the adjective οἷος (literally *of the sort to ...* ) with τε (elided) and the verb *to be*, both adjective and verb changing their endings as appropriate

# The uses of τίς/τις

• In the last passage you met:
    τίνες ἐστέ;          who are you (*pl*)?
And in the story about the Locrians in Chapter 3 you met:
    τις                  someone
    Λοκρός τις           a (certain) Locrian
These are parts of τις, an important pronoun/adjective (third declension in form) with a range of uses.

• In a question, and <u>with an acute accent on the first (or only) syllable</u>, it means
        *who? what? which?*
This is the *interrogative* use (asking a question):

|     |      | masculine/feminine | neuter     |                     |
|-----|------|--------------------|------------|---------------------|
| sg  | nom  | τίς                | τί         | who? which? what?   |
|     | acc  | τίν-α              | τί         |                     |
|     | gen  | τίν-ος             | τίν-ος     |                     |
|     | dat  | τίν-ι              | τίν-ι      |                     |
| pl  | nom  | τίν-ες             | τίν-α      |                     |
|     | acc  | τίν-ας             | τίν-α      |                     |
|     | gen  | τίν-ων             | τίν-ων     |                     |
|     | dat  | τίσι(ν)*           | τίσι(ν)*   |                     |

    * contracted from  τιν-σι(ν)  to aid pronunciation

• Elsewhere, usually without an accent or with an accent on the second syllable, it means
        *a (certain), some (one/thing)*
This is the *indefinite* use:

|     |      | masculine/feminine | neuter     |                              |
|-----|------|--------------------|------------|------------------------------|
| sg  | nom  | τις                | τι         | a (certain), some (one/thing)|
|     | acc  | τιν-ά              | τι         |                              |
|     | gen  | τιν-ός             | τιν-ός     |                              |
|     | dat  | τιν-ί              | τιν-ί      |                              |
| pl  | nom  | τιν-ές             | τιν-ά      |                              |
|     | acc  | τιν-άς             | τιν-ά      |                              |
|     | gen  | τιν-ῶν             | τιν-ῶν     |                              |
|     | dat  | τισί(ν)*           | τισί(ν)*   |                              |

    * contracted from  τιν-σι(ν) to aid pronunciation

• The form is regular third declension, with genitive stem  τιν- ; as often when a word has a neuter form, its nominative is a shortened form of the masculine. And as with all neuters, nominative and accusative are the same, and nominative and accusative plural end in alpha.

• The uses of τίς/τις provide one of the most obvious examples in Greek of an accent making a difference to the meaning of a word. Although (as we saw at the beginning of this chapter) it is not normally necessary to use accents when you write Greek, τίς/τις is an exception: the interrogative version should always be given its accent. Greek texts and passages are usually printed with accents, but even when they are not, an exception is made for this word.

• In both the interrogative and indefinite uses, τίς/τις can be used either as an adjective (with a noun) or as a pronoun (standing alone).

• The word order is very important. The interrogative version normally comes first in its clause. The indefinite version never comes first, and when used as an adjective must follow its noun.

As noted above, the interrogative version *always* has an accent in the first/only syllable; the indefinite version usually has no accent, or an accent on the second syllable. Occasionally the single-syllable parts of the indefinite τις *acquire* an accent from a following word, but in these rare cases confusion with the interrogative is avoided by word order and context.

• The four main uses therefore are:

τίς δοῦλος ἀποτρέχει;        *interrogative adjective*
Which slave is running away?

τίς ἀποτρέχει;        *interrogative pronoun*
Who is running away?

δυῦλός τις ἀποτρέχει.        *indefinite adjective*
A (certain) slave is running away.

ἀποτρέχει τις.        *indefinite pronoun*
Someone is running away.

• The indefinite adjective version is sometimes called the *indefinite article*, though as we have seen Greek commonly has the noun alone (e.g. δοῦλος) for *a slave*, keeping δοῦλός τις for a slightly more emphatic *a certain* slave, or to imply a contrast with *the* slave.

• If the indefinite adjective version is used with a noun which has an adjective as well, it normally comes between the noun and the adjective: e.g. νόμος τις νέος = *a certain new law.*

• Whilst the interrogative version naturally occurs in a question, it is of course possible for the indefinite version to be used *within* a question (which will usually have a *different* interrogative word, e.g. ἆρα; or ποῦ;).

• When the interrogative version is a pronoun, there is a clear distinction in English between *who?* for a person and *what?* for a thing. When it is an adjective, the English is usually *which ...?* for either (and of course the gender in Greek is, as with any adjective, determined by the gender of the noun).

Exercise 5.5

*Translate into English:*
1    τίς ἤκουσε τὰς βοάς;
2    τίνες στρατιῶται ἐδίωξαν τὸν ἵππον;
3    βουλήν τινα σοφὴν ἔχω.
4    τί λέγει ὁ θεός;
5    τίνι τῶν γερόντων δεῖπνον παρέσχες, ὦ δοῦλε;
6    ἆρα ἐθέλετε μῦθόν τινα ἀκούειν;
7    πολῖταί τινες ἐν τῇ ἀγορᾷ ἦσαν.
8    "τί ἐστι τὸ τοῦ γίγαντος ὄνομα;" εἶπεν ὁ διδάσκαλος.
9    ἔστι* δοῦλός τις ἐν τῷ ἱερῷ.
10   τί ζῷον τὸ μέγιστον σῶμα ἔχει;

> \* remember that if the verb *to be* starts the sentence it is usually translated *there is* etc: because it introduces something not mentioned before, it goes naturally with the indefinite τις

Exercise 5.6

*Translate into Greek:*
1    Who sent the letter?
2    Which horses ran away?
3    A certain village has a new temple.
4    What did the soldier take?
5    Something fell from the boat.

• Some more third-declension nouns:

| | | |
|---|---|---|
| ἀγών -ῶνος | ὁ | contest |
| ἄρχων -οντος | ὁ | ruler, magistrate |
| λέων -οντος | ὁ | lion |
| λιμήν -ένος | ὁ | harbour |
| ὄρνις -ιθος | ὁ/ἡ | bird |
| παῖς παιδός | ὁ/ἡ | boy, girl, child |
| πούς ποδός | ὁ | foot |

• Notice that some words, such as ὄρνις and παῖς here, are *common gender*: i.e. they can be either masculine or feminine. (The same is true of the second declension ἄνθρωπος = *man* or *woman,* according to context.)

• Notice again the importance of the genitive stem, and the fact that English derivatives are often formed from it.

• Notice that if the nominative ends -ων, the genitive most commonly ends -οντος (like γέρων), but some nouns have variants: e.g. -ωνος.

• As usual, slight adjustment is necessary with the dative plural to aid pronunciation. The dative plurals of these nouns are:

| | | |
|---|---|---|
| ἀγῶσι(ν) | for | -ωνσι(ν) |
| ἄρχουσι(ν) | | -οντσι(ν) |
| λέουσι(ν) | | -οντσι(ν) |
| λιμέσι(ν) | | -ενσι(ν) |
| ὄρνισι(ν) | | -ιθσι(ν) |
| παισί(ν) | | -δσι(ν) |
| ποσί(ν) | | -δσι(ν) |

It is not necessary however to learn them individually: just observe the patterns and you will usually be able to predict them.

Exercise 5.7

*Give one English derivative from:*
1    ὄρνις -ιθος
2    παῖς παιδός
3    πούς ποδός
4    ἀγών -ῶνος
5    ὄνομα -ατος

Excrcise 5.8

*Translate into English:*
1    οἱ παῖδες ἐν τοῖς ἀγῶσιν ἔτρεχον.
2    τίς ἐστιν ὁ τῆς κώμης ἄρχων;
3    ἡ παῖς τὸν ὄρνιθα διώκει.
4    τὰ πλοῖα ἐν τῷ λιμένι ἦν.
5    οἱ στρατιῶται ἔλαβον τὸν λέοντα.
6    φόβος τις ἐκώλυσε τὸν παῖδα.
7    τίνα νῆσον ἐφυλάσσετε, ὦ στρατιῶται;
8    ὁ λέων πόδας μεγίστους ἔχει.
9    ὁ ποιητὴς τοὺς παῖδας ἐδίδαξεν.
10   οἱ τῆς ὄρνιθος ὀφθαλμοὶ μικροί.

Exercise 5.9

*Translate into Greek:*
1    There was a certain sea-battle in the harbour.
2    The ruler of the island is an old man.
3    The girls were learning certain stories.
4    What is the name of the bird?
5    The horse has fine feet.

# The Cyclops (3)

νὺξ ἦν. ὅ τ᾽ Ὀδυσσεὺς καὶ οἱ <u>ἑταῖροι</u> ἐν τῷ <u>ἄντρῳ</u> ἔμενον. ὁ Πολύφημος <u>μετὰ</u> τῶν <u>μήλων</u> πρὸς τὸ ἄντρον προσέβαινεν. οἱ ἄνθρωποι τὸν Κύκλωπα <u>εἶδον</u>. ἐπεὶ ἐν τῷ ἄντρῳ <u>παρῆν</u>, <u>ἕτοιμοι</u> ἦσαν. ὁ Ὀδυσσεὺς τὸ <u>ῥόπαλον</u> εἶχεν· ἡ τοῦ ἄντρου θύρα νῦν <u>κλειστὴ</u> ἦν. ὁ Κύκλωψ <u>αὖθις</u> ἔλαβε δύο
5  τῶν ἑταίρων καὶ <u>ἔφαγεν</u>. ὁ δ᾽ Ὀδυσσεὺς <u>οἶνόν</u> τινα <u>κάλλιστον</u> ἐν τῷ πλοίῳ <u>ἐκόμισε</u>, δῶρον ξένου τινός· νῦν ἐν <u>ἀσκῷ</u> ἔφερε, καὶ τῷ Κύκλωπι εἶπεν, "οἶνον λάμβανε, καὶ μετὰ τὸ δεῖπνον <u>πῖνε</u>. οἶνον γὰρ κάλλιστον ἐν τῷ πλοίῳ φέρομεν." ὁ οὖν Πολύφημος τὸν οἶνον ἔλαβε καὶ ἔπινεν. ἔπειτα δ᾽ εἶπε, "κάλλιστος ὁ οἶνος, ὦ ξένε· αὖθις παρέχε. ἀλλὰ τί ἐστι τὸ <u>σὸν</u>
10  ὄνομα; δῶρον γὰρ ἐθέλω παρέχειν." ὁ οὖν Ὀδυσσεὺς οἶνον αὖθις παρέσχε καὶ εἶπε, "τὸ ὄνομα τὸ <u>ἐμὸν</u> Οὖτίς ἐστιν". "Οὖτιν οὖν <u>ὕστατον</u> <u>ἔδομαι</u>," εἶπεν ὁ Πολύφημος, "τοὺς <u>ἄλλους</u> πρότερον· <u>οὕτως</u> γὰρ δῶρον παρέχω".

| | | |
|---|---|---|
| | ἑταῖρος -ου ὁ | companion |
| | ἄντρον -ου τό | cave |
| | μετά | (+ *gen*) with  (+ *acc* = after) |
| | μῆλα -ων τά | sheep |
| | εἶδον  (*irregular second [strong]* | |
| | *aorist*) | I saw |
| | πάρειμι | I am present, I arrive |
| | ἕτοιμος -η -ον | ready |
| | ῥόπαλον -ου τό | club |
| | κλειστός -ή -όν | closed, shut |
| | αὖθις | again |
| 5 | ἐσθίω ἔφαγον | I eat |
| | οἶνος -ου ὁ | wine |
| | κάλλιστος -η -ον | very fine, excellent |
| | κομίζω ἐκόμισα | I bring |
| | ἀσκός -οῦ ὁ | wine-skin |
| | πίνω | I drink |
| | σός σή σόν | your (of you *sg*) (*used with the article, though this is not translated*) |
| 10 | ἐμός -ή -όν | my (*used similarly with the article*) |
| | Οὖτις (*accusative* Οὖτιν) | Noman (*invented name:* οὖτις = no-one) |
| | ὕστατον | last |
| | ἔδομαι (*irregular future*) | I shall eat |
| | ἄλλος -η -ο | other |
| | οὕτως | in this way |

ὁ δὲ Κύκλωψ νῦν <u>ἐμέθυε</u>, καὶ ὁ ὀφθαλμὸς <u>κλειστὸς</u> ἦν· <u>ὕπνος</u> γὰρ ἔλαβε
15 τὸν Πολύφημον. ὁ οὖν Ὀδυσσεὺς τὸ <u>ῥόπαλον</u> πρὸς τὸ <u>πῦρ</u> <u>αὖθις</u> ἔφερεν.
ἔπειτα δὲ <u>μετὰ</u> τῶν <u>ἑταίρων</u> <u>ἐνέβαλεν</u> εἰς τὸν τοῦ Κύκλωπος ὀφθαλμόν.
μεγίστη βοὴ ἦν. οἱ <u>ἄλλοι</u> Κύκλωπες πρὸς τὸ ἄντρον ἔδραμον. "τί ἐστιν, ὦ
Πολύφημε;" εἶπον οἱ Κύκλωπες, "τίς ἐστιν ὁ κίνδυνος; τίς <u>βλάπτει</u> <u>σε</u>;"
"<u>Οὖτις</u> βλάπτει με, Οὖτις ἐθέλει ἀποκτείνειν," εἶπεν ὁ Πολύφημος.
20 "κίνδυνος οὖν οὐκ ἔστιν, ἐπεὶ <u>οὖτις</u> βλάπτει, οὖτις ἐθέλει ἀποκτείνειν σε.
νόσον γάρ τινα ἀπὸ τῶν θεῶν ἔχεις," εἶπον οἱ Κύκλωπες, καὶ ἀπέβαινον.

ὁ δὲ Πολύφημος νῦν <u>τυφλὸς</u> ἦν, ἀλλ' <u>ἔτι</u> <u>οἷός τ' ἦν</u> <u>κυλίνδειν</u> τὸν λίθον.
ἐπεὶ δὲ ἡμέρα ἦν ὁ Κύκλωψ ἐξῆγαγε τὰ μῆλα. <u>ὑπὸ</u> <u>ἑκάστῳ</u> ἦν <u>εἷς</u> τῶν
ἑταίρων. καὶ ὁ μέγιστος <u>κριὸς</u> τὸν Ὀδυσσέα ἔφερεν. <u>οὕτως</u> οὖν ἐκ τοῦ
25 <u>ἄντρου</u> ἔφυγον καὶ πρὸς τὴν θάλασσαν ἔτρεχον. ἔπειτα δὲ τὰ <u>μῆλα</u> εἰς τὸ
πλοῖον ἤγαγον καὶ τὸ πλοῖον ἔλυσαν. ὁ δ' Ὀδυσσεὺς <u>ὕβρισε</u> τὸν
Πολύφημον· "ἆρα ἐθέλεις γιγνώσκειν τίς ὕβρισέ σε καὶ τὰ μῆλα <u>ἔκλεψεν</u>;
οὐ γὰρ Οὖτίς εἰμι <u>ἐγὼ</u> ἀλλ' ὁ Ὀδυσσεὺς ὁ <u>πολύτροπος</u>."

| | | |
|---|---|---|
| | μεθύω | I am drunk |
| | κλειστός -ή -όν | closed, shut |
| | ὕπνος -ου ὁ | sleep |
| 15 | ῥόπαλον -ου τό | club |
| | πῦρ πυρός τό | fire |
| | αὖθις | again |
| | μετά | (+ gen) with |
| | ἑταῖρος -ου ὁ | companion |
| | ἐμβάλλω ἐνέβαλον | I thrust in |
| | ἄλλος -η -ο | other |
| | βλάπτω | I harm |
| | σε | you (acc sg) |
| | Οὖτις | Noman |
| 20 | οὖτις | no-one |
| | τυφλός -ή -όν | blind |
| | ἔτι | still |
| | οἷός τ' εἰμί | I am able |
| | κυλίνδω | I roll |
| | ὑπό | (+ dat) under |
| | ἕκαστος -η -ον | each |
| | εἷς | one |
| | κριός -οῦ ὁ | ram |
| | οὕτως | in this way |
| 25 | ἄντρον -ου τό | cave |
| | μῆλα -ων τά | sheep |
| | ὑβρίζω ὕβρισα | I insult |
| | κλέπτω ἔκλεψα | I steal |
| | ἐγώ | I |
| | πολύτροπος | of many wiles, full of tricks (*recurrent Homeric adjective describing Odysseus*) |

83

# Cases taken by prepositions

In Chapter 1 you met these prepositions that are followed by the accusative case, indicating *motion towards*:

| | |
|---|---|
| εἰς | into |
| πρός | towards |

In Chapter 3 you met these prepositions that are followed by the genitive case, indicating *motion away from*:

| | |
|---|---|
| ἀπό | from |
| ἐκ (ἐξ) | out of |

and this preposition that is followed by the dative case, indicating *rest*:

| | |
|---|---|
| ἐν | in |

• This pattern of case usage applies to most prepositions. Some however can take more than one case; the thought-process determining the case is not always as obvious as in the examples above; and some uses of prepositions have special idiomatic meanings that cannot easily be guessed. But as always the common examples quickly become familiar. In Chapter 4 you met:

μετά + *accusative*  after

In this chapter you have met:

μετά + *genitive*  with

Another preposition taking both accusative and genitive is:

| | |
|---|---|
| διά + *accusative* | on account of* |
| διά + *genitive* | through |

* note however that the translation 'through' would often also be appropriate here (e.g. *She was absent through illness*; contrast *She was walking through the field* (<u>physically</u> through), which would need the genitive)

• Note the very common phrase:

διὰ τί;
why?  (*literally* on account of what?)

• Where a preposition takes only one case, it is given in wordlists in this book in the form:

ἀπό  from (+ *gen.*)

but if the case is given *before* the meaning, that is a signal that the preposition has one or more other meanings with one or more different cases:

μετά  (+ *gen*) with

Exercise 5.11

*Translate into English:*

1  διὰ τί αἱ παῖδες ἐκ τῆς οἰκίας ἐξέδραμον;
2  οἱ στρατιῶται ἐνθάδε μετὰ τῶν συμμάχων μένουσιν.
3  ὁ ἵππος διὰ τοῦ ποταμοῦ ἔτρεχεν.
4  μετὰ τὸ δεῖπνον οἱ πολῖται εἰς τὴν ἀγορὰν ἐκβαίνουσιν.

5       διὰ τὴν νόσον ὁ γέρων οὐ <u>πάρεστιν</u>.

πάρειμι = *I am present, I am here* is a compound of εἰμί and has the same endings

Exercise 5.12

*Translate into Greek:*
1       After the contest we found a very big prize.
2       The slave was running through the marketplace towards the sea.
3       What did the old man leave in the house?
4       On account of the war we do not have wine.
5       Why were the magistrates not suffering with the citizens?

## Personal pronouns and adjectives (first and second person singular)

• You met some of these in the last passage. The first person singular pronoun (*I, me*, etc: note that this is one of the places where English has nominative and accusative) in full is:

| | | |
|---|---|---|
| *nom* | ἐγώ | I |
| *acc* | ἐμέ *or* με | me |
| *gen* | ἐμοῦ *or* μου | of me |
| *dat* | ἐμοί *or* μοι | to/for me |

• The accusative, genitive and dative are found both with and without the initial epsilon. The version with the epsilon is used in slightly more emphatic positions (e.g. first word in a sentence); the version without the epsilon is used when the pronoun is felt to follow another word closely (e.g. πίστευέ μοι = *believe me!*). A word closely following and depending on another in this way is known technically as an *enclitic* (= 'leaning on'). Enclitics usually do not have an accent. The indefinite τις is commonly used as an enclitic.

• Note similarity to the Latin equivalent (*ego, me,* etc). As in Latin, the nominative is only used for emphasis or to draw a contrast, because the first person singular of a verb is normally sufficient to indicate the subject.

• The associated adjective (my) is:
            ἐμός -ή -όν (*masculine, feminine, neuter*)

This goes exactly like σοφός. Its gender is that of the thing possessed (not the possessor). It behaves like any other adjective, i.e. when used with a noun normally has the article as well (not translated in English), and is either sandwiched or has repeated article for the *bound* or *attributive* position (telling you *which one*):

            ἡ ἐμὴ οἰκία *or*
            ἡ οἰκία ἡ ἐμή
            my house

• The second person singular pronoun (*you* sg) is:

| | | |
|---|---|---|
| *nom* | σύ | you (*sg*) |
| *acc* | σέ | |
| *gen* | σοῦ | of you |
| *dat* | σοί | to/for you |

• Again the nominative is normally only used for emphasis.

• The other cases are often used as enclitics (closely following and depending on another word): they then usually lose their accent (but, unlike the equivalent parts of the first person pronoun, do not otherwise have a special form for the enclitic use).

• The associated adjective here is: σός, σή, σόν

This declines and is used in the same way as the first person adjective.

Exercise 5.13

*Translate into English:*
1    ἐγὼ μὲν ἔμεινα, σὺ δὲ ἔφυγες.
2    δεῖπνόν μοι πάρεχε, ὦ δοῦλε.
3    ἐμὲ θαυμάζουσιν οἱ πολῖται.
4    ἆρα γιγνώσκεις τὸ ἐμὸν ὄνομα;
5    αἱ σαὶ ἐπιστολαὶ ἔπειθόν με.
6    ὁ ἐμὸς ἵππος κάλλιστος.
7    οὐκ ἐθέλω μετὰ σοῦ εἰς κίνδυνον βαίνειν.
8    ὁ γίγας διώκει τὸ σὸν πλοῖον.
9    σὺ μὲν εἶ ὁ τοῦ δήμου ἄρχων, ἐγὼ δὲ οὔ.
10   τὸ ἔργον τὸ τῶν ἐμῶν δούλων χαλεπόν ἐστιν.

Exercise 5.14

*Translate into Greek:*
1    I admire your prizes.
2    My house has a small door.
3    Who chased your horse, old man?
4    I am a slave, but you are free.
5    *You* did not trust my friends.

Exercise 5.15

# The Cyclops (4)

*Odysseus tells the next part of the story:*

"ὁ δὲ Πολύφημος, ἐπεὶ τοὺς ἐμοὺς λόγους ἤκουσε, <u>πολλοὺς λίθους</u>
ἔβαλλεν (<u>ὑβριστικῶς</u> γὰρ εἶπον), ἀλλ' οὐχ <u>οἷός τ' ἦν</u> τὸ ἐμὸν πλοῖον
<u>καταδύειν</u>. ἔφυγον οὖν μετὰ <u>ὀλίγων ἑταίρων</u> ἀπὸ τῆς τοῦ Κύκλωπος
χώρας. καὶ πρὸς τὴν τῶν <u>αἰγῶν</u> νῆσον <u>ταχέως ἤλθομεν</u>· ἐκεῖ γὰρ οἱ ἄλλοι
5    ἑταῖροι ἔμενον. τὰ δὲ <u>μῆλα</u> ἐκ τοῦ πλοίου ἐλάβομεν. ἔπειτα δὲ τὰ <u>κρέα</u>
τοῖς ναύταις <u>ἐνείμαμεν</u>. ἐγὼ δὲ τῷ <u>Διὶ ἔθυσα</u> τὸν μέγιστον <u>κριόν</u>. ὁ μέντοι
Ζεὺς οὐκ ἤκουσε τὴν ἐμὴν <u>εὐχήν</u>. ὁ γὰρ <u>Ποσειδῶν</u> (ὁ τῆς θαλάσσης
θεός, ὁ τοῦ Πολυφήμου <u>πατήρ</u>, ὁ τοῦ Διὸς <u>ἀδελφός</u>) <u>περιοργὴς</u> ἦν, καὶ οἱ
θεοὶ ἤθελον τὰ πλοῖα <u>διαφθείρειν</u> καὶ τοὺς ἑταίρους ἀποκτείνειν. ἀλλὰ
10   τὴν νῆσον ἐλίπομεν, <u>χαίροντες</u> διότι ἐκ θανάτου νῦν ἐφύγομεν."

|          |                              |                     |
|----------|------------------------------|---------------------|
|          | πολλοί -αί -ά                 | many                |
|          | λίθος -ου ὁ                   | stone               |
|          | ὑβριστικῶς                    | arrogantly          |
|          | οἷός τ' εἰμί                  | I am able           |
|          | καταδύω                       | I sink (something)  |
|          | ὀλίγοι -αι -α                 | few                 |
|          | ἑταῖρος -ου ὁ                 | companion           |
|          | αἴξ αἰγός ὁ                   | goat                |
|          | ταχέως                        | quickly             |
|          | ἦλθον (*irregular second [strong]* | |
|          |   *aorist*)                   | I came              |
| 5        | μῆλα -ων τά                   | sheep               |
|          | κρέα -ων τά                   | meat                |
|          | νέμω ἔνειμα                   | I distribute        |
|          | Ζεύς (*irregular genitive* Διός) ὁ | Zeus            |
|          | θύω ἔθυσα                     | I sacrifice         |
|          | κριός -οῦ ὁ                   | ram                 |
|          | εὐχή -ῆς ἡ                    | prayer              |
|          | Ποσειδῶν -ῶνος ὁ              | Poseidon            |
|          | πατήρ -τρός ὁ                 | father              |
|          | ἀδελφός -οῦ ὁ                 | brother             |
|          | περιοργής                     | very angry          |
|          | διαφθείρω                     | I destroy           |
| 10       | χαίροντες*                    | rejoicing           |

\* this is the *present participle* of χαίρω = *I rejoice*: see the next page

# Present participle (1)

• A participle is a part of a verb used (normally) as an adjective, formed by putting noun/ adjective endings onto a verb stem. Greek makes very full use of participles, and often avoids longer and more complex clauses by doing so.

• The present active participle is literally translated *-ing*. This however needs care in English: *they fell about laughing* and *the laughing cavalier* involve participles (equivalent to *while laughing, who is laughing,* etc); but *laughing is good for you* is a different idiom (equivalent to a noun *laughter* or *the act of laughing*): this is not a participle. (In Greek it would be an infinitive, as we shall see later.)

• The present active participle in the masculine declines exactly like a third-declension noun such as γέρων:

| sg | nom | παύ-ων | stopping |
|----|-----|--------|----------|
|    | acc | παύ-οντα | |
|    | gen | παύ-οντος | |
|    | dat | παύ-οντι | |
| pl | nom | παύ-οντες | |
|    | acc | παύ-οντας | |
|    | gen | παυ-όντων | |
|    | dat | παύ-ουσι(ν)* | |

* as will be familiar by now, this is a contraction of  παυ-οντσι(ν)

• This is broadly comparable to a Latin present participle (e.g. *portans, portantis*) which is likewise third-declension (similar to the adjective *ingens*).

• The present participle does not tell you that the action is necessarily happening *now*, but rather *at the same time as* the action expressed by the main verb. If the main verb is past (as it commonly is in narrative), the present participle refers to something also happening in the past (and so may be translated like an imperfect tense).

• As we saw in the English examples above (*fell about laughing, laughing cavalier*) the participle often replaces a clause: a *when* or *while* clause (*temporal*, telling you when), or a *who* clause (*relative*, describing further, or specifying which one).

Examples:
> τρέχων ἔπεσον

literally *running, I fell* or (in better English, and because the main verb is past) *while I was running, I fell*;

> διδάσκοντες μανθάνομεν

literally *teaching, we learn* or (in better English, this time with present main verb) *while we are teaching, we learn*;

φεύγοντες ἀπέθανον
literally *escaping, they died* or *when they were escaping, they died.*


• When the participle is used with a noun, the word order and use of the article make an important difference to the meaning. Consider the difference between:

1:   The slave, while he was escaping, fell.
where we are being given information about the *circumstances* of the person under discussion: this in Greek is
ὁ δοῦλος φεύγων ἔπεσεν.

2:   The slave who was escaping fell.
*or*   The escaping slave fell (which may imply e.g. *but the other slave didn't*): we are being told an *attribute* of the slave in question, distinguishing him from others. This in Greek is
ὁ δοῦλος ὁ φεύγων ἔπεσεν.
*literally*
The slave the one escaping fell.
*i.e.*   The escaping slave fell.
*or*   The slave who was escaping fell.
(this is like the normal use of an adjective; we saw above that a participle is an adjective formed from a verb)


• With an ordinary adjective the sandwiched version (ὁ κακὸς δοῦλος) is the norm, with the repeated article version (ὁ δοῦλος ὁ κακός) available as an alternative. But with the participle, the repeated article version (ὁ δοῦλος ὁ φεύγων) is the norm (with the sandwiched version ὁ φεύγων δοῦλος possible in theory but very uncommon).

• To summarise - you need to distinguish two main uses of the participle with a noun:

1: circumstantial (e.g. what someone was doing at the time)
οἱ σύμμαχοι τρέχοντες βοὰς ἤκουσαν.
The allies while running heard shouts.
*or*   The allies when they were running heard shouts.

2: attributive/adjectival (describing the people, perhaps to distinguish them from others)
οἱ σύμμαχοι οἱ τρέχοντες βοὰς ἤκουσαν.
The allies who were running heard shouts.
(perhaps implying e.g. *but those who were standing still did not*)
This is the normal way Greek expresses what in English or Latin would be a relative clause: indeed a failsafe way of translating a participle after the article is to use a relative clause introduced by *who* or *which*.

• Although a participle may have become an adjective, or be replacing a clause, it remains a verb and so can for example still take an object, or a preposition phrase. This normally (especially with the attributive version) goes in front of the participle:

οἱ παῖδες οἱ τὸν ἵππον διώκοντες ἐθαύμασαν.
The boys who were chasing the horse were amazed.

ὁ στρατιώτης εἰς τὸ στρατόπεδον εἰστρέχων ἔπεσεν.
The soldier while running into the camp fell.
*or*, with better English word order,
    The soldier fell while running into the camp.

• As many of these examples have shown, there are often several possible English translations of a participle (*when* ..., *while* ..., etc). The important point is that Greek likes to have just one main verb in a sentence: other, subordinate ideas are commonly expressed by participles.

Exercise 5.16

*Translate into English:*
1    ὁ στρατηγὸς τὸν στρατὸν τάσσων βοὴν ἤκουσεν.
2    οἱ δοῦλοι οἱ φεύγοντες εἰς τὸν ποταμὸν εἰσέπεσον.
3    ἐλάβομεν τὸν λέοντα τὸν τοὺς ἀνθρώπους ἐσθίοντα.
4    ὁ ξένος ὁ τὸν ἵππον ἔχων ἔφυγεν.
5    κελεύσω τὸν δοῦλον τὸν λέγοντα ἀποβαίνειν.
6    οἱ στρατιῶται τὴν κώμην φυλάσσοντες ἀπέθανον.
7    τίνες εἰσὶν οἱ ναῦται οἱ τὸν λιμένα λείποντες;
8    πιστεύω τῷ κριτῇ τῷ σοφῶς λέγοντι.
9    ἐγὼ ηὗρον ἄνθρωπόν τινα τὸ ἐμὸν δεῖπνον ἐσθίοντα.
10   ὁ νεανίας ὁ τὴν χώραν γιγνώσκων χρήσιμός σοί ἐστιν.

Exercise 5.17

*Translate into Greek:*
1    The soldiers who are escaping are not wise.
2    While chasing the giant, the young man fell.
3    The teacher, while he was writing a letter, heard the shouts.
4    The lion died when it was eating the boy.
5    Who is the slave who is driving the horses?

• The present participle of the verb *to be* is simply the participle endings (with smooth breathing), so the masculine is:

| sg | nom | ὤν | being |
|----|-----|-----|-------|
|    | acc | ὄντα | |
|    | gen | ὄντος | |
|    | dat | ὄντι | |

| pl | nom | ὄντες | |
|----|-----|-------|---|
|    | acc | ὄντας | |
|    | gen | ὄντων | |
|    | dat | οὖσι(ν) | |

• With any participle, another possible translation of the circumstantial use is *because*:

ὁ δοῦλος ἐν τῇ οἰκίᾳ μένων οὐκ ἤκουσε τὰς βοάς.

The slave, because he stayed in the house, did not hear the shouts.

The translation *because* is often particularly appropriate with the participle of *to be*:

e.g.        ὁ παῖς ἀνδρεῖος ὢν οὐκ ἔφυγεν.
*literally*  The boy, being brave, did not run away.
*or*        The boy, because he was brave, did not run away.

However, the translation *who* is also often natural:

ὁ Περικλῆς στρατηγὸς ὢν ἔταξε τὸν στρατόν.

Pericles, who was general, drew up the army.

Exercise 5.18

*Translate into English:*
1    διὰ τί οἱ ναῦται ἀνδρεῖοι ὄντες ἔφυγον;
2    ὁ διδάσκαλος σοφὸς ὢν σοφῶς διδάσκει.
3    οἱ ξένοι σύμμαχοι ὄντες ἐφύλασσον τὸν λιμένα.
4    ὁ Ζεὺς θεὸς ὢν καλὰ δῶρα παρέχει.
5    οἱ πολῖται οἱ ἐν τῇ ἀγορᾷ παρόντες ἐθαύμασαν.

Exercise 5.19

*Translate into Greek:*
1    The ruler, because he was wise, wrote good laws.
2    The soldiers, being brave, guarded the citizens.
3    The boys, because they were bad, did not listen.
4    Polyphemus, who was a giant, ate two men.
5    Because it was dangerous, the river hindered the army.

Polyphemus: Πολύφημος ὁ
I hinder: κωλύω, *aorist* ἐκώλυσα

# Revision checkpoint

*Make sure you know:*
• first and second person singular pronouns and adjectives
• the declension of the present participle in the masculine, and the main ways it is used

Exercise 5.20

# The Bag of Winds

*After leaving the scene of the adventure with the Cyclops, Odysseus and his surviving men came to the floating island of Aeolia, ruled by Aeolus.*

"ὁ δ' <u>Αἴολος</u> καλῶς <u>ἐξένισεν ἡμᾶς</u>. καὶ ἐπεὶ τὴν νῆσον ἐλείπομεν, δῶρα <u>θαυμάσια</u> παρέσχεν· τοὺς γὰρ <u>ἀνέμους</u> ἐν <u>ἀσκῷ σκυτίνῳ ἐδέσμευσεν</u>. <u>ἐννέα</u> ἡμέρας ἀπὸ τῆς τοῦ Αἰόλου νήσου <u>ἐπλέομεν</u>. <u>τέλος</u> δὲ τὴν <u>Ἰθάκην</u> <u>εἴδομεν</u>. ἀλλ' <u>ὕπνος</u> ἔλαβέ με. ἔπειτα δὲ οἱ <u>ἑταῖροι</u> εἶπον, 'ὁ Ὀδυσσεύς,
5  ἀνθρώπων <u>πλουσίων</u> φίλος <u>ὤν</u>, <u>πολλὰ</u> δῶρα ἀεὶ ἔχει. καὶ ἀπὸ τῆς <u>Τροίας</u> <u>θησαυρὸν</u> φέρει. <u>ἡμεῖς</u> δ' οὐδὲν ἔχομεν. καὶ νῦν ὁ Αἴολος <u>ἄλλο</u> δῶρον παρέσχεν. ἆρα <u>χρυσὸς</u> ἐν τῷ ἀσκῷ ἔνεστιν;' τὸν οὖν ἀσκὸν ἔλυσαν. καὶ οἱ ἄνεμοι <u>εὐθὺς</u> ἐξέφυγον. <u>χειμὼν</u> μέγιστος τὰ πλοῖα ἀπὸ τῆς Ἰθάκης <u>πόρρω ἤνεγκεν</u>. ἐγὼ <u>ἐγρηγορὼς ἀθλιώτατος</u> ἦ. πρὸς οὖν τὴν τοῦ Αἰόλου

| | |
|---|---|
| Αἴολος -ου ὁ | Aeolus |
| ξενίζω ἐξένισα | I entertain |
| ἡμᾶς | us |
| θαυμάσιος -α -ον | amazing, wonderful |
| ἄνεμος -ου ὁ | wind |
| ἀσκός -οῦ ὁ | bag |
| σκύτινος -η -ον | (made of) leather |
| δεσμεύω ἐδέσμευσα | I fasten up |
| ἐννέα | nine |
| πλέω | I sail |
| τέλος | finally |
| Ἰθάκη -ης ἡ | Ithaca |
| εἶδον | (*irregular aorist*) I saw |
| ὕπνος -ου ὁ | sleep |
| ἑταῖρος -ου ὁ | companion |
| 5    πλούσιος -α -ον | wealthy |
| πολλοί -αί -ά | many |
| Τροία -ας ἡ | Troy |
| θησαυρός -οῦ ὁ | treasure |
| ἡμεῖς | we |
| ἄλλος -η -ο | another |
| χρυσός -οῦ ὁ | gold |
| εὐθύς | immediately |
| χειμών -ῶνος ὁ | storm |
| πόρρω | far off |
| ἤνεγκα | (*irregular aorist of* φέρω) I carried |
| ἐγρηρορώς | having woken up, on waking up |
| ἀθλιώτατος -η -ον | very miserable |

10 νῆσον <u>βραδέως</u> <u>ἐπανήλθομεν</u>. ὁ μέντοι Αἴολος θαυμάζων εἶπε, ἡπῶς πάρει, ὦ 'Οδυσσεῦ; ἆρα θεὸς κακὸς ἔπεμψέ σε; ἐγὼ γὰρ δῶρα παρέχων ἀπέπεμψά σε πρὸς τὴν 'Ιθάκην.' 'οἵ τε <u>ἑταῖροι</u> <u>αἴτιοί</u> εἰσιν, ὦ Αἴολε, καὶ ὁ <u>ὕπνος</u>. ἀλλὰ φίλος ὢν δῶρα <u>αὖθις</u> πάρεχε.' ὁ μέντοι Αἴολος εἶπεν, 'ἀπὸ τῆς νήσου εὐθὺς φεῦγε, ὦ <u>κάκιστε</u>. οὐ γὰρ παρέχομεν δῶρα ἀνθρώποις <u>εἰ</u>
15 οἱ θεοὶ ἐχθροί εἰσιν'. "

| | | |
|---|---|---|
| 10 | βραδέως | slowly |
| | ἐπανῆλθον | (*irregular aorist*) I returned |
| | ἑταῖρος -ου ὁ | companion |
| | αἴτιος -α -ον | to blame, responsible |
| | ὕπνος -ου ὁ | sleep |
| | αὖθις | again |
| | κάκιστος -η -ον | very bad, very wicked |
| | εἰ | if |

93

# Vocabulary checklist for Chapter 5

| | |
|---|---|
| ἀγρός -οῦ ὁ | field |
| ἀγών -ῶνος ὁ | contest |
| ἄλλος -η -ο | other, another |
| ἄνεμος -ου ὁ | wind |
| ἄπειμι *imperfect* ἀπῆν | I am away |
| ἄρχων -οντος ὁ | ruler, magistrate |
| βλάπτω ἔβλαψα | I harm, I damage |
| γέρων -οντος ὁ | old man |
| γίγας -αντος ὁ | giant |
| διά | (+ *acc*) on account of |
| | (+ *gen*) through |
| διὰ τί; | why? |
| ἐγγύς | near (+ *gen*) |
| ἐγώ | I |
| εἶδον | (*irregular aorist*) I saw |
| ἕκαστος -η -ον | each |
| ἐμβάλλω ἐνέβαλον | I throw in, I thrust in |
| ἐμός -ή -όν | my |
| ἔτι | still, yet |
| ἑτοῖμος -η -ον | ready |
| κάλλιστος -η -ον | very fine, very beautiful |
| κλέπτω ἔκλεψα | I steal |
| κύκλος -ος ὁ | circle |
| κωλύω ἐκώλυσα | I hinder |
| λέων -οντος ὁ | lion |
| λίθος -ου ὁ | stone |
| λιμήν -ένος ὁ | harbour |
| μετά | (+ *gen*) with |
| μόνον | only (*adverb*) |
| μόνος -η -ον | only, alone |
| μῶρος -α -ον | foolish, stupid |
| νύξ νυκτός ἡ | night |
| οἶνος -ου ὁ | wine |
| οἷός τ' εἰμί | I am able |
| ὀλίγοι -αι -α | few |
| ὄνομα -ατος τό | name |
| ὄρνις -ιθος ὁ/ἡ | bird |
| παῖς παιδός ὁ/ἡ | boy, girl, child |
| πάρειμι *imperfect* παρῆν* | I am here, I am present |
| πίνω ἔπιον | I drink |
| πόθεν; | where from? |
| πολλοί -αί -ά | many |
| πούς ποδός ὁ | foot |
| πῦρ πυρός τό | fire |

| | |
|---|---|
| σός σή σόν | your (of you *sg*) |
| σύ | you (*sg*) |
| σῶμα -ατος τό | body |
| τίς; τί; | who? what? which? |
| τις, τι | a (certain), someone, something |
| ὕπνος -ου ὁ | sleep |
| φύλαξ -ακος ὁ | guard |
| (50 words) | |

* in the compound form of εἰμί, the ending -ῆν (rather than -ῆ) is used for the imperfect first person singular

# Chapter 6

## Present participle (2)

• Here is the present participle in full, for all three genders:

stopping

|    |     | masculine | feminine | neuter |
|----|-----|-----------|----------|--------|
| sg | nom | παύ-ων | παύ-ουσ-α | παῦ-ον |
|    | acc | παύ-οντα | παύ-ουσ-αν | παῦ-ον |
|    | gen | παύ-οντος | παυ-ούσ-ης | παύ-οντος |
|    | dat | παύ-οντι | παυ-ούσ-ῃ | παύ-οντι |
| pl | nom | παύ-οντες | παύ-ουσ-αι | παύ-οντα |
|    | acc | παύ-οντας | παυ-ούσ-ας | παύ-οντα |
|    | gen | παυ-όντων | παυ-ουσ-ῶν | παυ-όντων |
|    | dat | παύ-ουσι(ν) | παυ-ούσ-αις | παύ-ουσι(ν) |

• As we have seen already, the masculine is identical to a third declension noun like γέρων. The neuter is a predictable neuter version of this: nominative a 'reduced' (short *o*) version of the masculine; nominative and accusative the same; nominative and accusative plural ending in alpha.

• The feminine adds -ουσ- to the verb stem and then is identical to a first declension noun like θάλασσα (the version of first declension where on a consonant stem the alpha ending changes to eta after the accusative).

• And the participle of the verb *to be* (εἰμί) in full, for all three genders:

being

|    |     | masculine | feminine | neuter |
|----|-----|-----------|----------|--------|
| sg | nom | ὤν | οὖσα | ὄν |
|    | acc | ὄντα | οὖσαν | ὄν |
|    | gen | ὄντος | οὔσης | ὄντος |
|    | dat | ὄντι | οὔσῃ | ὄντι |
| pl | nom | ὄντες | οὖσαι | ὄντα |
|    | acc | ὄντας | οὔσας | ὄντα |
|    | gen | ὄντων | οὐσῶν | ὄντων |
|    | dat | οὖσι(ν) | οὔσαις | οὖσι(ν) |

Exercise 6.1

*Translate into English:*

1   ἡ κόρη ἐπιστολὴν γράφουσα οὐκ ἤκουσε τὴν βοήν.
2   ἐγὼ τὸ τῆς κώμης ὄνομα χαλεπὸν ὂν οὐκ ἔμαθον.
3   αἱ παῖδες αἱ τὴν ἐμὴν οἰκίαν φυλάσσουσαι ἀνδρεῖαι ἦσαν.
4   θαυμάζομεν τὸ ἱερὸν ὡς* καλὸν ὄν.
5   τὸ ζῷον τὸ τὸν δοῦλον διῶκον μέγιστόν ἐστιν.
6   ἡ Ἀφροδίτη θεὰ οὖσα δῶρα τοῖς ἀνθρώποις παρέχει.
7   αἱ τοῦ διδασκάλου βίβλοι χρήσιμαι οὖσαι ἡμᾶς διδάσκουσιν.
8   ἆρα πιστεύεις τῇ Μούσῃ τῇ τοὺς ποιητὰς διδασκούσῃ;
9   ἐλάβομεν τὴν χώραν ὡς* χρησίμην οὖσαν.
10  ἆρα εἰσεδράμετε εἰς τὸ ἱερὸν τὸ τὴν μεγίστην θύραν ἔχον;

ἡμᾶς   us *(acc pl)*

* ὡς (literally *as*) with a present participle specifies that the meaning is *because* or *on the grounds that*

# Background: Alexander the Great

Alexander (356-323 BC) became in his short life the greatest general in Greek history. His father Philip II, king of Macedon in the northern mountains, had made himself leader (almost dictator) of the Greek city-states. Alexander inherited this role, and his father's ambition to lead an army against Persia to avenge the wrongs inflicted on Greece in the Persian Wars 150 years earlier.

Alexander also looked back even further for inspiration: to the Trojan War of Homer, on whose greatest hero Achilles he modelled himself. He spent the last ten years of his life creating the largest empire the world had yet seen, founding numerous cities named Alexandria after him, and penetrating as far as northern India.

Writers accompanied his campaign, and Alexander himself kept a diary. These works do not themselves survive. But we have numerous accounts from later Greek times which drew on contemporary sources. Some accounts are hostile, seeing Alexander as a tyrant corrupted by power. But the majority admire him as a supremely successful commander, a remarkable character, and a worthy heir of the Homeric heroes.

Exercise 6.2

# Alexander and Bucephalas

*The young Alexander acquires the horse that will serve him faithfully in his career of conquest.*

Φιλόνεικος* ὁ Θεσσαλός, ἵππων ἔμπορος ὤν, πρὸς τὴν Μακεδονίαν καὶ
τὰ τοῦ Φιλίππου βασίλεια ποτε ἦλθεν. ἵππον γὰρ μέγιστον καὶ κάλλιστον
εἶχεν. καὶ ὁ Φίλιππος εἶπε, "τί ἐστι τὸ τοῦ ἵππου ὄνομα;"
"Βουκεφάλας ἐστί, διότι κεφαλὴν μεγίστην ἔχει, ὥσπερ βοῦς."
5  "καὶ τίς ἡ τιμή;"
"τρία καὶ δέκα τάλαντα· ὁ γὰρ ἵππος ἄριστός ἐστιν."
ὁ μέντοι Βουκεφάλας καίπερ κάλλιστος ὢν ἄγριος ἦν· ὥστ' οὐδεὶς τῶν
τοῦ Φιλίππου δούλων καὶ φίλων οἷός τ' ἦν κατέχειν. ὁ οὖν Φίλιππος
ἐκέλευσε τὸν Φιλόνεικον ἀπάγειν τὸν ἵππον.

10  ἔπειτα δὲ βοή τις ἦν. ὁ γὰρ ᾿Αλέξανδρος, ἔτι παῖς ὤν, εἶπε τοῖς παροῦσι
"μωροί ἐστε. ὁ γὰρ Βουκεφάλας ἄριστός ἐστιν. διὰ τί ἀποπέμπει τὸν
ἵππον ὁ ἐμὸς πατήρ;" ὁ οὖν Φίλιππος εἶπε τῷ παιδί, "ἆρα σύ, νέος ὤν,

* note that the first time a proper name occurs, the usual definite article is often omitted

|  |  |  |
|---|---|---|
| | Φιλόνεικος -ου ὁ | Philoneikos |
| | Θεσσαλός -οῦ ὁ | Thessalian, man of Thessaly (*area of north-central Greece famous for horse-breeding*) |
| | ἔμπορος -ου ὁ | trader |
| | Μακεδονία -ας ἡ | Macedonia |
| | Φίλιππος -ου ὁ | Philip |
| | βασίλεια -ων τά | palace |
| | ποτε | (*not a question*) once |
| | ἦλθον | (*irreg aor*) I came |
| | Βουκεφάλας ὁ | Bucephalas |
| | κεφαλή -ῆς ἡ | head |
| | ὥσπερ | just as, like |
| | βοῦς ὁ | ox |
| 5 | τιμή -ῆς ἡ | (*here*) price |
| | τρία καὶ δέκα | thirteen |
| | τάλαντον -ου τό | talent (*very large unit of currency*) |
| | ἄριστος -η -ον | very good, excellent |
| | καίπερ | although, despite (*followed by participle*) |
| | ἄγριος -α -ον | wild |
| | ὥστε | and so, as a result |
| | οὐδείς | no-one, none |
| | κατέχω | I restrain |
| 10 | ᾿Αλέξανδρος -ου ὁ | Alexander |
| | πατήρ ὁ | father |
| | νέος -α -ον | (*here*) young |

οἷός τ' εἶ τὸν ἵππον κατέχειν; οἱ γὰρ ἐμοὶ φίλοι καὶ δοῦλοι, ἔμπειροι
ὄντες, οὐχ οἷοί τ' ἦσαν. ἀλλ' ὁ Βουκεφάλας πάρεστί σοι. κατέχε οὖν τὸν
15 ἵππον· εἰ δὲ μή, τὴν σὴν προπέτειαν κολάσω."

ὁ οὖν 'Αλέξανδρος τῷ ἵππῳ εὐθὺς προσέδραμεν. τὴν δὲ ἡνίαν ἔλαβε, καὶ
τὸν ἵππον πρὸς τόν ἥλιον ἐπέστρεψεν. ἔπειτα δὲ τὴν κεφαλὴν ψήχων
ἀνέβαινεν. πρότερον μὲν γὰρ ἡ σκιὰ φόβον παρεῖχε, νῦν δὲ ἥσυχος ἦν
ὁ Βουκεφάλας. καὶ ὁ 'Αλέξανδρος ἐπισταμένως ἵππευσεν. ὁ οὖν Φίλιππος,
20 περιχαρὴς ὤν, εἶπεν, "ὦ παῖ, δεῖ σε ἄλλην βασιλείαν εὑρίσκειν. ἡ γὰρ
Μακεδονία οὐχ ἱκανή."

|  |  |  |
|---|---|---|
|  | κατέχω | I restrain |
|  | ἔμπειρος -ον | experienced |
| 15 | εἰ δὲ μή | but if not, otherwise |
|  | προπέτεια -ας ἡ | rashness |
|  | κολάζω *future* κολάσω | I punish |
|  | εὐθύς | immediately |
|  | ἡνία -ας ἡ | bridle |
|  | ἥλιος -ου ὁ | sun |
|  | ἐπιστρέφω ἐπέστρεψα | I turn (something) |
|  | κεφαλή -ῆς ἡ | head |
|  | ψήχω | I stroke |
|  | ἀναβαίνω | I mount, I get on (a horse *etc*) |
|  | σκιά -ᾶς ἡ | shadow |
|  | ἥσυχος -ον | calm |
|  | ἐπισταμένως | skilfully |
|  | ἱππεύω ἵππευσα | I ride |
| 20 | περιχαρής | delighted |
|  | δεῖ σε | it is necessary for you (to, + *infinitive*) |
|  | βασιλεία -ας ἡ | kingdom |
|  | ἱκανός -ή -όν | enough, sufficient |

Exercise 6.3

## Alexander seeks Revenge

*Alexander, after assuming power (at the age of twenty), explicitly links his heroic ancestry and his desire to punish the aggressors in the Persian Wars of 490-479 BC.*

ἐπεὶ δ' ἐχθρός τις τὸν Φίλιππον ἀπέκτεινεν, ὁ Ἀλέξανδρος, ἔτι νεανίας
ὤν, τὴν ἀρχὴν παρέλαβεν. τοὺς οὖν στρατηγοὺς συνέλεξεν· ἔπειτα δ'
εἶπε, "στρατὸν μέγιστον πρὸς Ἀσίαν ἄξω. ὁ γὰρ Ἀχιλλεύς, στρατιώτης
ἀνδρεῖος καὶ πρόγονός μοι, ἐν τῇ Ἀσίᾳ δόξαν ἔλαβεν. καὶ ἐγὼ τοὺς
5   βαρβάρους κολάζειν ἔθελω. οἱ γὰρ βάρβαροι τοὺς Ἕλληνας τρισὶν
ἐμβολαῖς πάλαι ἔβλαψαν."

| | |
|---|---|
| ἐχθρός -οῦ ὁ | (*as noun*) enemy |
| ἀρχή -ῆς ἡ | rule, power |
| παραλαμβάνω παρέλαβον | I succeed to, I take over |
| συλλέγω συνέλεξα | I gather together |
| Ἀσία -ας ἡ | Asia |
| Ἀχιλλεύς ὁ | Achilles (*greatest Greek hero of the Trojan War*) |
| πρόγονος -ου ὁ | ancestor |
| δόξα -ης ἡ | glory |
| 5   βάρβαροι -ων οἱ | barbarians |
| κολάζω | I punish |
| Ἕλληνες -ων οἱ | Greeks |
| τρισί(ν) | three (*dat pl*) |
| ἐμβολή -ῆς ἡ | invasion |
| πάλαι | long ago |

## More uses of the definite article (1)

• As we have seen, the definite article is used with a noun:
οἱ ποιηταί
*either*    the poets (*the ones we are talking about*)
*or*        poets (*as a class*)

• It can also be used with an adjective:
οἱ σοφοί
the wise (*as a class*), wise men

τὸ ἀγαθόν
the good (*as an abstraction*), that which is good, goodness

• And so too with a participle:
οἱ τρέχοντες
those who are running, the ones running, the runners

100

This is like the attributive use
οἱ δοῦλοι οἱ τρέχοντες
the slaves who are running
but leaving the noun to be supplied (from gender, context, etc): in effect, the participle itself (like the adjective in the previous example) has become a noun. This is a very common Greek usage.

• Here too the participle can take an object or preposition phrase, which is sandwiched:
οἱ τὸν ἵππον διώκοντες
those chasing the horse, the men chasing the horse

αἱ εἰς τὴν κώμην τρέχουσαι
the women running into the village

Exercise 6.4

*Translate into English:*
1    ἐλάβομεν τοὺς φεύγοντας.
2    οἱ τὸν ποταμὸν φυλάσσοντες ἀνδρεῖοι ἦσαν.
3    τίς ἐστιν ἡ λέγουσα;
4    ἆρα θαυμάζεις τὸ καλόν;
5    οὐκ ἤκουσα τὰς τῆς τρεχούσης βοάς.
6    ὁ τοὺς παῖδας διδάσκων σοφός ἐστιν.
7    πολλὰ ἐλέγομεν τῷ τὸν στρατὸν τάσσοντι.
8    ὁ τὰ πλοῖα ἐξάγων ἐστὶ στρατηγός.
9    ἡ τὴν βουλὴν ἔχουσα ἐν τῇ ἐκκλησίᾳ οὐκ ἦν.
10   τί ἐστι τὸ τοῦ φεύγοντος ὄνομα;

Exercise 6.5

*Translate into Greek:*
1        The woman* who was running fell into the sea.
2        The temple, being very big, has two doors.
3        Who are the men* driving the horse?
4        The girl while writing a letter stopped the work.
5        The soldier chased the women* who were running away.

* no words for *woman, men,* etc are needed in these sentences: just use the participle with the appropriate ending (preceded by the appropriate part of the definite article)

# More uses of the definite article (2)

• You have seen the definite article used with a noun:

    οἱ διδάσκαλοι         (the) teachers

and with an adjective:

    οἱ ἀνδρεῖοι          the brave, (the) brave men

and with a participle:

    οἱ τρέχοντες        those (who are) running, the runners

• It can also be used with an adverb:

    οἱ νῦν                men now, people* of today
                             * the masculine is often used inclusively

    ἡ ἐκεῖ                the woman there

    τὰ ἐνθάδε           things here, affairs here

A noun (e.g. *men, woman, things*) is understood each time from the number and gender of the article. Another common adverb often used like this is πάλαι = long ago:

    οἱ πάλαι           people (of) long ago, men of old

• The same thing can be done with a preposition phrase:

    οἱ ἐν τῇ νήσῳ       the people on the island

    αἱ ἐν τῇ κώμῃ      the women in the village

    τὰ ἐν τῷ λιμένι     the events* in the harbour

    * Context will usually indicate the most appropriate translation of the neuter (e.g. *things, affairs, events*). Something comparable is done when neuter adjectives occur with neither article nor noun, e.g. κακὰ ἔπαθον = *they suffered bad things.*

These examples can be thought of as open or incomplete sandwiches, i.e. οἱ ἐν τῇ νήσῳ represents οἱ ἐν τῇ νήσῳ (ἄνθρωποι). You need to look ahead to see whether or not a noun to complete the sandwich is coming (e.g. οἱ ἐν τῇ νήσῳ δοῦλοι); if it is not, you make an appropriate inference from the gender of the article, and context. Compare also the common expression τὰ τοῦ πολέμου = *the affairs of war, warfare, military matters*: a similarly unfinished genitive sandwich.

Exercise 6.6

*Translate into English:*

1      οἱ ἐν τῇ ἐκκλησίᾳ ἤκουσαν τοὺς τοῦ στρατηγοῦ λόγους.
2      τίς ἐστιν ὁ λέγων;
3      αἱ τὴν κώμην φυλάσσουσαι ἔπαυσαν τὸν πόλεμον.
4      ὁ ἄγγελος ἔλεγε τὰ <u>περὶ</u> τῆς ναυμαχίας.
        περί  (+ *gen*) about, concerning

5     οἱ μὲν πάλαι ἀνδρεῖοι ἦσαν, οἱ δὲ νῦν σοφοί.
6     ἀρα εἶδες τὴν τὸν ἐμὸν ἵππον διώκουσαν;
7     πῶς ἔμαθες τὰ τοῦ πολέμου;
8     ὁ τὸ δεῖπνον ἐσθίων δοῦλός ἐστιν.
9     αἱ ἐν τῇ νήσῳ ἐφύλασσον τὰ πλοῖα.
10    οἱ πολλάκις φεύγοντες οὐκ εἰσιν ἀνδρεῖοι.

Exercise 6.7

*Translate into Greek:*
*(no words needed for* men, women, things *etc: these are expressed by appropriate part of the article)*
1     The men in the village were guarding the gate.
2     Who is the woman in the road?
3     The events in the war produced fear.
4     The man guarding the boats is a stranger.
5     The people in the assembly believed the messenger.

Exercise 6.8

# Alexander and Hope

καὶ ἐπεὶ ὁ Ἀλέξανδρος ἤθελε τὸν στρατὸν πρὸς Ἀσίαν ἄγειν, πάντα τὰ
χρήματα τοῖς φίλοις πρῶτον ἔνειμεν. ὁ οὖν Περδίκκας, φίλος τις τοῦ
Ἀλεξάνδρου, εἶπεν αὐτῷ, "ὦ βασιλεῦ, πάντα τὰ χρήματα ἡμῖν ἔνειμας.
ἀλλὰ τί σοι λοιπόν ἐστιν;" "ἡ ἐλπίς," εἶπεν ὁ Ἀλέξανδρος. ὁ οὖν
5  Περδίκκας ἐπεὶ ἤκουσε τὸν τοῦ Ἀλεξάνδρου λόγον εἶπεν αὐτῷ, "πρὸς
Ἀσίαν καὶ πρὸς πόλεμον στρατεύων, ἐθέλω τὴν σὴν ἐλπίδα ἔχειν μᾶλλον
ἢ τὰ σὰ χρήματα".

| | |
|---|---|
| Ἀσία -ας ἡ | Asia |
| πάντα | all |
| χρήματα -ων τά | money |
| νέμω ἔνειμα | I distribute |
| Περδίκκας ὁ | Perdiccas |
| αὐτῷ | to him |
| βασιλεύς ὁ (*voc* βασιλεῦ) | king |
| πάντα | all |
| ἡμῖν | to us |
| λοιπός -ή -όν | left, remaining |
| ἐλπίς -ίδος ἡ | hope |
| 5  αὐτῷ | to him |
| στρατεύω | I march, I go on a campaign |
| μᾶλλον ἤ | rather than |

Exercise 6.9 (Revision)

*Translate into English:*
1    ὁ τοῦ πολέμου κίνδυνος μέγιστος νῦν ἐστιν.
2    ἡ θάλασσα, χαλεπὴ οὖσα, ἐκώλυσε τὸν ἄγγελον.
3    ἆρα ὁ τοὺς παῖδας <u>παιδεύων</u> δοῦλός ἐστιν;
4    ὁ στρατιώτης εἰς τὸν ποταμὸν εἰσέπεσεν.
5    ἐθαυμάσαμεν τὰς σοφῶς λεγούσας.
6    τίνες εἰσὶν οἱ εἰς τὴν ἀγορὰν τρέχοντες;
7    δοῦλός τις ἐν τῇ ὁδῷ ἐστιν.
8    ὁ περὶ τῆς ναυμαχίας λόγος μακρὸς ἦν.
9    οἱ στρατιῶται οἱ φεύγοντες ἵππον τινὰ ηὗρον.
10   τὸ σὸν πλοῖον ἐν τῷ λιμένι οὐκ ἔστιν, ὦ νεανία.


παιδεύω   I train, I educate

Exercise 6.10

*Translate into Greek:*
1    The man writing the letter is wise.
2    The men of old used to suffer bad things.
3    The woman in the house did not hear the words of the general.
4    Night stopped the events* of the day.
5    The people there were guarding the women in the village.


*no word for *events* is needed: just *the things of the day* (using the neuter article)


# Revision checkpoint

*Make sure you know:*
• the declension and uses of the present participle
• the use of the definite article with adjectives, participles, adverbs, and preposition phrases

Exercise 6.11

# Alexander at Troy

*Alexander reaches the site of Achilles' heroic exploits.*

ὁ δ' Ἀλέξανδρος, τὸν στρατὸν πρὸς τὴν <u>Ἀσίαν</u> ἄγων, πρὸς χώραν
τινὰ <u>προσῆλθεν</u>· ἐνθάδε ἡ <u>Τροία πάλαι</u> ἦν. ὁ οὖν Ἀλέξανδρος πρῶτον
μὲν τῷ <u>Πριάμῳ ἔθυσε</u>, διὰ φόβον τῆς <u>ὀργῆς αὐτοῦ</u>. καὶ οἱ τῆς χώρας
<u>ἔνοικοι</u> εἶπον, "ἦν πάλαι ἄλλος Ἀλέξανδρος. ὁ γὰρ <u>Πάρις</u>, ὁ τοῦ
5  Πριάμου <u>υἱός</u>, ἄλλο ὄνομα εἶχεν· <u>ὥστ'</u> Ἀλέξανδρος ἦν, <u>ὥσπερ</u> σύ. ἔχομεν
ἔτι νῦν τὴν τοῦ Ἀλεξάνδρου <u>λύραν</u>. ἆρ' ἐθέλεις <u>ἰδεῖν</u>;" ὁ μέντοι
Ἀλέξανδρος εἶπεν, "οὐ τὴν τοῦ Ἀλεξάνδρου λύραν ἀλλὰ τὸν τοῦ
<u>Ἀχιλλέως τάφον</u> ἐθέλω ἰδεῖν. ὁ γὰρ Ἀχιλλεὺς <u>ἥρως</u> μέγιστος ἦν καὶ
<u>πρόγονός</u> μοι." ἔπειτα δὲ πρὸς τὸν τοῦ Ἀχιλλέως τάφον ἔδραμεν. καὶ
10  <u>στέφανον</u> <u>ἐπὶ</u> τοῦ τάφου λείπων εἶπεν, "ὦ Ἀχιλλεῦ, πρόγονος ἐμός,
σύμμαχος ἐν τῷ πολέμῳ <u>ἴσθι</u>."

|  |  |  |
|---|---|---|
|  | Ἀσία -ας ἡ | Asia |
|  | προσῆλθον | (*irreg aor*) I came to |
|  | Τροία -ας ἡ | Troy |
|  | πάλαι | long ago |
|  | Πρίαμος -ου ὁ | Priam (*King of Troy at the time of the Trojan War*) |
|  | θύω ἔθυσα | I sacrifice |
|  | ὀργή -ῆς ἡ | anger |
|  | αὐτοῦ | his, of him |
|  | ἔνοικος -ου ὁ | inhabitant |
|  | Πάρις ὁ | Paris (*prince of Troy whose abduction of Helen started the Trojan War*) |
| 5 | υἱός -οῦ ὁ | son |
|  | ὥστε | and so, as a result |
|  | ὥσπερ | just as, like |
|  | λύρα -ας ἡ | lyre (*musical instrument resembling simple harp*) |
|  | ἰδεῖν | to see |
|  | Ἀχιλλεύς -έως* (*voc* -εῦ) ὁ | Achilles (*greatest Greek hero in the Trojan War*) |
|  | τάφος -ου ὁ | tomb |
|  | ἥρως ὁ | hero |
|  | πρόγονος -ου ὁ | ancestor |
| 10 | στέφανος -ου ὁ | wreath, garland |
|  | ἐπί | (+ *gen*) on |
|  | ἴσθι | be! (*sg imperative of* εἰμί) |

\* note that with nouns of this type (which will be explained fully in Chapter 9) the
third-declension genitive singular -ος is lengthened to -ως

# The uses of αὐτός (1)

• You have already seen αὐτός = *himself,* αὐτοῦ = *his/of him,* αὐτούς = *them* (masc acc pl). These are parts of αὐτός, an extremely important word with a range of uses. Here is its declension in full:

|    |     | masculine | feminine | neuter |
|----|-----|-----------|----------|--------|
| sg | nom | αὐτ-ός    | αὐτ-ή    | αὐτ-ό  |
|    | acc | αὐτ-όν    | αὐτ-ήν   | αὐτ-ό  |
|    | gen | αὐτ-οῦ    | αὐτ-ῆς   | αὐτ-οῦ |
|    | dat | αὐτ-ῷ     | αὐτ-ῇ    | αὐτ-ῷ  |
|    |     |           |          |        |
| pl | nom | αὐτ-οί    | αὐτ-αί   | αὐτ-ά  |
|    | acc | αὐτ-ούς   | αὐτ-άς   | αὐτ-ά  |
|    | gen | αὐτ-ῶν    | αὐτ-ῶν   | αὐτ-ῶν |
|    | dat | αὐτ-οῖς   | αὐτ-αῖς  | αὐτ-οῖς |

• The declension in all three genders is like the adjective σοφός, except that (like the article, and most pronouns) the neuter nominative and accusative singular ends -o rather than -ον.

• It has *three* separate meanings, according to context and word order:
  (1)  self (compare *auto-* in English);
  (2)  same;
  (3)  him/her/it/them

• The meaning is *self* when αὐτός is used with article + noun but *not sandwiched*:
  ὁ στρατηγὸς αὐτός = the general himself*

• The meaning is *same* when αὐτός is sandwiched with article + noun:
  ὁ αὐτὸς στρατηγός = the same general*

* Note that in both uses the word order is normally the same as the equivalent English (though with the first example αὐτὸς ὁ στρατηγός is also possible: the crucial point is that it is not sandwiched).

• The meaning is *him/her/it/them* (according to number and gender) when αὐτός is used on its own and is *not in the nominative*:

  διδάσκομεν αὐτούς.
  We teach them.

  πιστεύω αὐτῇ.
  I trust her.

Exercise 6.12

*Translate into English:*
1   ὁ γίγας αὐτὸς ἔφαγε τοὺς ἀνθρώπους.
2   δύο παῖδες τὸ αὐτὸ ὄνομα ἔχουσιν.
3   ὁ ξένος νῦν πάρεστιν, ἀλλὰ τίς φυλάσσει αὐτόν;
4   ὁ αὐτὸς στρατηγὸς ἔτασσε τούς τε στρατιώτας καὶ τοὺς ναύτας.
5   οἱ θεοὶ αὐτοὶ τὰ δῶρα παρέχουσιν.
6   αὐτὴ ἡ παῖς διώξει τὸν ἵππον.
7   εἴδομεν αὐτοὺς φεύγοντας.
8   ἐθέλω εὑρίσκειν τὴν αὐτὴν ὁδόν.
9   οἱ λόγοι αὐτοὶ οὐ χαλεποί εἰσιν.
10  ὁ αὐτὸς ἵππος ἔφερεν αὐτούς.

Exercise 6.13

*Translate into Greek:*
1   I led him into the camp.
2   We were speaking the same words.
3   The judge himself taught me.
4   Who persuaded her to listen?
5   The house itself has two doors.


# The uses of αὐτός (2)

All the uses of αὐτός you will meet come into one of the three categories described above: it is important to be clear about the distinction between them.

Note the following further points about each:

(1) αὐτός = *self* is not necessarily third person: if it is nominative, its person is determined by the person ending of the verb (to which it adds emphasis). So for example:
   ἆρα τὸν δοῦλον ἔλυσας αὐτός, ὦ γέρον;
   Did you release the slave yourself, old man?

(2) αὐτός = *same* is an adjective, as in the example above (ὁ αὐτὸς στρατηγός = *the same general*, parallel to e.g. ὁ σοφὸς στρατηγός = *the wise general*). Like any adjective, it can be used with the article alone (as a sort of incomplete sandwich), to make a noun: so for example ὁ αὐτός = *the same man*, τὰ αὐτά = *the same things*. The crucial point here is that αὐτός coming immediately after the article always means 'same'.

(3) αὐτόν etc (alone and *not* in the nominative) = *him/her/it/them* in contrast is always a pronoun and is always third person.

107

Exercise 6.14

# Alexander's Leadership

*Several versions of this story exist, set at different stages in his career, but the point is always to explain why Alexander's troops (enduring great hardship and long absence from home) remained so devoted to him.*

ὁ τοῦ Ἀλεξάνδρου στρατὸς διὰ χώρας τινὸς <u>θερμῆς</u> ἔβαινεν. οἱ δὲ στρατιῶται <u>ὕδωρ</u> οὐκ εἶχον. καὶ ὁ Ἀλέξανδρος αὐτός, <u>καίπερ</u> κακὰ πάσχων, <u>ἐφ'</u> ἵππον <u>ἀναβαίνειν</u> οὐκ ἤθελεν. οἱ οὖν στρατιῶται οἱοί τ' ἦσαν τὴν <u>δίψαν</u> <u>φέρειν</u>, ἐπεὶ εἶδον τὸν στρατηγὸν τὰ αὐτὰ πάσχοντα.
5 ἔπειτα δέ τινες τῶν στρατιωτῶν ἀπὸ τῆς ὁδοῦ ἀπέδραμον· ἤθελον γὰρ ὕδωρ εὑρίσκειν. καὶ <u>πηγήν</u> τινα μικρὰν <u>τέλος</u> ηὗρον, ὕδωρ <u>ὀλίγον</u> ἔχουσαν. ἐπεὶ οὖν τὸ ὕδωρ <u>συνέλεξαν</u>, ἐν <u>κόρυθι</u> <u>βραδέως</u> ἔφερον, <u>ὥσπερ</u> ἆθλον ἀγαθὸν ὄν. ἐπεὶ δὲ τὸν στρατὸν <u>αὖθις</u> εἶδον, οἱ τὴν κόρυθα φέροντες τὸ ὕδωρ τῷ Ἀλεξάνδρῳ παρέσχον. ὁ μέντοι Ἀλέξανδρος εἶπεν
10 αὐτοῖς, "ὦ φίλοι, τοῦ δώρου <u>χάριν ἔχω</u>. ἀλλ' οὐχ οἷός τ' εἰμὶ πίνειν. οἱ γὰρ στρατιῶται, ὕδωρ οὐκ ἔχοντες, τὰ αὐτὰ κακὰ πάσχουσιν." καὶ ὁ Ἀλέξανδρος τὴν κόρυθα <u>εὐθὺς</u> <u>κατέβαλεν</u>.

| | θερμός -ή -όν | hot |
|---|---|---|
| | ὕδωρ -ατος τό | water |
| | καίπερ | although (+ *participle*) |
| | ἐφ' | = ἐπί (*elided*) (+ *acc, here*) on, onto |
| | ἀναβαίνω | I get up, I mount |
| | δίψα -ης ἡ | thirst |
| | φέρω | (*here*) I bear, I put up with |
| 5 | πηγή -ῆς ἡ | spring |
| | τέλος | finally |
| | ὀλίγος -η -ον | a little, a small amount of |
| | συλλέγω συνέλεξα | I collect (something) |
| | κόρυς -υθος ἡ | helmet |
| | βραδέως | slowly |
| | ὥσπερ | as if |
| | αὖθις | again |
| 10 | χάριν ἔχω | I am grateful (for, + *gen*) |
| | εὐθύς | immediately |
| | καταβάλλω κατέβαλον | I throw down |

# Aorist participle (1)

• The aorist active participle of verbs with a *first (weak) aorist* declines in the masculine exactly like a third declension noun such as γίγας. The endings are added to the *aorist stem*: i.e. normally the present stem plus sigma (but *without the augment*, which is used only for the tense itself):

| sg | nom | παύσ-ας | having stopped (see notes below) |
|----|-----|---------|----------|
|    | acc | παύσ-αντα |  |
|    | gen | παύσ-αντος |  |
|    | dat | παύσ-αντι |  |

| pl | nom | παύσ-αντες |
|----|-----|-----------|
|    | acc | παύσ-αντας |
|    | gen | παυσ-άντων |
|    | dat | παύσ-ασι(ν)* |

* as will be familiar by now, this is a contraction of παυσ-αντσι(ν)

• The aorist participle is used to indicate a single action (rather than a process), and normally one which *has already happened* at the time of the action described in the main verb of the sentence. (This is the same principle we saw with the present participle, where the tense of the participle is *in relation to* that of the main verb.)

• The literal translation of the aorist participle (the way to think of it before recasting it into better English) is thus normally e.g. *having stopped*.

• If the main narrative is in the past, it will often be appropriate to translate the aorist participle like a pluperfect: *having done X, they did Y* comes out as *when they had done X, they did Y*. This is comparable to the way a present participle is often translated like an imperfect: *(while) doing X, they (suddenly) did Y* comes out as *when they were doing X, they did Y*.

• The uses of the aorist participle, the effect of the article, and the possible introductory words in translation (*when ..., who ...* etc) are similar to those of the present participle, except that *while ...* is replaced by *after ... *.

Exercise 6.15

*Translate into English:*
1    ὁ δοῦλος λύσας τὸν ἵππον πρὸς τὴν οἰκίαν προσέδραμεν.
2    ἆρα πιστεύεις τῷ τὴν ἐπιστολὴν γράψαντι;
3    ὁ παῖς τὰς βοὰς ἀκούσας πρὸς τὴν σὴν οἰκίαν ἔφυγεν.
4    τίς ἐστιν ὁ στρατηγὸς ὁ τοὺς στρατιώτας τάξας;
5    ὁ τὴν ἐπιστολὴν πέμψας ἐστὶ σύμμαχος.
6    θαυμάζομεν τὸν τοὺς παῖδας διδάξαντα.
7    δῶρον παρέχω τῷ τὸν δοῦλον διώξαντι.
8    ὁ ποιητὴς ὁ τὸν δῆμον πείσας τιμὴν ἔχει.
9    οἱ ναῦται, τὰ πλοῖα δύο ὥρας φυλάξαντες, ἀπέδραμον.
10   πιστεύομεν τῷ τὴν ναυμαχίαν παύσαντι.

• Here is the first (weak) aorist participle in full, for all three genders:

|    |     | masculine | femimine | neuter |
|----|-----|-----------|----------|--------|
| sg | nom | παύσ-ας | παύσ-ασ-α | παῦσ-αν |
|    | acc | παύσ-αντα | παύσ-ασ-αν | παῦσ-αν |
|    | gen | παύσ-αντος | παυσ-άσ-ης | παύσ-αντος |
|    | dat | παύσ-αντι | παυσ-άσ-η | παῦσ-αντι |
| pl | nom | παύσ-αντες | παύσ-ασ-αι | παύσ-αντα |
|    | acc | παύσ-αντας | παυσ-άσ-ας | παύσ-αντα |
|    | gen | παυσ-άντων | παυσ-ασ-ῶν | παυσ-άντων |
|    | dat | παύσ-ασι(ν) | παυσ-άσ-αις | παύσ-ασι(ν) |

• As we have already seen, the masculine is identical to a third-declension noun such as γίγας.

• As with the present participle, the neuter here too is third declension, and a predictable variant of the masculine: its nominative a shortened version of the stem; nominative and accusative the same; nominative and accusative plural ending in alpha.

• Also as with the present participle, the feminine adds another syllable to the verb stem (this time -ασ-) and then is identical to a first-declension noun like θάλασσα.

• Both present and aorist participles are thus '3-1-3' in declension: i.e. the masculine is third, the feminine is first, and the neuter is third. The formula could be more fully expressed as 3(m)-1(f)-3(n), but because the masculine-feminine-neuter order is conventional, 3-1-3 is enough.

## The adjective πᾶς

• Adjectives you have seen so far, e.g. σοφός, are (to use a similar formula) 2-1-2 in declension: i.e. the masculine is second, the feminine is first, and the neuter is second declension. (Like Latin *bonus*.) There are also third-declension adjectives. An extremely common one is πᾶς = *all* (also *each, every*). This is identical in formation to a first (weak) aorist participle. It is likewise 3-1-3 in declension. Here it is in full:

|    |     | masculine | femimine | neuter |
|----|-----|-----------|----------|--------|
| sg | nom | πᾶς | πᾶσ-α | πᾶν |
|    | acc | πάντ-α | πᾶσ-αν | πᾶν |
|    | gen | παντ-ός | πάσ-ης | παντ-ός |
|    | dat | παντ-ί | πάσ-η | παντ-ί |
| pl | nom | πάντ-ες | πᾶσ-αι | πάντ-α |
|    | acc | πάντ-ας | πάσ-ας | πάντ-α |
|    | gen | πάντ-ων | πασ-ῶν | πάντ-ων |
|    | dat | πᾶσι(ν) | πάσ-αις | πᾶσι(ν) |

• When used (as it commonly is) with a noun and the article, πᾶς does not sandwich:
e.g.     πάντες οἱ πολῖται
         all the citizens  (*same order as English*)
or       οἱ πολῖται πάντες (*with the same meaning*)

• Like any adjective, it can also be used alone (leaving a noun to be understood from the number, gender, and context):
e.g.     πάντες ἔφυγον.
         They all ran away.

         πάντα μανθάνει.
         He learns all things (*or* everything).

• The presence of the article in the singular usually indicates that the meaning is *the whole (of)* rather than *every*:
e.g.     πάντα τὸν μῦθον μανθάνω.
            I learn the whole story.
Contrast:
         πάντα μῦθον μανθάνω.
         I learn every story.

• A high percentage of English words beginning *pan-* or *pant-* are derivatives of πᾶς.

Exercise 6.16

*Give the English meaning, and the Greek word joined to* pan(t), *in:*
1        pandemic
2        Pandora
3        pantheism
4        pantograph
5        pantophobia

Exercise 6.17

*Translate into English:*
1        ἡ κόρη ἡ πάντας τοὺς ἵππους λύσασα <u>οὐκέτι</u> ἐν τῇ κώμῃ ἐστίν.
2        τίνες εἰσὶν οἱ τὸν δῆμον πείσαντες;
3        ἔχω τὸ τόξον τὸ τὸν πόλεμον παῦσαν.
4        πολλάκις διδάξας ἀεὶ μανθάνω.
5        αἱ τὴν κώμην φυλάξασαι ἀνδρεῖαί εἰσιν.
6        ἆρα πιστεύεις παντὶ τῷ μύθῳ;
7        ἡ θεά, τὰς βοὰς ἀκούσασα, ἄγγελον ἔπεμψεν.
8        οἱ παῖδες εἰς πάντα κίνδυνον εἰσέπιπτον.
9        τί ἐστι τὸ ὄνομα τῆς τὴν ἐπιστολὴν γραψάσης;
10       οἱ τοὺς <u>πολεμίους</u> διώξαντες σύμμαχοί εἰσιν.
οὐκέτι   no longer              πολέμιοι -ων οἱ  enemy (*in war;* ἐχθρός *is used for a personal enemy*)

Exercise 6.18

*Translate into Greek:*
1    They have all the gifts.
2    The soldiers, after guarding the island for five days, were no longer willing to
        remain.
3    The woman who had written the letter was not in the house.
4    Those who have heard the story trust the messenger.
5    I want to find the man who has released the lions.


# Revision checkpoint

*Make sure you know:*
• the declension and three main uses of αὐτός
• the declension and meaning of the first (weak) aorist participle (all three genders)
• the declension and use of πᾶς


Exercise 6.19

## Alexander and the Gordian Knot (1)

*This story has become proverbial for solving a difficulty by drastic means.*

ὁ δ' Ἀλέξανδρος <u>εἰσῆλθεν</u> εἰς <u>τόπον</u> τινά, <u>Γόρδιον</u> ὀνόματι. ὁ τόπος
ὄνομα ἔχει ἀπὸ ἀνθρώπου τινὸς τῶν <u>πάλαι</u>. ὁ γὰρ <u>Γόρδιος πένης</u> ἦν.
οἰκίαν μικρὰν ἐν τοῖς ἀγροῖς εἶχεν. ἦν δ' αὐτῷ <u>υἱός</u>, <u>Μίδας</u> ὀνόματι.
<u>πόλις</u> δέ τις <u>ἐγγὺς</u> ἦν, καὶ ἐκεῖ <u>στάσις</u> μεγίστη ἐν τοῖς πολίταις. οἱ μέντοι
5    πολῖται ἐθαύμασαν <u>μαντεῖον</u> τῶν θεῶν ἀκούσαντες· "<u>ἅμαξα</u> ἄξει <u>ὑμῖν</u>
<u>σωτῆρα</u>· καὶ <u>βασιλεὺς</u> ὢν τὰ ἐν ὑμῖν κακὰ παύσει". ἐπεὶ δὲ οἱ πολῖται

| | | |
|---|---|---|
| | εἰσῆλθον | (*irreg aor*) I came in |
| | τόπος -ου ὁ | place |
| | Γόρδιον -ου τό | Gordium |
| | πάλαι | long ago |
| | Γόρδιος -ου ὁ | Gordius |
| | πένης -ητος ὁ | poor man |
| | υἱός -οῦ ὁ | son |
| | Μίδας ὁ | Midas |
| | πόλις ἡ | city |
| | ἐγγύς | nearby |
| | στάσις ἡ | civil strife, revolution |
| 5 | μαντεῖον -ου τό | oracle, oracular response |
| | ἅμαξα -ης ἡ | cart |
| | ὑμῖν | you (*dat pl*) |
| | σωτήρ -ῆρος ὁ | saviour, deliverer |
| | βασιλεύς ὁ | king |

περὶ τοῦ <u>μαντείου</u> ἔτι ἔλεγον, ὁ Μίδας <u>καρπὸν</u> φέρων ἐν τῇ τοῦ Γορδίου <u>ἁμάξῃ</u> εἰς τὴν ἀγορὰν <u>εἰσῆλθεν</u>. οἱ δὲ πολῖται εἶπον, "ὦ ξένε, ὦ <u>βασιλεῦ</u>, <u>εἰς καιρὸν</u> <u>ἦλθες</u>." ὁ οὖν Μίδας, βασιλεὺς νῦν ὤν, τὰ τῶν πολιτῶν κακὰ
10  <u>παύσας</u>, τὴν ἅμαξαν ἐν τῷ ἱερῷ ἔλιπεν ὡς <u>χαριστήριον</u>.

| | |
|---|---|
| περί | (+ *gen*) about, concerning |
| μαντεῖον -ου τό | oracle, oracular response |
| καρπός -οῦ ὁ | produce, harvest |
| ἅμαξα -ης ἡ | cart |
| εἰσῆλθον | (*irreg aor*) I came in |
| βασιλεύς ὁ (*voc* βασιλεῦ) | king |
| εἰς καιρόν | at just the right time |
| ἦλθον | (*irreg aor*) I came |
| 10  χαριστήριον -ου τό | thank-offering |

## Aorist participle (2)

• The aorist participles you have seen so far (e.g. παύσας) are of verbs with a *first* (or *weak*) aorist: normally adding sigma to the stem, and with an alpha in most bits both of the tense itself and of the participle.

• Verbs with a *second* (or *strong*) aorist (e.g. λαμβάνω), as we saw, form the aorist *tense* by borrowing the endings of the *imperfect* tense and putting them onto a special *aorist stem* (very often a shortened version of the present stem):

| e.g. | imperfect | ἐλάμβανον |
|---|---|---|
| | aorist | ἔλαβον |

Verbs with a second aorist form their aorist *participle* by borrowing the endings of the *present participle* and putting them onto the *aorist stem* (again *without the augment*, which is used only for the tense itself).

| e.g. | present participle | λαμβάνων |
|---|---|---|
| | aorist participle | λαβών |

• Here is the second (strong) aorist participle in full, for all three genders:

| | | *masculine* | *feminine* | *neuter* |
|---|---|---|---|---|
| *sg* | *nom* | λαβ-ών | λαβ-οῦσ-α | λαβ-όν |
| | *acc* | λαβ-όντα | λαβ-οῦσ-αν | λαβ-όν |
| | *gen* | λαβ-όντος | λαβ-ούσ-ης | λαβ-όντος |
| | *dat* | λαβ-όντι | λαβ-ούσ-η | λαβ-όντι |
| | | | | |
| *pl* | *nom* | λαβ-όντες | λαβ-οῦσ-αι | λαβ-όντα |
| | *acc* | λαβ-όντας | λαβ-ούσ-ας | λαβ-όντα |
| | *gen* | λαβ-όντων | λαβ-ουσ-ῶν | λαβ-όντων |
| | *dat* | λαβ-οῦσι(ν) | λαβ-ούσ-αις | λαβ-οῦσι(ν) |

113

• This works for verbs with a fairly regular or predictable aorist stem:

e.g.     present participle          μανθάνων
         aorist participle           μαθών

and for verbs with a completely irregular aorist stem:

e.g.     present participle          τρεχών
         aorist participle           δραμών

So long as you know, or look up, the aorist tense, the formation of the aorist participle should cause no difficulty. There is a list of aorist tenses and stems on page 129 below.

Excercise 6.20

*Translate into English:*
1        ὁ γίγας, δέκα ναύτας λαβών, ἔφαγε πάντας.
2        κακὰ παθόντες, ἐκ τῆς ναυμαχίας ἐφύγομεν.
3        οἱ πάντας τοὺς λόγους μαθόντες σοφοί εἰσιν.
4        αἱ παῖδες, τὸ δεῖπνον φαγοῦσαι, ἐν τῇ οἰκίᾳ ἔμενον.
5        τίς ἐστιν ὁ δοῦλος ὁ εἰς τὸν ποταμὸν εἰσπεσών;
6        ὁ στρατηγὸς ὁ τὸν στρατὸν ἄγων σοφός τε καὶ ἀγαθός ἐστιν.
7        οἱ στρατιῶται, πρὸς τὸ στρατόπεδον προσδραμόντες, φόβον
           οὐκέτι εἶχον.
8        αἱ τὸν ἄγγελον εὑροῦσαι πρὸς τὴν ἀγορὰν προσήγαγον αὐτόν.
9        οἱ ἐν τῷ πολέμῳ ἀποθανόντες ἀνδρεῖοι ἦσαν.
10      τὴν βίβλον ἀποβαλὼν οὐκέτι μανθάνω.

Exercise 6.21

*Translate into Greek:*
1        The boys, having taken the gift, ran away.
2        The woman who had found the letter was in the agora.
3        After leading the army out of danger, the general found a friendly village.
4        When I had learned the words I threw away the book.
5        The man who has eaten the dinner is a slave.

# Alexander and the Gordian Knot (2)

καὶ μετὰ πολλὰς <u>γενεὰς</u> ἡ τοῦ <u>Γορδίου</u> <u>ἄμαξα</u> ἐν τῷ ἱερῷ ἔτι ἦν, καὶ
τιμὴν μεγίστην εἶχεν. πρῶτον μὲν γὰρ <u>παλαιὰ</u> ἦν, καὶ ἐν αὐτῇ <u>εἰσῆλθεν</u>
ὁ <u>Μίδας</u> ὡς <u>βασιλεύς·</u> ἔπειτα δὲ ἐν τῷ τοῦ <u>ζυγοῦ</u> <u>δεσμῷ</u> ἦν <u>ἄμμα</u> δεινόν
τε καὶ <u>πολύπλοκον</u>, <u>ὥστ'</u> <u>οὐδεὶς</u> οἷός τ' ἦν λύειν· καὶ λόγος τις ἐν τοῖς
5  πολίταις ἦν· "ὁ τὸ ἄμμα λύσας βασιλεὺς τῆς <u>Ἀσίας</u> <u>ἔσται</u>". ὁ οὖν
Ἀλέξανδρος τὸν λόγον ἀκούσας εἰς τὸ ἱερὸν εἰσῆλθεν. τὴν δὲ ἄμαξαν
καὶ τὸ ἄμμα εἶδεν. καὶ <u>μάχαιραν</u> λαβὼν τὸ ἄμμα ἔλυσεν· <u>ἀπάτη</u> ἦν,
ἀλλὰ <u>μεγαλοπρεπής</u>.

|  | γενεά -ᾶς ἡ | generation |
|---|---|---|
|  | Γόρδιος -ου ὁ | Gordius |
|  | ἄμαξα -ης ἡ | cart |
|  | παλαιός -ά -όν | ancient |
|  | εἰσῆλθον | (*irreg aor*) I came in |
|  | Μίδας ὁ | Midas |
|  | βασιλεύς ὁ | king |
|  | ζυγόν -οῦ τό | yoke |
|  | δεσμός -οῦ ὁ | fastening |
|  | ἄμμα -ατος τό | knot |
|  | πολύπλοκος -ον | intricate |
|  | ὥστε | with the result that |
|  | οὐδείς | no-one |
| 5 | Ἀσία -ας ἡ | Asia |
|  | ἔσται | he will be |
|  | μάχαιρα -ας ἡ | small sword |
|  | ἀπάτη -ης ἡ | cheating |
|  | μεγαλοπρεπής | magnificent |

# Numerals

You have already seen several (e.g. δύο *two*; δέκα *ten*). Here are the cardinal numbers 1 to
10:

| εἷς μία ἕν (ἑν-) | one |
|---|---|
| δύο | two |
| τρεῖς τρία | three |
| τέσσαρες τέσσαρα | four |
| πέντε | five |
| ἕξ | six |
| ἑπτά | seven |
| ὀκτώ | eight |
| ἐννέα | nine |
| δέκα | ten |

• Only 1 to 4 change their endings; the others are indeclinable.

• *One* is 3-1-3 in declension (i.e. masculine and neuter are third declension, with stem ἑν-; feminine is first declension like χώρα):

|     | masculine | feminine | neuter |     |
| --- | --- | --- | --- | --- |
| nom | εἷς | μία | ἕν | one |
| acc | ἕνα | μίαν | ἕν | |
| gen | ἑνός | μιᾶς | ἑνός | |
| dat | ἑνί | μιᾷ | ἑνί | |

The breathing (and accent, or absence of it) distinguish between:

|     |     |     |
| --- | --- | --- |
|     | εἷς | one (*masculine nom*) |
| and | εἰς | into (*prep + acc*) |

Also between:

|     |     |     |
| --- | --- | --- |
|     | ἕν | one (*neuter nom/acc*) |
| and | ἐν | in (*prep + dat*) |

• *Two* changes in the genitive and dative, but is the same for all genders:

| nom | δύο | two |
| --- | --- | --- |
| acc | δύο | |
| gen | δυοῖν | |
| dat | δυοῖν | |

(These endings are a fossilised remainder of the *dual*, a set of forms widely used in earlier Greek for both nouns and verbs when referring to *two* of anything: the plural was used originally for three or more.)

• *Three* is third declension (but just 3-3, not 3-1-3: i.e. there is no separate feminine: this is unlike *one*, and unlike the third declension participles and adjectives you have seen so far - though like a common pattern in Latin, e.g. *ingens, portans*).

|     | masc/fem | neuter |
| --- | --- | --- |
| nom | τρεῖς | τρία |
| acc | τρεῖς | τρία |
| gen | τριῶν | τριῶν |
| dat | τρισί(ν) | τρισί(ν) |

• *Four* is third declension (3-3) in just the same way:

|     | masc/fem | neuter |
| --- | --- | --- |
| nom | τέσσαρες | τέσσαρα |
| acc | τέσσαρας | τέσσαρα |
| gen | τεσσάρων | τεσσάρων |
| dat | τέσσαρσι(ν) | τέσσαρσι(ν) |

The corresponding ordinal numbers (the adjectival ones, telling you the *order* things come in) are:

| | |
|---|---|
| πρῶτος -η -ον | first |
| δεύτερος -α -ον | second |
| τρίτος -η -ον | third |
| τέταρτος -η -ον | fourth |
| πέμπτος -η -ον | fifth |
| ἕκτος -η -ον | sixth |
| ἕβδομος -η -ον | seventh |
| ὄγδοος -η -ον | eighth |
| ἔνατος -η -ον | ninth |
| δέκατος -η -ον | tenth |

• These decline like ordinary 2-1-2 adjectives: thus πρῶτος goes like σοφός (with eta in the feminine), whilst δεύτερος goes like φίλιος (with alpha in the feminine).

• Note though that ὄγδοος goes like σοφός even though its stem ends in a vowel: this is because after the first omicron there was originally a consonant called *digamma* (a *w* sound), which had dropped out of the written alphabet before classical times but may still have been partly sounded. Its presence can be inferred from the parallel Latin word *octavus*. There are many other examples of this: e.g. οἶνος originally started with a digamma (compare Latin *vinum*, and English *wine*).

• The ordinal numbers are also used like any adjective. When they have the article (where *the* would be used in English) it is sandwiched or repeated.

## Expressing time (2)

We saw in Chapter 2 that *time how long* is expressed by the accusative:

> τρεῖς ὥρας ἐτρέχομεν.
> We were running for three hours.

Time *within which* is expressed by the genitive:

> τὸν στρατὸν τριῶν ἡμερῶν πέμψομεν.
> We shall send the army within three days.

*Time when* (e.g. the hour at which, day on which) is expressed by the dative:

> τῇ τετάρτῃ ἑσπέρᾳ τοὺς συμμάχους εἴδομεν.
> On the fourth evening we saw the allies.

The accusative and genitive versions naturally go with cardinal (ordinary) numbers, the dative version with an ordinal number. Different expressions of time may be contrasted within the same sentence:

οἱ στρατιῶται τέσσαρας ἡμέρας ἐφύλασσον τὴν κωμην, ἀλλὰ τῇ πέμπτῃ ἔφυγον.

The soldiers were guarding the village for four days, but on the fifth (day) they ran away.

• Contrast the situation in Latin, where *time how long* is expressed by the accusative (as in Greek), but *time within which* and *time when* are both expressed by the ablative. Notice how (here, as often) Greek makes more or clearer distinctions, despite having fewer cases available.

Exercise 6.23

*Translate into English:*
1 τρεῖς ἡμέρας ἐμένομεν, ἀλλὰ τῇ τετάρτῃ ἐφύγομεν.
2 ὁ πρῶτος ἀγὼν μακρός τε καὶ χαλεπός ἐστιν.
3 ἡ δευτέρα νίκη ἔπαυσε τὸν πόλεμον.
4 ἡ παῖς ὀλίγων ὡρῶν πάσας τὰς ἐπιστολὰς γράψει.
5 πέντε πλοῖα ἐν τῷ λιμένι ἦν.
6 ὁ δοῦλος αὐτὸς ηὗρε τὴν δευτέραν θύραν.
7 αἱ ἐν τῇ νήσῳ πλοῖον εἶδον τῇ ὀγδόῃ ἑσπέρᾳ.
8 τί ἐστι τὸ τρίτον ἆθλον;
9 ὁ στρατηγὸς τὴν ἑβδόμην πύλην ἐφύλασσεν.
10 δέκα στρατιῶται μετὰ δυοῖν ἵππων τὸν ἄγγελον πρὸς τὴν κώμην προσήγαγον.


Exercise 6.24

*Translate into Greek:*
1 The second assembly sent an army.
2 The soldiers were in very great danger for three days.
3 We sent one messenger and one letter.
4 Five boys were carrying the two bodies.
5 Will the gods prevent a second sea-battle within four days?

Exercise 6.25

*Explain the derivation of:*
1 pentathlon
2 trilogy
3 henotheism
4 octopus
5 Deuteronomy

# The use of οὐδείς

This pronoun/adjective meaning *no-one, nothing, no* (i.e. *not any*) is simply the word οὐδέ *not even* joined onto the appropriate part of the word *one* (thus literally *not even one*). The epsilon on the end of οὐδέ is elided before the epsilon at the beginning of the masculine and neuter parts of *one*, e.g. οὐδέ + εἷς = οὐδείς (and the rough breathing on εἷς disappears).

Hence in full:

|     | masculine | feminine  | neuter  |
|-----|-----------|-----------|---------|
| nom | οὐδ-είς   | οὐδε-μία  | οὐδ-έν  |
| acc | οὐδ-ένα   | οὐδε-μίαν | οὐδ-έν  |
| gen | οὐδ-ενός  | οὐδε-μιᾶς | οὐδ-ενός |
| dat | οὐδ-ενί   | οὐδε-μιᾷ  | οὐδ-ενί |

• It is very common as a pronoun:

> οὐδεὶς ἤκουσε τὴν βοήν.
> No-one heard the shout.

> οὐδὲν ἐν τῷ πλοίῳ ηὕρομεν.
> We found nothing in the boat.

If the pronoun is followed by a genitive plural, the translation *none (of ... )* is appropriate:

> οὐδεὶς τῶν δούλων ἐφύλασσε τὴν θύραν.
> None of the slaves was guarding the door.

• It is also often used as an adjective, where the translation *no ...* is appropriate:

> οὐδεμίαν βουλὴν ἔχομεν.
> We have no plan.

> οὐδένα δοῦλον εἶδον.
> They saw no slave.

• As a masculine or feminine pronoun it corresponds to Latin *nemo*, as a neuter pronoun to Latin *nihil*, and as an adjective to Latin *nullus -a -um*.

Exercise 6.26

*Translate into English:*
1    οὐδεὶς ἐν τῇ ἀγορᾷ παρῆν.
2    οὐδεμία τῶν κορῶν εἶδε τὸ πλοῖον.
3    οὐδένα στρατηγὸν νῦν ἔχομεν.

4      ὁ δοῦλος οὐδενὶ δεῖπνον παρέχειν ἐθέλει.

5      οὐδὲν ἐν τῷ ἱερῷ ἐστιν.

## Exercise 6.27

*Translate into Greek:*

1      I sent no-one to the harbour.
2      No slave took the second book.
3      We heard no shout.
4      Nothing will prevent the battle.
5      The messenger himself trusts no-one.

## Exercise 6.28
### Alexander's Trust

*There were several actual or alleged plots against Alexander's life, but observers were impressed by how he continued to trust people, and his own judgement.*

ὁ δ' Ἀλέξανδρος ἐν τῇ Ταρσῷ ποτε παρῆν. ἐκεῖ λουτρὸν καλὸν ἦν.
ὁ μέντοι Ἀλέξανδρος ἀπὸ τοῦ ποταμοῦ νόσον τινὰ δεινὴν ἔλαβεν. καὶ
θανάτου κίνδυνος ἦν· οὐδεὶς γὰρ οἷός τ' ἦν σῴζειν αὐτόν. ἦν μέντοι
ἰατρός τις, ὀνόματι Φίλιππος· καὶ πάντες αὐτῷ ἐπίστευον. ὁ δὲ Φίλιππος
5  ἤθελε φάρμακόν τι τῷ Ἀλεξάνδρῳ παρέχειν. ὁ οὖν βασιλεὺς ἐπένευσε,
καὶ ὁ Φίλιππος τὸ φάρμακον ἐν κύλικι παρεσκεύαζεν. ἔπειτα δὲ
στρατηγός τις ἐπιστολὴν ἔπεμψεν. ἐν δὲ τῇ ἐπιστολῇ εἶπε τῷ Ἀλεξάνδρῳ
ὅτι οἱ ἐχθροί, χρήματα παράσχοντες, ἔπεισαν τὸν Φίλιππον ἀποκτείνειν
τὸν Ἀλέξανδρον. ἐπεὶ δὲ ὁ ἰατρὸς παρῆν, ὁ βασιλεὺς τὴν κύλικα λαβὼν
10  ἔφηνε τὴν ἐπιστολήν. ἅμα οὖν ὁ μὲν Ἀλέξανδρος ἔπινεν, ὁ δὲ Φίλιππος
τὴν ἐπιστολὴν ἀνεγίγνωσκεν.

|  |  |  |
|---|---|---|
|  | Ταρσός -οῦ ἡ | Tarsus (*city in modern southern Turkey*) |
|  | ποτε | once (*'indefinite' use, not asking a question*) |
|  | λουτρόν -οῦ τό | bathing-place |
|  | σῴζω | I save |
|  | ἰατρός -οῦ ὁ | doctor |
|  | Φίλιππος -ου ὁ | Philip |
| 5 | φάρμακον -ου τό | drug |
|  | βασιλεύς ὁ | king |
|  | ἐπινεύω ἐπένευσα | I consent |
|  | κύλιξ -ικος ἡ | cup |
|  | παρασκευάζω | I prepare |
|  | ὅτι | that |
|  | ἐχθρός -οῦ ὁ | (personal) enemy |
|  | χρήματα -ων τά | money |
| 10 | φαίνω ἔφηνα | I show, I reveal |
|  | ἅμα | at the same time |
|  | ἀναγιγνώσκω | I read |

# Personal pronouns and adjectives (first and second person plural)

You have already met the first and second person singular pronouns and their associated adjectives (pronouns shown with nom/acc/gen/dat, adjectives with m/f/n endings):

ἐγώ, ἐμέ (με), ἐμοῦ (μου), ἐμοί (μοι)     I
ἐμός -ή -όν                                my

σύ, σέ, σοῦ, σοί                          you (*sg*)
σός, σή, σόν                              your (of you *sg*)

The first person plural pronoun is a slight variant of third declension:

| | | |
|---|---|---|
| *nom* | ἡμεῖς | we |
| *acc* | ἡμᾶς | |
| *gen* | ἡμῶν | |
| *dat* | ἡμῖν | |

The associated adjective is:

ἡμέτερος -α -ον          our

The second person plural pronoun is very similar:

| | | |
|---|---|---|
| *nom* | ὑμεῖς | you (*pl*) |
| *acc* | ὑμᾶς | |
| *gen* | ὑμῶν | |
| *dat* | ὑμῖν | |

As is the associated adjective:

ὑμέτερος -α -ον          your (of you *pl*)

• To remember which is which, note that the word for *we* has a long *e* sound, and the word for *you* (pl) a long *u* sound.

• As with other pronouns and possessive adjectives, these are most often used for emphasis or to draw a contrast. (The person ending on the verb of course normally suffices to indicate e.g. *we* as subject; and the article with a noun can often be *translated* as a possessive, because it applies to *the one naturally applicable*.) Where possessive adjectives are used, they have the article as well (sandwiched or repeated - but not translated).

Exercise 6.29

*Translate into English:*
1   ἡμεῖς μὲν σοφοί ἐσμεν, ὑμεῖς δὲ ἀνδρεῖοι.
2   πάντες φυλάσσομεν τὴν ἡμετέραν κώμην.
3   τίς τὸ δεῖπνον ὑμῖν παρέσχεν;
4   ὁ ἄγγελος ἡμᾶς φεύγοντας οὐκ εἶδεν.
5   οὐχ ἡ ἐμὴ βουλὴ ἀλλ' ἡ ὑμετέρα πείσει τοὺς πολίτας.

Exercise 6.30

*Translate into Greek:*
1   Our soldiers are always brave.
2   We were waiting, but you (*pl*) ran away.
3   The general provides horses for us.
4   Who found your house, friends?
5   The lion did not eat us.


# Possessive dative

As well as saying e.g.
βουλὴν ἔχομεν
for *we have a plan*, it is also possible - and very common - to say
βουλή ἐστιν ἡμῖν
(literally *there is to us a plan*) with the same meaning.

Likewise,
ὁ κριτὴς καλὴν οἰκίαν ἔχει
and     καλὴ οἰκία τῷ κριτῇ ἐστιν
are both good Greek for *the judge has a fine house* - the possessive dative is in fact more
idiomatic (the more natural way the language would express the idea). This is possible in
Latin too (e.g. *est mihi canis*, literally *there is a dog to me*, for *I have a dog*), but less
common.

Exercise 6.31

*Translate into English:*
1   ὑμῖν εἰσιν ἀνδρεῖοι σύμμαχοι.
2   ἔστι μοι ἄθλον κάλλιστον.
3   ἆρα ἵππος τῷ ἀγγέλῳ ἦν;
4   τῷ στρατηγῷ αὐτῷ πολλὰ ἔργα ἐστίν.
5   ἦσαν τῷ διδασκάλῳ δέκα βίβλοι.

Exercise 6.32

*Translate into Greek (using the possessive dative):*
1       I have two horses.
2       The poet has a fine voice.
3       You (*pl*) have a wise general.
4       We had a very great victory.
5       Which boat do the boys have?


Exercise 6.33

# Alexander's Kindness

*This is one of many stories illustrating Alexander's concern for his troops.*

οἱ τοῦ ᾿Αλεξάνδρου στρατιῶται δι᾿ ὕλης μεγίστης ἐστράτευον. πολλοὶ δὲ
διὰ τὴν χιόνα ἤδη ἀπέθανον, καὶ ἀθυμία τοῖς ἄλλοις ἦν. ὁ μέντοι
βασιλεύς, τοὺς πλανήτας συλλέξας ἐκέλευσεν αὐτοὺς πολλὰ δένδρα
κόψαντας στρατόπεδόν τε καὶ πῦρ παρασκευάζειν. καὶ δι᾿ ὀλίγου ἦν τοῖς
5      στρατιώταις στρατόπεδόν τε καλὸν καὶ πῦρ μέγιστον. καὶ πάντες τὰ
σώματα ἐγγὺς τοῦ πυρὸς ἐθέρμαινον. μετὰ δὲ πολλὰς ὥρας στρατιώτης
τις τὰ ὅπλα μόλις φέρων εἰς τὸ στρατόπεδον ὑπὸ νύκτα εἰσῆλθεν
ἡμιθνής. ὁ δ᾿ ᾿Αλέξανδρος, ἐπεὶ τὸν στρατιώτην εἶδε, τὴν ἕδραν εὐθὺς
ἔλιπεν. τὰ δὲ ὅπλα ἀπὸ τοῦ στρατιώτου ἀπολαβών, ἐκέλευσεν αὐτὸν ἐγγὺς
10     τοῦ πυρὸς καθίζειν. ὁ οὖν στρατιώτης ἐκάθισεν, οὐκ ἐπιγιγνώσκων τὸν

| | | |
|---|---|---|
| | ὕλη -ης ἡ | forest |
| | στρατεύω ἐστράτευσα | I march, I make an expedition |
| | χιών -όνος ἡ | snow |
| | ἤδη | already |
| | ἀθυμία -ας ἡ | despondency, despair |
| | βασιλεύς ὁ | king |
| | πλανήτης -ου ὁ | wanderer, straggler |
| | συλλέγω συνέλεξα | I gather (people/things) together |
| | κόπτω ἔκοψα | I cut (down) |
| | παρασκευάζω παρεσκεύασα | I prepare |
| | δι᾿ ὀλίγου | soon, in a short time |
| 5 | θερμαίνω | I warm |
| | μόλις | with difficulty, scarcely |
| | ὑπὸ νύκτα | just before nightfall |
| | εἰσῆλθον | (*irreg aor*) I came in |
| | ἡμιθνής | half-dead |
| | ἕδρα -ας ἡ | seat |
| | εὐθύς | immediately |
| | ἀπολαμβάνω ἀπέλαβον | I take ... from |
| 10 | καθίζω ἐκάθισα | I sit |
| | ἐπιγιγνώσκω | I recognise |

Ἀλέξανδρον. ὕπνος δ' εὐθὺς ἔλαβεν αὐτόν. ὕστερον δ' ἐγρηγορὼς ὑγιεινὸς μὲν ἦν, περίφοβος δὲ ὡς ἐν τῇ βασιλικῇ ἕδρᾳ καθίζων· καὶ ἤθελε τὴν ἕδραν εὐθὺς λείπειν.

ὁ μέντοι Ἀλέξανδρος πᾶσιν εἶπεν, "ἆρα γιγνώσκετε, ὦ φίλοι, ὅτι ὑμῖν μέν
15 ἐστιν ἀγαθὴ τύχη, τοῖς δὲ πολεμίοις κακή. ὁ γὰρ τῶν Περσῶν βασιλεύς, εἴ τις ἐν τῇ βασιλικῇ ἕδρᾳ καθίζει, θανάτῳ κολάζει αὐτόν. τῷ οὖν βαρβάρῳ θάνατον φέρει ἡ ἕδρα· σοὶ δέ, ὦ στρατιῶτα, βίον τε καὶ σωτηρίαν."

| | |
|---|---|
| ὕστερον | later |
| ἐγρηγορὼς | having woken up |
| ὑγιεινός -ή -όν | healthy |
| περίφοβος -ον | terrified |
| βασιλικός -ή -όν | royal |
| ἕδρα -ας ἡ | seat |
| ὅτι | that |
| 15 τύχη -ης ἡ | luck, fortune |
| πολέμιοι -ων οἱ | enemy (in war) |
| Πέρσαι -ῶν οἱ | Persians |
| βασιλεύς ὁ | king |
| εἰ | if |
| κολάζω ἐκόλασα | I punish |
| βάρβαρος -ου ὁ | barbarian |
| σωτηρία -ας ἡ | safety, deliverance |

# Future participle

For the large number of verbs that form their future by adding sigma to the stem (e.g. παύω becomes παύσω), the future participle is very simple - putting the present participle endings after the sigma:

| | | masculine | feminine | neuter | |
|---|---|---|---|---|---|
| sg | nom | παύσ-ων | παύσ-ουσα | παῦσ-ον | about to stop |
| | acc | παύσ-οντα | παύσ-ουσαν | παῦσ-ον | |
| | gen | παύσ-οντος | παυσ-ούσης | παύσ-οντος | |
| | dat | παύσ-οντι | παυσ-ούσῃ | παύσ-οντι | |
| | | | | | |
| pl | nom | παύσ-οντες | παύσ-ουσαι | παύσ-οντα | |
| | acc | παύσ-οντας | παυσ-ούσας | παύσ-οντα | |
| | gen | παυσ-όντων | παυσ-ουσῶν | παυσ-όντων | |
| | dat | παύσ-ουσι(ν) | παυσ-ούσαις | παύσ-ουσι(ν) | |

• The future participle is thus identical to the present participle, with the insertion of the sigma throughout.

• Verbs which make some adjustment to a consonant stem to add the sigma of course do so here too: e.g. διώξων, πέμψων.

• The future participle is thus for many verbs only one letter different from
participle. Parts of it are also only one letter different from the first (weak) aori
(which also of course has the sigma): e.g.

λύσοντες *future*; λύσαντες *first (weak) aorist.*

• The literal meaning of the future participle is *(being) about to ...* , but this is rarely good
English. As with other participles, translations involving words such as *when, while* and *who*
are often appropriate (but always with some indication that the action described in the
participle is *still to happen*). As always, the tense of the participle is *in relation to the tense
of the main verb*. Thus a future participle in a sentence with a present main verb may be
translated e.g.

when he is going to do X, he does Y

while he is about to do *X*, he does Y

Similarly, a future participle in a sentence with a past main verb may come out as

when he was going to do X, he did Y

while he was about to do *X*, he did Y

Like any participle, it can also be used with the article:

οἱ διδάξοντες

those who are/were*going to teach

(*depending on tense of main verb)

• The future participle alone can express an idea of purpose: *about to do X* may well imply
*intending* or *aiming* to do it. But this meaning can be specified more clearly by putting ὡς
(literally *as*) in front of the future participle:

ὁ ἄγγελος πάρεστιν ὡς πείσων τὸν δῆμον.

The messenger is here (in order) to persuade the people.

This is a very common and simple way of expressing purpose.


Exercise 6.34

*Translate into English:*

1    ὁ δοῦλος, τὸν ἵππον λύσων, βοὴν ἤκουσεν.
2    ἡ τὴν βίβλον γράψουσα σοφή ἐστιν.
3    ὁ στρατηγὸς βουλὴν ἔλαβεν ὡς τὴν ναυμαχίαν παύσων.
4    ὁ γέρων, τὸν παῖδα διδάξων, τοὺς λόγους πρῶτον ἔμαθεν.
5    τὴν νίκην τὴν τὸν πόλεμον παύσουσαν νῦν ἔχομεν.
6    οἱ ξένοι παρῆσαν ὡς τὰ ἱερὰ θαυμάσοντες.
7    τίς ἐστιν ὁ τοὺς πολίτας ἀποτρέχειν κελεύσων;
8    τὸν στρατὸν τάξοντες, οἱ στρατηγοὶ τοὺς φεύγοντας εἶδον.
9    δοῦλον ἔπεμψα ὡς τοὺς παῖδας διώξοντα.
10    οἱ ναῦται οἱ τὸν λιμένα φυλάξοντες παρῆσαν.

guard the gate, the soldier hears a shout.

prevent the danger.

speak, the messenger does not eat.

is going to teach the children was waiting for two hours.

river in order to release our horses.

## Focusing the sense of participles

We saw above that the future participle alone can express purpose, but that this sense can be specified more clearly by putting ὡς in front of it. This principle - of inserting a word to focus on one of the possible meanings a participle already has - is seen in other contexts too.

• When put in front of a present or aorist participle, ὡς narrows the meaning to *as, since* or *on the grounds that*.

• Conversely, καίπερ in front of any participle gives the sense *although* or *despite*. (Participles basically describe *circumstances applying* to whatever happens in the main part of the sentence. Often they are circumstances that cause or explain it - hence translations like *as, since* - but they can also be circumstances which might have tended to prevent it.)

Exercise 6.36

*Translate into English:*
1    καίπερ δεινὰ παθών, ἐν τῷ ἀγῶνι μόνος ἔδραμον.
2    ἆρα ἔλιπες τὴν νῆσον ὡς περὶ τῶν ἐκεῖ ἀκούσας, ὦ ναυτά;
3    οἱ πολέμιοι πάρεισιν ὡς τοὺς ἡμετέρους ἀγροὺς βλάψοντες.
4    θαυμάζω τὸν ξένον ὡς λέοντα ἀποκτείναντα.
5  ❡  τὸ ὕδωρ καίπερ κακὸν ὂν πάντες ἐπίομεν ὡς οὐδὲν ἄλλο ἔχοντες.

## More uses of the definite article (3)

In Chapter 3 you met the particles μέν and δέ, used to express a contrast:

> οἱ μὲν ναῦται ἔμειναν, οἱ δὲ στρατιῶται ἔφυγον.
> The sailors stayed, but the soldiers ran away.

These particles are also very common with just the definite article, leaving a noun to be understood from the number and gender:

> αἱ μὲν ἔμειναν, αἱ δὲ ἔφυγον.
> Some (women) stayed, (but) others ran away.

126

They are also very common with a partitive genitive (as in English *one of, some of*):

οἱ μὲν τῶν δούλων ἐν τῇ οἰκίᾳ εἰσίν, οἱ δὲ ἐν τῇ ὁδῷ.
Some of the slaves are in the house, others in the street.

τὰς μὲν τῶν βίβλων ἀπέβαλον, τὰς δὲ ἔτι ἔχω.
I threw away some of the books, but I still have others.

The same idiom is also found in the singular:

ὁ μὲν τῶν παίδων ἔμεινεν, ὁ δὲ ἔφυγεν.
One of the boys stayed, (but) the other ran away.

Note that before translating the article followed by μέν you must look ahead to see whether there is a noun agreeing with it, or whether the article is being used alone (i.e. as a *pronoun*) in one of the idioms just described.

Exercise 6.37

*Translate into English:*
1    οἱ μὲν τῶν γερόντων σοφοί εἰσιν, οἱ δὲ μῶροι.
2    τὴν μὲν τῶν ἐπιστολῶν ἐγὼ ἔγραψα, τὴν δὲ οὔ.
3    τῶν δώρων τὰ μὲν ἐλάβομεν, τὰ δὲ ἐλίπομεν.
4    διὰ τί τοῖς μὲν τῶν παίδων δεῖπνον παρέσχες, τοῖς δὲ οὐδέν;
5    οἱ μὲν τῷ ἀγγέλῳ πιστεύουσιν, οἱ δὲ διώκουσιν αὐτὸν ἐκ τῆς κώμης.

Exercise 6.38

*Translate into Greek:*
1    Some (men) speak, others listen.
2    Some of the slaves were running away, but others stayed.
3    Some of the gifts are beautiful, others are not.
4    I sent some of the boys to the village, others to the harbour.
5    One of the girls was guarding the house, the other was running away.

# Revision checkpoint

*Make sure you know:*
• all present and aorist participles
• numerals (cardinal and ordinal) 1 -10
• expressions of time (accusative, genitive and dative)
• the use of οὐδείς
• first and second person plural pronouns and possessives
• the possessive dative
• the future participle, and the uses of ὡς and καίπερ to focus the sense of participles
• the use of the definite article with μέν and δέ

Exercise 6.39

# Alexander's Ambition

*After conquering Asia Minor, Alexander won a major victory over the Persians at Issus in the north-east corner of the Mediterranean in 333 BC. This was in itself sufficient to avenge their attacks on Greece 150 years earlier. Alexander's refusal of the generous peace terms offered showed however that he now aimed to conquer the whole of the vast Persian empire. Before his second major victory at Gaugamela on the River Tigris in 331, his sacking of the Persian palace at Persepolis, and his more exploratory expedition further east, Alexander paid a formative visit to an oracle in the North African desert.*

ὁ Ἀλέξανδρος ἐν τῇ διὰ τῆς ἐρημίας ὁδῷ πρὸς τὸ τοῦ Ἄμμωνος
μαντεῖον ἦλθεν. τοῖς μὲν γὰρ τῶν ἀνθρώπων ὁ τῶν θεῶν βασιλεὺς καὶ
πατὴρ Ζεύς ἐστιν ὀνόματι, τοῖς δὲ Ἄμμων ἢ ἄλλος τις. τὸ οὖν τοῦ Διὸς
ὄνομα ἐν τῇ Λιβύῃ Ἄμμων ἐστίν. ἐπεὶ δὲ ὁ Ἀλέξανδρος πρὸς τὸ
5   μαντεῖον ἦλθεν, ὁ ἱερεύς, τὴν γλῶσσαν κακῶς μαθών, ἤθελεν Ἑλληνιστὶ
λέγειν αὐτῷ "ὦ παίδιον". οὐ μέντοι "ὦ παίδιον" ὀρθῶς εἶπεν, ἀλλ᾽
"ὦ παίδιος", ἀντὶ τοῦ νῦ τὸ σίγμα λέγων. ὁ δ᾽ Ἀλέξανδρος ἔχαιρε διότι
ὁ ἱερεύς, ὡς ἐπίστευεν, εἶπεν αὐτῷ "ὦ παῖ Διός". ἐπεὶ οὖν ἐν τῷ πολέμῳ
τῷ ἐπὶ τοὺς Πέρσας ὁ Ἀλέξανδρος νίκην ἔσχεν, ἐκέλευσε τοὺς
10  στρατιώτας αὐτὸν ὡς θεὸν προσαγορεύειν. καὶ πολλοὶ τῶν ἐν τῷ στρατῷ
ἕτοιμοι ἦσαν τὸν Ἀλέξανδρον οὕτως προσαγορεύειν. Λακεδαιμόνιος δέ τις
εἶπε μόνον, "εἰ ὁ Ἀλέξανδρος ἐθέλει θεὸς εἶναι, ἔστω θεός".

| | | |
|---|---|---|
| | ἐρημία -ας ἡ | desert |
| | Ἄμμων -ωνος ὁ | Ammon (*Egyptian god equated to Zeus*) |
| | μαντεῖον -ου τό | oracle |
| | ἦλθον | (*irreg aor*) I came |
| | βασιλεύς ὁ | king |
| | πατήρ ὁ | father |
| | Ζεύς ὁ | Zeus |
| | ἤ | or |
| | Διός | (*irreg gen of* Ζεύς) |
| | Λιβύη -ης ἡ | Libya (*north Africa*) |
| 5 | ἱερεύς ὁ | priest |
| | γλῶσσα -ης ἡ | tongue, language |
| | Ἑλληνιστί | in Greek |
| | παιδίον -ου τό | child (*diminutive of* παῖς, *implying* small *and/or* dear) |
| | ὀρθῶς | correctly |
| | ἀντί | instead of (+ *gen*) |
| | χαίρω | I rejoice, I am happy |
| 10 | ἐπί | (+ *acc*) against |
| | Πέρσαι -ων οἱ | Persians |
| | προσαγορεύω | I address |
| | οὕτως | in this way |
| | Λακεδαιμόνιος -ου ὁ | Spartan (*the Spartans were famous for short but devastating comments*) |
| | εἰ | if |
| | εἶναι | to be (*infinitive of* εἰμί) |
| | ἔστω | let him be |

# Round-up of verbs and their aorist formation

Verbs you have met in this book, with their aorist tense and aorist stem:

| present | aorist | aorist stem | meaning |
|---|---|---|---|
| ἀγγέλλω | ἤγγειλα | ἀγγειλ- | I report, I announce |
| ἄγω | ἤγαγον | ἀγαγ- | I lead |
| ἀκούω | ἤκουσα | ἀκουσ- | I hear, I listen (to) |
| ἀποθνήσκω | ἀπέθανον | ἀποθαν- | I die |
| ἀποκτείνω | ἀπέκτεινα | ἀποκτειν- | I kill |
| βάλλω | ἔβαλον | βαλ- | I throw |
| βλάπτω | ἔβλαψα | βλαψ- | I harm, I damage |
| γράφω | ἔγραψα | γραψ- | I write |
| διδάσκω | ἐδίδαξα | διδαξ- | I teach |
| διώκω | ἐδίωξα | διωξ- | I chase, I pursue |
| ἐθέλω | ἠθέλησα | ἐθελησ- | I wish, I am willing |
| ἐλαύνω | ἤλασα | ἐλασ- | I drive |
| ἐσθίω | ἔφαγον | φαγ- | I eat |
| εὑρίσκω | ηὗρον | εὑρ- | I find |
| ἔχω | ἔσχον | σχ- | I have |
| θάπτω | ἔθαψα | θαψ- | I bury |
| θαυμάζω | ἐθαύμασα | θαυμασ- | I am amazed (at), I admire |
| κελεύω | ἐκέλευσα | κελευσ- | I order |
| κλέπτω | ἔκλεψα | κλεψ- | I steal |
| κωλύω | ἐκώλυσα | κωλυσ- | I hinder, I prevent |
| λαμβάνω | ἔλαβον | λαβ- | I take |
| λέγω | ἔλεξα | λεξ- | I speak, I say |
| | _or_ εἶπον | εἰπ- | |
| λείπω | ἔλιπον | λιπ- | I leave |
| λύω | ἔλυσα | λυσ- | I release |
| μανθάνω | ἔμαθον | μαθ- | I learn |
| μένω | ἔμεινα | μειν | I stay, I remain; I wait for |
| παιδεύω | ἐπαίδευσα | παιδευσ- | I train, I educate |
| παρασκευάζω | παρεσκεύασα | παρασκευασ- | I prepare |
| παρέχω | παρέσχον | παρασχ- | I produce, I provide |
| πάσχω | ἔπαθον | παθ- | I suffer |
| παύω | ἔπαυσα | παυσ- | I stop |
| πείθω | ἔπεισα | πεισ- | I persuade |
| πέμπω | ἔπεμψα | πεμψ- | I send |
| πίνω | ἔπιον | πι- | I drink |
| πίπτω | ἔπεσον | πεσ- | I fall |
| πιστεύω | ἐπίστευσα | πιστευσ- | I trust, I believe (+ _dat_) |
| στρατεύω | ἐστράτευσα | στρατευσ- | I march, I go on an expedition |
| τάσσω | ἔταξα | ταξ- | I draw up, I arrange |
| τρέχω | ἔδραμον | δραμ- | I run |
| φαίνω | ἔφηνα | φην- | I show |
| φέρω | ἤνεγκα | ἐνεγκ- | I carry |
| | _or_ ἤνεγκον | | |
| φεύγω | ἔφυγον | φυγ- | I run away, I flee |
| φυλάσσω | ἐφύλαξα | φυλαξ- | I guard |

• The aorist is by far the commonest tense of a Greek verb. The aorist stem enables you to form the aorist participle, which also plays a major part in any historical narrative or continuous story set in the past (a very high percentage of passages of course come into this category). Remember that the aorist tense has the augment, but the aorist participle does not. So for example:

| verb | aorist tense | aorist participle |
|------|------|------|
| πέμπω | ἔπεμψα | πέμψας |
| βάλλω | ἔβαλον | βαλών |

• Many of the aorists in the list above are predictable. We saw in Chapter 4 the important distinction between *first (weak)* and *second (strong)* aorist. To recap, and explain a few exceptions/irregularities:

(1) *First (weak) aorist* usually adds sigma to the present tense stem, then puts on a set of endings with the characteristic vowel alpha (-α, -ας, -ε[ν], -αμεν, -ατε, -αν). Adding sigma to a stem ending in a consonant such as gamma, kappa or pi (see διδάσκω, διώκω, πέμπω) simply results in writing one of the so-called 'double consonants' (xi or psi). Note however that if the stem ends in lambda or nu (as with ἀγγέλλω, μένω), something different happens: no sigma is added, but (by way of compensation) the vowel in the stem is lengthened or strengthened into a diphthong:

| ἀγγέλλω | aorist | ἤγγειλα |
|------|------|------|
| μένω | aorist | ἔμεινα |

However ἀποκτεινω has a diphthong in the stem already, which it simply keeps:

| ἀποκτείνω | aorist | ἀπέκτεινα |
|------|------|------|

(2) *Second (strong) aorist* usually shortens or telescopes the present stem, then puts on the same endings as the imperfect tense (-ον, -ες, -ε[ν], -ομεν, -ετε, -ον):

| λαμβάνω | aorist | ἔλαβον |
|------|------|------|

Sometimes the aorist stem is changed rather more:

| πίπτω | aorist | ἔπεσον |
|------|------|------|

And sometimes it seems completely unrelated:

| τρέχω | aorist | ἔδραμον |
|------|------|------|

The compensation for this complication is that the very irregular forms tend to be very common words, which quickly become familiar.

• Note that λέγω has both a regular first (weak) aorist ἔλεξα *and* an irregular second (strong) aorist εἶπον: the latter is much more commonly found.

• Note that φέρω has an irregular aorist with the stem ἐνεγκ-, which can be conjugated either as a first (weak) aorist ἤνεγκα, or as a second (strong) aorist ἤνεγκον.

• Excluded from the list above are βαίνω and γιγνώσκω. They form their aorists in a different way, which will be explained later.

• Compound verbs form their aorist in the same way as the equivalent simple verb. Remember that the aorist tense of a compound has the augment after the prefix (whilst the participle of course does not have the augment at all). So for example:

| compound verb | | aorist tense | aorist participle |
|---|---|---|---|
| I send towards | προσπέμπω | προσέπεμψα | προσπέμψας |
| I throw away | ἀποβάλλω | ἀπέβαλον | ἀποβαλών |

• The verb εἰμί = *I am* does not have an aorist. Because it usually refers to a continuing state, the imperfect is its only past tense. The verb *to be* also has compounds (where the ending for the first person of the imperfect is -ην rather than -η):

| compound verb | | imperfect tense |
|---|---|---|
| I am away | ἄπειμι | ἀπῆν |
| I am here | πάρειμι | παρῆν |

• You have also met two important second (strong) aorists of irregular verbs of which you have not yet seen the present tense:

| aorist tense | aorist stem | |
|---|---|---|
| εἶδον | ἰδ- | I saw |
| ἦλθον | ἐλθ- | I came, I went |

Exercise 6.40

*Translate into English:*

1  ὁ ἀπὸ τῆς νήσου ἄγγελος δεινὰ ἤγγειλε περὶ τῶν ἐκεῖ.
2  ὁ δοῦλος τὰ ἡμέτερα χρήματα κλέψας πρὸς τὸ πλοῖον ἤνεγκεν.
3  οἱ ἐν τῇ κώμῃ ἀπήλασαν τοὺς ἵππους ἀπὸ τοῦ πυρός.
4  ὁ παῖς καίπερ ἐν τῷ ἀγῶνι πεσὼν μετὰ ὀλίγας ὥρας αὖθις ἔδραμεν.
5  οἱ σύμμαχοι ἦλθον ὡς τοὺς ἐν τῷ δεσμωτηρίῳ λύσοντες.
6  ἡ τὴν ἐπιστολὴν γράψασα τῇ δευτέρᾳ ἡμέρᾳ ηὗρε τὸν νεκρόν.
7  ἆρα νῦν ἐστιν ὑμῖν βουλή τις, ὦ πολῖται;
8  οἱ μὲν τῶν πολεμίων τοὺς ἀγροὺς ἔβλαψαν, οἱ δὲ τὰς οἰκίας.
9  ὁ ξένος τά τε ἱερὰ καὶ τὴν ἀγορὰν θαυμάσας τέλος ἀπῆλθεν.
10  τίς εἶδε τοὺς τὸν οἶνον πιόντας;

Exercise 6.41

*Translate into Greek:*

1  When they had killed the animals, the sailors ate dinner.
2  The old man chased the boys out of the field.
3  After waiting for three days, the woman who had prepared the plan told the general everything*.
4  The slave who had chased my horse finally ran away.
5  Although they had guarded the village bravely, the people there did not wait for the army.

* *literally* said all things to the general

131

Exercise 6.42

## Alexander and Dionysus

*In making his expedition into the farthest reaches of the then known world, Alexander saw himself as emulating the god Dionysus who in myth had likewise pursued a career of travel and conquest.*

ἐπεὶ δὲ ὁ Ἀλέξανδρος πρὸς τὴν <u>Νῦσαν</u> προσέβαινεν, οἱ <u>Νυσαῖοι</u>
ἐξέπεμψαν ἀγγέλους· "ὦ <u>βασιλεῦ</u>, οἱ Νυσαῖοι ἐθέλουσιν ἐλεύθεροι μένειν.
<u>σῷζε</u> οὖν τὴν <u>αὐτονομίαν</u> αὐτῶν διὰ τὸν <u>Διόνυσον</u>. ὁ γὰρ θεὸς <u>κτίστης</u>
τῆς Νύσης ἦν. ἐπεὶ γὰρ νίκην ἔλαβε τῶν Ἰνδῶν, ἔκτισε τὴν Νῦσαν ὡς
5   <u>μνημεῖον</u> τῆς νίκης <u>τοῖς ἐσομένοις</u> λείψων. τῷ δ' αὐτῷ <u>τρόπῳ</u> <u>καὶ</u> σὺ
αὐτὸς ἔκτισας τὴν τ' Ἀλεξάνδρειαν τὴν Ἐσχάτην καὶ ἄλλην
Ἀλεξάνδρειαν ἐν τῇ τῶν Αἰγυπτίων γῇ, καὶ ἄλλας πολλάς· τὰς μὲν
ἔκτισας <u>ἤδη</u>, τὰς δὲ κτίσεις <u>ἀνὰ χρόνον</u>. ἀεὶ δ' ἐλεύθεραν τὴν Νῦσαν
ἔχομεν, διὰ τὴν αὐτονομίαν <u>πολιτεύοντες</u> ἐν <u>κόσμῳ</u>. ἔστι δὲ <u>καὶ</u>
10  <u>τεκμήριόν</u> τι τοῦ Διονύσου τὴν Νῦσαν κτίσαντος· <u>κισσὸς</u> γὰρ οὐκ <u>ἄλλη</u>
τῆς τῶν Ἰνδῶν γῆς ἀλλ' ἐνθάδε μόνον <u>θάλλει</u>."

| | | |
|---|---|---|
| | Νῦσα -ης ἡ | Nysa (*city in northern India [modern Pakistan]; exact location uncertain*) |
| | Νυσαῖοι -ων οἱ | people of Nysa |
| | βασιλεύς ὁ (*voc* βασιλεῦ) | king |
| | σῴζω | I save, I preserve |
| | αὐτονομία -ας ἡ | independence |
| | Διόνυσος -ου ὁ | Dionysus (*god of wine, the theatre and ecstatic experience*) |
| | κτίστης -ου ὁ | founder |
| | Ἰνδοί -ῶν οἱ | Indians |
| | κτίζω ἔκτισα | I found, I establish |
| 5 | μνημεῖον -ου τό | memorial, monument |
| | τοῖς ἐσομένοις | to those yet to be, to future generations |
| | τρόπος -ου ὁ | way |
| | καί | (*here*) also |
| | Ἀλεξάνδρεια -ας ἡ | Alexandria |
| | ἔσχατος -η -ον | farthest (*here as proper name, of the most distant of the thirty cities Alexander founded [in modern Tajikistan]*) |
| | Αἰγύπτιοι -ων οἱ | Egyptians |
| | ἤδη | already |
| | ἀνὰ χρόνον | in due course |
| | πολιτεύω | I govern |
| | κόσμος -ου ὁ | order |
| | καί | (*here*) also |
| 10 | τεκμήριον -ου τό | piece of evidence, proof |
| | κισσός -οῦ ὁ | ivy (*sacred to Dionysus, and worn in garlands by his worshippers*) |
| | ἄλλη | elsewhere |
| | θάλλω | I flourish |

τοὺς οὖν τῶν ἀγγέλων λόγους <u>ἡδέως</u> ἀκούσας ὁ Ἀλέξανδρος ἐκέλευσε
τὸν τῆς Νύσης ἄρχοντα <u>τετρακοσίους</u> τῶν <u>ἀρίστων</u> πέμπειν ὡς
στρατιώτας. ὁ δ' ἄρχων εἶπεν, "οὐχ οἷοί τ' ἐσμὲν τὴν Νῦσαν ἐν <u>κόσμῳ</u>
15  πολιτεύειν <u>εἰ πλεῖστοι</u> ἄριστοι ἄπεισιν. ἀπάγε οὖν <u>ἀντὶ</u> τῶν τετρακοσίων
ἀρίστων <u>διπλασίους</u> τῶν κακῶν. <u>οὕτως</u> οὖν <u>κατελθὼν</u> εὑρήσεις τὴν
Νῦσαν ἐν τῷ αὐτῷ κόσμῳ οὖσαν."

| | | |
|---|---|---|
| | ἡδέως | gladly |
| | τετρακόσιοι -αι -α | four hundred |
| | ἄριστος -η -ον | best, excellent |
| | κόσμος -ου ὁ | order |
| 15 | εἰ | if |
| | πλεῖστοι -αι -α | very many |
| | ἀντί | instead of (+ *gen*) |
| | διπλάσιοι -αι -α | twice as many |
| | οὕτως | in this way |
| | κατῆλθον | (*irregular aorist*) I returned |

Exercise 6.43

## Alexander, Homer and Fame

*As we saw in Exercise 6.11, Alexander claimed descent from Achilles. He modelled his behaviour on that of the Homeric hero.*

ὁ Ἀλέξανδρος ἔτι παῖς ὢν τὴν <u>Ἰλιάδα</u> πολλάκις <u>ἀνεγίγνωσκεν</u>. ἦν δ' αὐτῷ
<u>ἐπωνυμία</u> "<u>Ἀχιλλεύς</u>". ἦν δὲ <u>καὶ</u> τῷ διδασκάλῳ αὐτοῦ ἐπωνυμία "<u>Χείρων</u>",
διότι ὁ <u>κένταυρος</u> τὸν Ἀχιλλέα <u>ἐπαίδευσεν</u>. ἐπεὶ δὲ <u>βασιλεὺς</u> καὶ
στρατηγὸς ἦν, ὁ Ἀλέξανδρος τὴν τ' Ἰλιάδα μετὰ τοῦ <u>ἐγχειριδίου</u> ἀεὶ <u>ὑπὸ</u>
5  τῷ <u>προσκεφαλαίῳ</u> εἶχεν. καὶ τοὺς <u>Πέρσας</u> ἐν μάχῃ <u>τρέψας</u> ἔλαβε πολλὰ
<u>ἆθλα</u> καὶ <u>θήκην</u> τινὰ τοῦ <u>Δαρείου</u> <u>τιμίαν</u> οὖσαν· καὶ ἐν τῇ θήκῃ τὴν

| | | |
|---|---|---|
| | Ἰλιάς -άδος ἡ | the *Iliad* |
| | ἀναγιγνώσκω | I read |
| | ἐπωνυμία -ας ἡ | nickname |
| | Ἀχιλλεύς -έως ὁ | Achilles |
| | καί | (*here*) also |
| | Χείρων -ωνος ὁ | Cheiron (*unusually kindly and wise centaur, tutor of Achilles and other heroes*) |
| | κένταυρος -ου ὁ | centaur (*mythical creature: horse with man's head and shoulders*) |
| | παιδεύω ἐπαίδευσα | I train, I educate |
| | βασιλεύς ὁ | king |
| | ἐγχειρίδιον -ου τό | dagger |
| | ὑπό | (+ *dat*) under |
| 5 | προσκεφάλαιον -ου τό | pillow |
| | Πέρσαι -ῶν οἱ | Persians |
| | τρέπω ἔτρεψα | I rout, I cause to run away |
| | θήκη -ης ἡ | chest |
| | Δάρειος -ου ὁ | Darius (*the Third, king of Persia*) |
| | τίμιος -α -ον | valuable |

Ἰλιάδα ἐφύλασσεν. καὶ ἐπεὶ εἰσέδραμέ <u>ποτε</u> ἄγγελός τις <u>μετέωρος</u>, ὁ
Ἀλέξανδρος εἶπεν αὐτῷ, "διὰ τί <u>οὕτω</u> μετέωρος εἶ; ἆρα <u>Ὅμηρος</u> <u>αὖθις</u>
<u>ἔμψυχός</u> ἐστιν;" τὸν γὰρ Ἀχιλλέα <u>ἐμακάριζε</u> διότι Ὅμηρος περὶ αὐτοῦ
10  <u>ᾖδεν</u>. καὶ ποιητής τις κακὸς τῷ Ἀλεξάνδρῳ ποτὲ εἶπε, "<u>ποίημα</u> περὶ σοῦ
γράψω <u>ὥσπερ</u> Ὅμηρος περὶ Ἀχιλλέως". ὁ δ' Ἀλέξανδρος <u>ὑπέλαβε</u>,
"<u>μᾶλλον</u> ἐθέλω Θερσίτης ἐν τῇ Ἰλιάδι <u>εἶναι</u> <u>ἢ</u> <u>Ἀγαμέμνων</u> ἐν τῷ σῷ
ποιήματι". ὁ δὲ <u>Καλλισθένης</u>, <u>λογογράφος</u> τις περὶ τοῦ Ἀλεξάνδρου
γράψας, εἶπεν, "ἐν ἐμοί ἐστιν ἡ τοῦ Ἀλεξάνδρου <u>δόξα</u>". πολλοὶ μέντοι
15  καὶ <u>τότε</u> καὶ <u>ὕστερον</u> περὶ τοῦ Ἀλεξάνδρου ἔγραφον. καὶ λέγουσιν ὅτι
ναῦται φωνήν τινα δεινὴν <u>ἐνίοτε</u> ἀκούουσι, "ποῦ ἐστιν ὁ Ἀλέξανδρος ὁ
<u>μέγας</u>;" λέγουσαν. καὶ <u>ἀντιλέγουσιν</u>, "ὁ Ἀλέξανδρος ἔμψυχός ἐστι καὶ
<u>βασιλεύει</u>".

|  |  |  |
|---|---|---|
| | ποτε | once (*'indefinite' use, not asking a question*) |
| | μετέωρος -ον | excited |
| | οὕτω | so |
| | Ὅμηρος -ου ὁ | Homer |
| | αὖθις | again |
| | ἔμψυχος -ον | alive |
| | μακαρίζω | I envy, I regard (someone) as fortunate |
| 10 | ᾄδω *imperfect* ᾖδον | I sing |
| | ποίημα -ατος τό | poem |
| | ὥσπερ | just like |
| | ὑπολαμβάνω ὑπέλαβον | I reply |
| | μᾶλλον | rather, more |
| | Θερσίτης ὁ | Thersites (*a ridiculous and despicable common soldier in the* Iliad) |
| | εἶναι | to be (*infinitive of* εἰμί) |
| | ἤ | than |
| | Ἀγαμέμνων ὁ | Agamemnon (*supreme commander of the Greek forces in the* Iliad) |
| | Καλλισθένης ὁ | Callisthenes |
| | λογογράφος -ου ὁ | historian |
| | δόξα -ης ἡ | glory, reputation |
| 15 | τότε | then, at that time |
| | ὕστερον | later |
| | ἐνίοτε | sometimes |
| | μέγας | great |
| | ἀντιλέγω | I say in reply |
| | βασιλεύω | I reign, I am king |

# Revision checkpoint

*Make sure you know:*
• regular and irregular aorists
• the various ways in which aorists are formed
• how the aorist participle is formed from the aorist stem

# Vocabulary checklist for Chapter 6

| | |
|---|---|
| ἀγγέλλω ἤγγειλα | I report, I announce |
| αὖθις | again |
| αὐτός -ή -ό | self; same; (not nom) him, her, it |
| δεξιός -ά -όν | right (hand side) |
| εἶναι | to be (infinitive of εἰμί) |
| εὐθύς | immediately |
| ἐχθρός -οῦ ὁ | (personal) enemy |
| Ζεύς Διός ὁ | Zeus |
| ἦλθον | (irregular aorist) I came, I went |
| ἡμεῖς | we |
| ἡμέτερος -α -ον | our |
| θάπτω ἔθαψα | I bury |
| καίπερ | although, despite (being) (+ participle) |
| μάχη -ης ἡ | battle |
| μισθός -οῦ ὁ | payment, wages |
| νεκρός -οῦ ὁ | corpse, dead body |
| ὀλίγος -η -ον | a little, a small amount (of) |
| ὀργή -ῆς ἡ | anger |
| οὐδείς οὐδεμία οὐδέν (οὐδεν-) | no-one, nothing, no (i.e. not any) |
| οὐκέτι | no longer |
| οὐρανός -οῦ ὁ | sky, heaven |
| παιδεύω ἐπαίδευσα | I train, I educate |
| πάλαι | long ago, in the past |
| παρασκευάζω παρεσκεύασα | I prepare, get (something) ready |
| πᾶς πᾶσα πᾶν (παντ-) | all, every |
| περί | (+ gen) about, concerning |
| πολέμιοι -ων οἱ | enemy (in war) |
| στρατεύω ἐστράτευσα | I march, I make an expedition |
| συλλέγω συνέλεξα | I collect, I gather |
| τὰ τοῦ πολέμου | the affairs of war, warfare, military matters |
| τέλος | finally |
| τόπος -ου ὁ | place |
| ὕδωρ -ατος τό | water |
| ὑμεῖς | you (pl) |
| ὑμέτερος -α -ον | your (of you pl) |
| ὑπό | (+ dat) under |
| χρήματα -ων τά | money |
| ὡς | (+ future participle) in order to |
| | (+ present or aorist participle) as, since, on the grounds that |

| | |
|---|---|
| εἷς μία ἕν (ἑν-) | one |
| δύο | two |
| τρεῖς τρία | three |
| τέσσαρες τέσσαρα | four |
| πέντε | five |
| ἕξ | six |
| ἑπτά | seven |
| ὀκτώ | eight |
| ἐννέα | nine |
| δέκα | ten |
| | |
| πρῶτος -η -ον | first |
| δεύτερος -α -ον | second |
| τρίτος -η -ον | third |
| τέταρτος -η -ον | fourth |
| πέμπτος -η -ον | fifth |
| ἕκτος -η -ον | sixth |
| ἕβδομος -η -ον | seventh |
| ὄγδοος -η -ον | eighth |
| ἔνατος -η -ον | ninth |
| δέκατος -η -ον | tenth |

(57 words)

# Reference Grammar

## The definite article

|  |  | masculine | feminine | neuter |  |
|---|---|---|---|---|---|
| sg | nom | ὁ | ἡ | τό | the |
|  | acc | τόν | τήν | τό |  |
|  | gen | τοῦ | τῆς | τοῦ |  |
|  | dat | τῷ | τῇ | τῷ |  |
|  |  |  |  |  |  |
| pl | nom | οἱ | αἱ | τά |  |
|  | acc | τούς | τάς | τά |  |
|  | gen | τῶν | τῶν | τῶν |  |
|  | dat | τοῖς | ταῖς | τοῖς ✓ |  |

## Nouns: first declension

Pattern of endings for singular:

|  |  |  |  |  |
|---|---|---|---|---|
| nom | -η | or | -α | (adds -ς if masculine) |
| acc | -ην | or | -αν |  |
| gen | -ης | or | -ας | (changes to -ου if masculine) |
| dat | -η | or | -ᾳ |  |

All plurals are -αι, -ας, -ων, -αις

|  |  | feminine: |  |  | masculine: |  |
|---|---|---|---|---|---|---|
|  |  | honour | country | sea | judge | young man |
| sg | nom | τιμ-ή | χώρ-α | θάλασσ-α | κριτ-ής | νεανί-ας |
|  | acc | τιμ-ήν | χώρ-αν | θάλασσ-αν | κριτ-ήν | νεανί-αν |
|  | gen | τιμ-ῆς | χώρ-ας | θαλάσσ-ης | κριτ-οῦ | νεανί-ου |
|  | dat | τιμ-ῇ | χώρ-ᾳ | θαλάσσ-η | κριτ-ῇ | νεανί-ᾳ |
|  |  |  |  |  | (voc κριτ-ά) | (voc νεανί-α) |
|  |  |  |  |  |  |  |
| pl | nom | τιμ-αί | χῶρ-αι | θάλασσ-αι | κριτ-αί | νεανί-αι |
|  | acc | τιμ-άς | χώρ-ας | θαλάσσ-ας | κριτ-άς | νεανί-ας |
|  | gen | τιμ-ῶν | χωρ-ῶν | θαλασσ-ῶν | κριτ-ῶν | νεανι-ῶν |
|  | dat | τιμ-αῖς | χώρ-αις | θαλάσσ-αις | κριτ-αῖς | νεανί-αις |

# Nouns: second declension:

|    |     | masculine:*<br>word | neuter:<br>gift |
|----|-----|------------------|--------------|
| sg | nom | λόγ-ος           | δῶρ-ον       |
|    | acc | λόγ-ον           | δῶρ-ον       |
|    | gen | λόγ-ου           | δώρ-ου       |
|    | dat | λόγ-ῳ            | δώρ-ῳ        |
|    |     | (voc λόγ-ε)      |              |
| pl | nom | λόγ-οι           | δῶρ-α        |
|    | acc | λόγ-ους          | δῶρ-α        |
|    | gen | λόγ-ων           | δώρ-ων       |
|    | dat | λόγ-οις          | δώρ-οις      |

* feminine nouns such as βίβλος = *book* are identical in declension

# Nouns: third declension (pattern of endings)

| sg | nom | (wide range of possibilities) | |
|----|-----|------------------|--------------|
|    | acc | stem + α         | for masc and fem; same as nom if neuter |
|    | gen | stem + ος        |              |
|    | dat | stem + ι         |              |
| pl | nom | stem + ες        | for masc and fem; stem + α if neuter |
|    | acc | stem + ας        | for masc and fem; stem + α if neuter |
|    | gen | stem + ων        |              |
|    | dat | stem + σι(ν)*    |              |

* movable nu is added if the next word begins with a vowel, or at the end of a sentence

# Nouns: third declension (examples)

| sg | nom | φύλαξ             | guard (stem φυλακ-) |
|----|-----|------------------|--------------|
|    | acc | φύλακ-α          |              |
|    | gen | φύλακ-ος         |              |
|    | dat | φύλακ-ι          |              |
| pl | nom | φύλακ-ες         |              |
|    | acc | φύλακ-ας         |              |
|    | gen | φυλάκ-ων         |              |
|    | dat | φύλαξι(ν)        | *dat pl represents* φυλακ-σι(ν) |

| sg | nom | γέρων | old man (stem γεροντ-) | (*voc* γέρον) |
|----|-----|-------|------------------------|---------------|
|    | acc | γέροντ-α |  |  |
|    | gen | γέροντ-ος |  |  |
|    | dat | γέροντ-ι |  |  |

| pl | nom | γέροντ-ες |  |
|----|-----|-----------|--|
|    | acc | γέροντ-ας |  |
|    | gen | γερόντ-ων |  |
|    | dat | γέρουσι(ν) | *dat pl represents* γεροντ-σι(ν) |

| sg | nom | γίγας | giant (stem γιγαντ-) |
|----|-----|-------|----------------------|
|    | acc | γίγαντ-α |  |
|    | gen | γίγαντ-ος |  |
|    | dat | γίγαντ-ι |  |

| pl | nom | γίγαντ-ες |  |
|----|-----|-----------|--|
|    | acc | γίγαντ-ας |  |
|    | gen | γιγάντ-ων |  |
|    | dat | γίγασι(ν) | *dat pl represents* γιγαντ-σι(ν) |

These three examples are all masculine, but feminine nouns e.g. νύξ, νυκτός (stem νυκτ-) = *night* decline in the same way.

Third declension neuter noun:

| sg | nom | σῶμα | body (stem σωματ-) |
|----|-----|------|--------------------|
|    | acc | σῶμα |  |
|    | gen | σώματ-ος |  |
|    | dat | σώματ-ι |  |

| pl | nom | σώματ-α |  |
|----|-----|---------|--|
|    | acc | σώματ-α |  |
|    | gen | σωμάτ-ων |  |
|    | dat | σώμασι(ν) | *dat pl represents* σωματ-σι(ν) |

# Adjectives

σοφός = wise

|    |     | masculine | feminine | neuter |
|----|-----|-----------|----------|--------|
| sg | nom | σοφ-ός   | σοφ-ή    | σοφ-όν |
|    | acc | σοφ-όν   | σοφ-ήν   | σοφ-όν |
|    | gen | σοφ-οῦ   | σοφ-ῆς   | σοφ-οῦ |
|    | dat | σοφ-ῷ    | σοφ-ῇ    | σοφ-ῷ  |
|    |     |           |          |        |
| pl | nom | σοφ-οί   | σοφ-αί   | σοφ-ά  |
|    | acc | σοφ-ούς  | σοφ-άς   | σοφ-ά  |
|    | gen | σοφ-ῶν   | σοφ-ῶν   | σοφ-ῶν |
|    | dat | σοφ-οῖς  | σοφ-αῖς  | σοφ-οῖς |

This is exactly the same as τιμή, λόγος and δῶρον.

As with the nouns, there is a variant form of the feminine singular if the stem ends with a vowel or rho:

φιλίος = friendly

| sg | nom | φιλί-α  |
|----|-----|---------|
|    | acc | φιλί-αν |
|    | gen | φιλί-ας |
|    | dat | φιλί-ᾳ  |

This is exactly the same as the singular of χώρα.

The adjective πᾶς, πᾶσα, πᾶν (παντ-) = all declines like the first (weak) aorist participle.

# Pronouns

τίς

In a question, and with an acute accent on the iota:

|     |     | masculine/feminine | neuter |     |
| --- | --- | --- | --- | --- |
| sg  | nom | τίς | τί | who? which? what? |
|     | acc | τίν-α | τί |     |
|     | gen | τίν-ος | τίν-ος |     |
|     | dat | τίν-ι | τίν-ι |     |
|     |     |     |     |     |
| pl  | nom | τίν-ες | τίν-α |     |
|     | acc | τίν-ας | τίν-α |     |
|     | gen | τίν-ων | τίν-ων |     |
|     | dat | τίσι(ν)* | τίσι(ν)* |     |

\* contracted from τιν-σι(ν) to aid pronunciation

Elsewhere, usually without an accent, or with an accent on the second syllable:

|     |     | masculine/feminine | neuter |     |
| --- | --- | --- | --- | --- |
| sg  | nom | τις | τι | a (certain), some (one/thing) |
|     | acc | τιν-ά | τι |     |
|     | gen | τιν-ός | τιν-ός |     |
|     | dat | τιν-ί | τιν-ί |     |
|     |     |     |     |     |
| pl  | nom | τιν-ές | τιν-ά |     |
|     | acc | τιν-άς | τιν-ά |     |
|     | gen | τιν-ῶν | τιν-ῶν |     |
|     | dat | τισί(ν)* | τισί(ν)* |     |

\* contracted from τιν-σι(ν) to aid pronunciation

αὐτος

Three uses and meanings:
(1) self (*not sandwiched if used with article and noun*)
(2) (the) same (*coming immediately after the article*)
(3) him, her, it, them (*pronoun, not used in the nominative*)

|     |     | masculine | feminine | neuter |
| --- | --- | --- | --- | --- |
| sg  | nom | αὐτ-ός | αὐτ-ή | αὐτ-ό |
|     | acc | αὐτ-όν | αὐτ-ήν | αὐτ-ό |
|     | gen | αὐτ-οῦ | αὐτ-ῆς | αὐτ-οῦ |
|     | dat | αὐτ-ῷ | αὐτ-ῇ | αὐτ-ῷ |
|     |     |     |     |     |
| pl  | nom | αὐτ-οί | αὐτ-αί | αὐτ-ά |
|     | acc | αὐτ-ούς | αὐτ-άς | αὐτ-ά |
|     | gen | αὐτ-ῶν | αὐτ-ῶν | αὐτ-ῶν |
|     | dat | αὐτ-οῖς | αὐτ-αῖς | αὐτ-οῖς |

οὐδείς

|      | masculine | feminine | neuter   |
|------|-----------|----------|----------|
| nom  | οὐδείς    | οὐδεμία  | οὐδέν    |
| acc  | οὐδένα    | οὐδεμίαν | οὐδέν    |
| gen  | οὐδενός   | οὐδεμιᾶς | οὐδενός  |
| dat  | οὐδενί    | οὐδεμιᾷ  | οὐδενί   |

no-one, nothing, no (= not any)
(*m/n stem* οὐδεν-)

First and second person pronouns:

| nom  | ἐγώ        | I |
|------|------------|---|
| acc  | ἐμέ, με     |   |
| gen  | ἐμοῦ, μου   |   |
| dat  | ἐμοί, μοι   |   |

| nom  | ἡμεῖς | we |
|------|-------|----|
| acc  | ἡμᾶς  |    |
| gen  | ἡμῶν  |    |
| dat  | ἡμῖν  |    |

| nom  | σύ  | you (*sg*) |
|------|-----|------------|
| acc  | σέ  |            |
| gen  | σοῦ |            |
| dat  | σοί |            |

| nom  | ὑμεῖς | you (*pl*) |
|------|-------|------------|
| acc  | ὑμᾶς  |            |
| gen  | ὑμῶν  |            |
| dat  | ὑμῖν  |            |

# Numeral declensions

|      | masculine | feminine | neuter  |     |
|------|-----------|----------|---------|-----|
| nom  | εἷς       | μία      | ἕν      | one |
| acc  | ἕνα       | μίαν     | ἕν      |     |
| gen  | ἑνός      | μιᾶς     | ἑνός    |     |
| dat  | ἑνί       | μιᾷ      | ἑνί     |     |

|      | all genders |     |
|------|-------------|-----|
| nom  | δύο         | two |
| acc  | δύο         |     |
| gen  | δυοῖν       |     |
| dat  | δυοῖν       |     |

|       | masc/fem    | neuter      |       |
|-------|-------------|-------------|-------|
| nom   | τρεῖς       | τρία        | three |
| acc   | τρεῖς       | τρία        |       |
| gen   | τριῶν       | τριῶν       |       |
| dat   | τρισί(ν)    | τρισί(ν)    |       |

|       | masc/fem       | neuter         |      |
|-------|----------------|----------------|------|
| nom   | τέσσαρες       | τέσσαρα        | four |
| acc   | τέσσαρας       | τέσσαρα        |      |
| gen   | τεσσάρων       | τεσσάρων       |      |
| dat   | τέσσαρσι(ν)    | τέσσαρσι(ν)    |      |

# Prepositions

|           | + accusative      | + genitive | + dative |
|-----------|-------------------|------------|----------|
| ἀπό       |                   | from       |          |
| διά       | on account of     | through    |          |
| εἰς       | into              |            |          |
| ἐκ (ἐξ*)  |                   | out of     |          |
| ἐν        |                   |            | in       |
| μετά      | after             | with       |          |
| περί      |                   | about      |          |
| πρός      | to, towards       |            |          |
| ὑπό       |                   |            | under    |

\* before a word starting with a vowel

143

# Verbs: overview of tenses

*present*   *sg*          *pl*
1           παύ-ω         παύ-ομεν
2           παύ-εις       παύ-ετε
3           παύ-ει        παύ-ουσι(ν)

*imperative (sg)* παῦε, *(pl)* παύετε                    *infinitive* παύειν

*future*
1           παύσ-ω        παύσ-ομεν
2           παύσ-εις      παύσ-ετε
3           παύσ-ει       παύσ-ουσι(ν)

*imperfect*
1           ἔ-παυ-ον      ἐ-παύ-ομεν
2           ἔ-παυ-ες      ἐ-παύ-ετε
3           ἔ-παυ-ε(ν)    ἔ-παυ-ον

*first (weak) aorist*
1           ἔ-παυσ-α      ἐ-παύσ-αμεν
2           ἔ-παυσ-ας     ἐ-παύσ-ατε
3           ἔ-παυσ-ε(ν)   ἔ-παυσ-αν

*second (strong) aorist*
1           ἔ-λαβ-ον      ἐ-λάβ-ομεν
2           ἔ-λαβ-ες      ἐ-λάβ-ετε
3           ἔ-λαβ-ε(ν)    ἔ-λαβ-ον


# The verb *to be*:

*present*
1           εἰμί          ἐσμέν
2           εἶ            ἐστέ
3           ἐστί(ν)       εἰσί(ν)

*imperfect*
1           ἦ *(or* ἦν)   ἦμεν
2           ἦσθα          ἦτε
3           ἦν            ἦσαν

*participle* ὤν οὖσα ὄν *(m/n stem* ὀντ-)            *infinitive* εἶναι
(like the <u>endings</u> of an ordinary present participle: see next page)

# Participles:

Present, future, and second (strong) aorist participles all use the same endings.
Here is the present participle:

stopping

|    |     | *masculine* | *feminine* | *neuter* |
|----|-----|-------------|------------|----------|
| sg | nom | παύ-ων | παύ-ουσ-α | παῦ-ον |
|    | acc | παύ-οντα | παύ-ουσ-αν | παῦ-ον |
|    | gen | παύ-οντος | παυ-ούσ-ης | παύ-οντος |
|    | dat | παύ-οντι | παυ-ούσ-ῃ | παύ-οντι |
| pl | nom | παύ-οντες | παύ-ουσ-αι | παύ-οντα |
|    | acc | παύ-οντας | παυ-ούσ-ας | παύ-οντα |
|    | gen | παυ-όντων | παυ-ουσ-ῶν | παυ-όντων |
|    | dat | παύ-ουσι(ν) | παυ-ούσ-αις | παύ-ουσι(ν) |

From this it is easy to form the future participle:

about to stop

παύσων  παύσουσα  παῦσον

*stem (for masc and neut):* παυσοντ-

And the second (strong) aorist participle (for verbs with a second [strong] aorist):

having taken

λαβών  λαβουσα  λαβόν

*stem (for masc and neut):* λαβοντ-

The first (weak) aorist participle (for verbs with a first [weak] aorist) is a little different, but works on the same principle (3-1-3 declensions), and - like the first (weak) aorist tense - has the characteristic alpha.

having stopped

|    |     | *masculine* | *femimine* | *neuter* |
|----|-----|-------------|------------|----------|
| sg | nom | παύσ-ας | παύσ-ασ-α | παῦσ-αν |
|    | acc | παύσ-αντα | παύσ-ασ-αν | παῦσ-αν |
|    | gen | παύσ-αντος | παυσ-άσ-ης | παύσ-αντος |
|    | dat | παύσ-αντι | παυσ-άσ-ῃ | παύσ-αντι |
| pl | nom | παύσ-αντες | παύσ-ασ-αι | παύσ-αντα |
|    | acc | παύσ-αντας | παυσ-άσ-ας | παύσ-αντα |
|    | gen | παυσ-άντων | παυσ-ασ-ῶν | παυσ-άντων |
|    | dat | παύσ-ασι(ν) | παυσ-άσ-αις | παύσ-ασι(ν) |

# Appendix: Words easily confused

| | |
|---|---|
| ἀποθνήσκω | I die |
| ἀποκτεινω | I kill |
| | |
| εἰς | into |
| εἷς | one (*m*) |
| | |
| ἐν | in |
| ἕν | one (*n*) |
| | |
| ἐξ | out of |
| ἕξ | six |
| | |
| ἐπεί | when, since |
| ἔπειτα | then, next |
| | |
| ἤθελον | I was willing, I wanted (*imperfect of* ἐθέλω) |
| ἦλθον | I came, I went (*irreg aor*) |
| | |
| ἡμεῖς | we |
| ὑμεῖς | you (*pl*) |
| | |
| ἡμέτερος | our |
| ὑμέτερος | your (of you *pl*) |
| | |
| ναύτης | sailor |
| ναυτικόν | fleet |
| | |
| νῆσος | island |
| νόμος | law, custom |
| νόσος | disease, illness |
| | |
| πολέμιοι | enemy |
| πόλεμος | war |
| πολίτης | citizen |
| | |
| στρατηγός | general, commander |
| στρατιώτης | soldier |
| στρατόπεδον | camp |
| στρατός | army |

# Vocabulary

## English to Greek

*Verbs are usually given with present and aorist.*
*Nouns are given with nominative, genitive, and article to show gender.*
*Adjectives are given with masculine, feminine, and neuter.*
*\* = comes second word in sentence, clause or phrase.*

| | |
|---|---|
| able, I am | οἱος τ' εἰμι |
| about | περι (+ gen) |
| account of, on | δια (+ acc) |
| admire, I | θαυμαζω ἐθαυμασα |
| after (*preposition*) | μετα (+ acc) |
| after (*introducing a clause*) | (*use an aorist participle*) |
| again | αὐθις |
| agora | ἀγορα -ας ἡ |
| all | πας πασα παν (παντ-) |
| ally | συμμαχος -ου ὁ |
| alone | μονος -η -ον |
| although | καιπερ (+ *participle*) |
| always | ἀει |
| am, I | εἰμι |
| amazed (at), I am | θαυμαζω ἐθαυμασα |
| and | και |
| anger | ὀργη -ης ἡ |
| animal, creature | ζῳον -ου το |
| announce, I | ἀγγελλω ἠγγειλα |
| another | ἀλλος -η -ο |
| arms, armour | ὁπλα -ων τα |
| army | στρατος -ου ὁ |
| arrange, I | τασσω ἐταξα |
| as | ὡς |
| assembly | ἐκκλησια -ας ἡ |
| at first | πρωτον |
| Athenian | ᾿Αθηναιος -α -ον |
| away, I am | ἀπειμι *imperfect* ἀπην |
| | |
| bad | κακος -η -ον |
| battle | μαχη -ης ἡ |
| be, to | εἰναι |
| beautiful | καλος -η -ον |
| beautiful, very | καλλιστος -η -ον |
| because | διοτι (*or use a participle*) |
| before, previously | προτερον |
| believe, I | πιστευω ἐπιστευσα (+ dat) |
| big, very | μεγιστος -η -ον |
| bird | ὀρνις -ιθος ὁ/ἡ |

147

| | |
|---|---|
| boat | πλοιον -ου το |
| body | σωμα -ατος το |
| body, dead | νεκρος -ου ὁ |
| book | βιβλος -ου ἡ |
| both ... and | τε* ... και |
| bow | τοξον -ου το |
| boy | παις παιδος ὁ |
| brave | ἀνδρειος -α -ον |
| bring, I | φερω ἠνεγκα *or* ἠνεγκον |
| bury, I | θαπτω ἐθαψα |
| but | ἀλλα, δε* |

| | |
|---|---|
| came, I | ἠλθον (*irregular aorist*) |
| camp | στρατοπεδον -ου το |
| can, I | οἱος τ' εἰμι |
| carry, I | φερω ἠνεγκα *or* ἠνεγκον |
| certain, a | τις τι (τιν-) |
| chase, I | διωκω ἐδιωξα |
| child | παις παιδος ὁ/ἡ |
| circle | κυκλος -ου ὁ |
| citizen | πολιτης -ου ὁ |
| clever | σοφος -η -ον |
| collect (something), I | συλλεγω συνελεξα |
| commander | στρατηγος -ου ὁ |
| community | δημος -ου ὁ |
| concerning | περι (+ *gen*) |
| contest | ἀγων -ωνος ὁ |
| corpse | νεκρος -ου ὁ |
| council | βουλη -ης ἡ |
| country, land | χωρα -ας ἡ |
| custom | νομος -ου ὁ |

| | |
|---|---|
| damage, I | βλαπτω ἐβλαψα |
| danger | κινδυνος -ου ὁ |
| dangerous | χαλεπος -η -ον |
| day | ἡμερα -ας ἡ |
| dead body | νεκρος -ου ὁ |
| death | θανατος -ου ὁ |
| deed | ἐργον -ου το |
| despite (being) | καιπερ (+ *participle*) |
| die, I | ἀποθνησκω ἀπεθανον |
| difficult | χαλεπος -η -ον |
| dinner | δειπνον -ου το |
| disease | νοσος -ου ἡ |
| door | θυρα -ας ἡ |
| draw up, I | τασσω ἐταξα |
| drink, I | πινω ἐπιον |

| | |
|---|---|
| drive, I | ἐλαυνω ἠλασα |
| | |
| each | ἑκαστος -η -ον |
| earth | γη γης ἡ |
| eat | ἐσθιω ἐφαγον |
| educate, I | παιδευω ἐπαιδευσα |
| eight | ὀκτω |
| eighth | ὀγδοος -η -ον |
| enemy (personal) | ἐχθρος -ου ὁ |
| enemy (in war) | πολεμιοι -ων οἱ |
| evening | ἑσπερα -ας ἡ |
| every | πας πασα παν (παντ-) |
| expedition, I make an | στρατευω ἐστρατευσα |
| experience, I | πασχω ἐπαθον |
| eye | ὀφθαλμος -ου ὁ |
| | |
| fall, I | πιπτω ἐπεσον |
| fall into, I | εἰσπιπτω εἰσεπεσον |
| fear | φοβος -ου ὁ |
| few | ὀλιγοι -αι -α |
| field | ἀγρος -ου ὁ |
| fifth | πεμπτος -η -ον |
| finally | τελος |
| find, I | εὑρισκω ηὑρον |
| fine | καλος -η -ον |
| fine, very | καλλιστος -η -ον |
| fire | πυρ πυρος το |
| first (adj) | πρωτος -η -ον |
| first (adv), at first | πρωτον |
| five | πεντε |
| flee, I | φευγω ἐφυγον |
| fleet | ναυτικον -ου το |
| foolish | μωρος -α -ον |
| foot | πους ποδος ὁ |
| for | γαρ* |
| foreigner | ξενος -ου ὁ |
| four | τεσσαρες τεσσαρα |
| fourth | τεταρτος -η -ον |
| free | ἐλευθερος -α -ον |
| friend | φιλος -ου ὁ |
| friendly | φιλιος -α -ον |
| from | ἀπο (+ gen) |
| from where? | ποθεν; |
| | |
| gate | πυλη -ης ἡ |
| gather (something), I | συλλεγω συνελεξα |

| | |
|---|---|
| general | στρατηγος -ου ὁ |
| get to know, I | γιγνωσκω |
| giant | γιγας -αντος ὁ |
| gift | δωρον -ου το |
| girl | κορη -ης ἡ, παις παιδος ἡ |
| go, I | βαινω |
| go away, I | ἀποβαινω |
| go out, I | ἐκβαινω |
| go to(wards), I | προσβαινω |
| god | θεος -ου ὁ |
| goddess | θεα -ας ἡ |
| good | ἀγαθος -η -ον |
| great, very | μεγιστος -η -ον |
| guard | φυλαξ -ακος ὁ |
| guard, I | φυλασσω ἐφυλαξα |

| | |
|---|---|
| harbour | λιμην -ενος ὁ |
| harm, I | βλαπτω ἐβλαψα |
| have, I | ἐχω ἐσχον |
| hear, I | ἀκουω ἠκουσα (+ *acc of thing, gen of person*) |
| heaven | οὐρανος -ου ὁ |
| her | αὐτην |
| here | ἐνθαδε |
| here, I am | παρειμι *imperfect* παρην |
| him | αὐτον |
| hinder, I | κωλυω ἐκωλυσα |
| honour | τιμη -ης ἡ |
| horse | ἱππος -ου ὁ |
| hostile | ἐχθρος -α -ον |
| hour | ὡρα -ας ἡ |
| house | οἰκια -ας ἡ |
| how? | πως; |
| however | μεντοι* |
| human being | ἀνθρωπος -ου ὁ/ἡ |

| | |
|---|---|
| I | ἐγω |
| illness | νοσος -ου ἡ |
| immediately | εὐθυς |
| in | ἐν (+ *dat*) |
| in order to | ὡς (+ *future participle*) |
| in this way | οὑτω(ς) |
| into | εἰς (+ *acc*) |
| island | νησος -ου ἡ |
| it | αὐτο |

| | |
|---|---|
| journey | ὁδος -ου ἡ |

150

| | |
|---|---|
| judge | κριτης -ου ὁ |
| justice | δικαιοσυνη -ης ἡ |

| | |
|---|---|
| kill, I | ἀποκτεινω ἀπεκτεινα |
| know, I get to | γιγνωσκω |

| | |
|---|---|
| land | χωρα -ας ἡ |
| law | νομος -ου ὁ |
| lead, I | ἀγω ἠγαγον |
| lead out, I | ἐξαγω ἐξηγαγον |
| lead to(wards), I | προσαγω προσηγαγον |
| learn, I | μανθανω ἐμαθον |
| leave, I | λειπω ἐλιπον |
| letter | ἐπιστολη -ης ἡ |
| life | βιος -ου ὁ |
| lion | λεων -οντος ὁ |
| listen (to), I | ἀκουω ἠκουσα (+ acc of thing, gen of person) |
| little (of), a | ὀλιγος -η -ον |
| long | μακρος -α -ον |
| long ago | παλαι |

| | |
|---|---|
| magistrate | ἀρχων -οντος ὁ |
| man, human being | ἀνθρωπος -ου ὁ |
| many | πολλοι -αι -α |
| march, I | στρατευω ἐστρατευσα |
| marketplace | ἀγορα -ας ἡ |
| messenger | ἀγγελος -ου ὁ |
| military matters | τα του πολεμου |
| money | χρηματα -ων τα |
| Muse (goddess of poetry etc) | μουσα -ης ἡ |
| my | ἐμος -η -ον |

| | |
|---|---|
| name | ὀνομα -ατος το |
| near | ἐγγυς (+ gen) |
| new | νεος -α -ον |
| next | ἐπειτα |
| night | νυξ νυκτος ἡ |
| nine | ἐννεα |
| ninth | ἐνατος -η -ον |
| no ... , not any | οὐδεις οὐδεμια οὐδεν (οὐδεν-) |
| no longer | οὐκετι |
| no-one | οὐδεις οὐδεμια (οὐδεν-) |
| not | οὐ (οὐκ before smooth breathing, οὐχ before rough breathing) |
| nothing | οὐδεν (οὐδεν-) |
| now | νυν |

| | |
|---|---|
| often | πολλακις |
| old man | γερων -οντος ὁ |
| on account of | δια (+ *acc*) |
| on the one hand ... on the other | μεν* ... δε* |
| one | εἱς μια ἑν (ἑν-) |
| only (*adj*) | μονος -η -ον |
| only (*adv*) | μονον |
| order, I | κελευω ἐκελευσα |
| order to, in | ὡς (+ *future participle*) |
| other | ἀλλος -η -ο |
| our | ἡμετερος -α -ον |
| out of | ἐκ (ἐξ *before vowel*) (+ *gen*) |

| | |
|---|---|
| past, in the | παλαι |
| payment | μισθος -ου ὁ |
| peace | εἱρηνη -ης ἡ |
| people, community | δημος -ου ὁ |
| persuade, I | πειθω ἐπεισα |
| place | τοπος -ου ὁ |
| plan | βουλη -ης ἡ |
| poet | ποιητης -ου ὁ |
| prepare, I | παρασκευαζω παρεσκευασα |
| present, I am | παρειμι *imperfect* παρην |
| prevent, I | κωλυω ἐκωλυσα |
| previously | προτερον |
| prison | δεσμωτηριον -ου το |
| prize | ἀθλον -ου το |
| produce, I | παρεχω παρεσχον |
| provide, I | παρεχω παρεσχον |
| public square | ἀγορα -ας ἡ |
| pursue, I | διωκω ἐδιωξα |

| | |
|---|---|
| ready | ἑτοιμος -η -ον |
| ready, I get (something) | παρασκευαζω παρεσκευασα |
| reason | λογος -ου ὁ |
| release, I | λυω ἐλυσα |
| remain, I | μενω ἐμεινα |
| report, I | ἀγγελλω ἠγγειλα |
| right (hand side) (*adj*) | δεξιος -α -ον |
| river | ποταμος -ου ὁ |
| road | ὁδος -ου ἡ |
| ruler | ἀρχων -οντος ὁ |
| run, I | τρεχω ἐδραμον |
| run away, I | φευγω ἐφυγον, ἀποτρεχω ἀπεδραμον |
| run out, I | ἐκτρεχω ἐξεδραμον |
| run to(wards), I | προστρεχω προσεδραμον |

| | |
|---|---|
| said, I | εἰπον (*used as aorist of* λέγω) |
| sailor | ναυτης -ου ὁ |
| same, the | ὁ αὐτος, ἡ αὐτη, το αὐτο |
| saw, I | εἰδον |
| say, I | λεγω ἐλεξα *or* εἰπον |
| sea | θαλασσα -ης ἡ |
| sea-battle | ναυμαχια -ας ἡ |
| second | δευτερος -α -ον |
| self | αὐτος -η -ο |
| send, I | πεμπω ἐπεμψα |
| send to(wards), I | προσπεμπω προσεπεμψα |
| seven | ἑπτα |
| seventh | ἑβδομος -η -ον |
| shout | βοη -ης ἡ |
| show, I | φαινω φηνα |
| since | ἐπει (*or use a participle*) |
| six | ἑξ |
| sixth | ἑκτος -η -ον |
| sky, heaven | οὐρανος -ου ὁ |
| slave | δουλος -ου ὁ |
| sleep | ὑπνος -ου ὁ |
| small | μικρος -α -ον |
| small amount (of) | ὀλιγος -η -ον |
| so | οὑτω(ς) |
| soldier | στρατιωτης -ου ὁ |
| someone | 'ιις (τιν-) |
| something | τι (τιν-) |
| speak, I | λεγω ἐλεξα *or* εἰπον |
| stay, I | μενω ἐμεινα |
| steal, I | κλεπτω ἐκλεψα |
| still | ἐτι |
| stone | λιθος -ου ὁ |
| stop, I | παυω ἐπαυσα |
| story (myth, fable) | μυθος -ος ὁ |
| story (factual or historical) | λογος -ου ὁ |
| strange | δεινος -η -ον |
| stranger | ξενος -ου ὁ |
| stupid | μωρος -α -ον |
| suffer, I | πασχω ἐπαθον |
| supper | δειπνον -ου το |
| | |
| take, I | λαμβανω ἐλαβον |
| teach, I | διδασκω ἐδιδαξα |
| teacher | διδασκαλος -ου ὁ |
| temple | ἱερον -ου το |
| ten | δεκα |
| tenth | δεκατος -η -ον |
| terrible | δεινος -η -ον |

| | |
|---|---|
| the | ὁ ἡ το |
| them | αὐτους -ας |
| then, next | ἐπειτα |
| there | ἐκει |
| therefore | οὖν* |
| third | τριτος -η -ον |
| three | τρεις τρια |
| through | δια (+ *gen*) (+ *acc* = on account of) |
| throw, I | βαλλω ἐβαλον |
| throw away, I | ἀποβαλλω ἀπεβαλον |
| throw in, I | ἐμβαλλω ἐνεβαλον |
| throw out, I | ἐκβαλλω ἐξεβαλον |
| time | χρονος -ου ὁ |
| towards | προς (+ *acc*) |
| train, I | παιδευω ἐπαιδευσα |
| tree | δενδρον -ου το |
| trust, I | πιστευω ἐπιστευσα (+ *dat*) |
| two | δυο |
| | |
| under | ὑπο (+ *dat*) |
| useful | χρησιμος -η -ον |
| | |
| very fine, very beautiful | καλλιστος -η -ον |
| very great | μεγιστος -η -ον |
| victory | νικη -ης ἡ |
| village | κωμη -ης ἡ |
| voice | φωνη -ης ἡ |
| | |
| wages | μισθος -ου ὁ |
| wait (for), I | μενω ἐμεινα |
| war | πολεμος -ου ὁ |
| warfare | τα του πολεμου |
| water | ὑδωρ -ατος το |
| way, road | ὁδος -ου ἡ |
| way, in this | οὑτω(ς) |
| we | ἡμεις |
| weapons | ὁπλα -ων τα |
| went, I | ἠλθον (*irregular aorist*) |
| what? | τί; (τίν-;) |
| when? | ποτε; |
| when, since | ἐπει (*or use a participle*) |
| where? | που; |
| where from? | ποθεν; |
| which? | τίς; τί; (τίν-;) |
| while | (*use a present participle*) |
| who? | τίς; (τίν-;) |

| | |
|---|---|
| why? | δια τί; |
| willing, I am | ἐθελω ἠθελησα |
| wind | ἀνεμος -ου ὁ |
| wine | οἰνος -ου ὁ |
| wisdom | σοφια -ας ἡ |
| wise | σοφος -η -ον |
| wish, I | ἐθελω ἠθελησα |
| with | μετα (+ gen) |
| word | λογος -ου ὁ |
| work | ἐργον -ου το |
| write, I | γραφω ἐγραψα |
| | |
| yet, still | ἐτι |
| you (sg) | συ |
| you (pl) | ὑμεις |
| young man | νεανιας -ου ὁ |
| your (of you sg) | σος ση σον |
| your (of you pl) | ὑμετερος -α -ον |
| | |
| Zeus | Ζευς Διος ὁ |

# Greek to English

*Verbs are usually given with present and aorist.*
*Nouns are given with nominative, genitive, and article to show gender.*
*Adjectives are given with masculine, feminine, and neuter.*
*\* = comes second word in sentence, clause or phrase.*

chapter:

| | | |
|---|---|---|
| ἀγαγ- | (*aorist stem of* ἄγω) | |
| ἀγαθός -ή -όν | good | (3) |
| ἀγγέλλω ἤγγειλα | I report, I announce | (6) |
| ἄγγελος -ου ὁ | messenger | (1) |
| ἀγορά -ᾶς ἡ | agora, marketplace, public square | (2) |
| ἀγρός -οῦ ὁ | field | (5) |
| ἄγω ἤγαγον | I lead | (1) |
| ἀγών -ῶνος ὁ | contest | (5) |
| ἀεί | always | (3) |
| Ἀθηναῖος -α -ον | Athenian | (3) |
| ἆθλον -ου τό | prize | (2) |
| ἀκούω ἤκουσα | I hear, I listen to (+ *acc of thing, gen of person*) | (1) |
| ἀλλά | but | (2) |
| ἄλλος -η -ο | other, another | (5) |
| ἀνδρεῖος -α -ον | brave | (3) |
| ἄνεμος -ου ὁ | wind | (5) |
| ἄνθρωπος -ου ὁ/ἡ | man, human being; (*as feminine*) woman | (2) |
| ἄπειμι *imperfect* ἀπῆν | I am away | (5) |
| ἀπό | from (+ *gen*) | (3) |
| ἀποβάλλω ἀπέβαλον | I throw away | (4) |
| ἀποθνήσκω ἀπέθανον | I die | (3) |
| ἀποκτείνω ἀπέκτεινα | I kill | (2) |
| ἆρα; | (*introduces an open question, e.g.* Is it ... ?) | (3) |
| ἄρχων -οντος ὁ | ruler, magistrate | (5) |
| αὖθις | again | (6) |
| αὐτός -ή -ό | self; (*after definite article*) the same; (*not nom*) him, her, it | (6) |
| βαίνω | I go | (1) |
| βαλ- | (*aorist stem of* βάλλω) | |
| βάλλω ἔβαλον | I throw | (4) |
| βίβλος -ου ἡ | book | (4) |
| βίος -ου ὁ | life | (2) |
| βλάπτω ἔβλαψα | I harm, I damage | (5) |
| βοή -ῆς ἡ | shout | (1) |
| βουλή -ῆς ἡ | plan; council | (1) |

156

| | | |
|---|---|---|
| γάρ* | for | (3) |
| γέρων -οντος ὁ | old man | (5) |
| γῆ γῆς ἡ | earth | (1) |
| γίγας -αντος ὁ | giant | (5) |
| γιγνώσκω | I get to know | (3) |
| γράφω ἔγραψα | I write | (1) |

| | | |
|---|---|---|
| δέ* | but; and | (3) |
| δεινός -ή -όν | strange, terrible | (3) |
| δεῖπνον -ου τό | dinner | (4) |
| δέκα | ten | (2) |
| δέκατος -η -ον | tenth | (6) |
| δένδρον -ου τό | tree | (2) |
| δεξιός -ά -όν | right (hand side) (adj) | (6) |
| δεσμωτήριον -ου τό | prison | (2) |
| δεύτερος -α -ον | second | (6) |
| δῆμος -ου ὁ | people, community | (2) |
| διά | (+ acc) on account of | (5) |
| | (+ gen) through | (5) |
| διὰ τί; | why? | (5) |
| διδάσκαλος -ου ὁ | teacher | (1) |
| διδάσκω ἐδίδαξα | I teach | (1) |
| δικαιοσύνη -ης ἡ | justice | (1) |
| Διός | (irregular genitive of Ζεύς) | |
| διότι | because | (3) |
| διώκω ἐδίωξα | I chase, I pursue | (1) |
| δοῦλος -ου ὁ | slave | (1) |
| δραμ- | (aorist stem of τρέχω) | |
| δύο | two | (4) |
| δῶρον -ου τό | gift | (2) |

| | | |
|---|---|---|
| ἔβαλον | (aorist of βάλλω) | |
| ἕβδομος -η -ον | seventh | (6) |
| ἐγγύς | (+ gen) near | (5) |
| ἐγώ | I | (5) |
| ἔδραμον | (aorist of τρέχω) | |
| ἐθέλω ἠθέλησα | I wish, I am willing | (3) |
| εἶδον | I saw (irregular aorist) | (5) |
| εἰμί imperfect ἦ (or ἦν) | I am | (2) |
| εἶναι | to be (infinitive of εἰμί) | (6) |
| εἶπον | I said (irregular aorist of λέγω) | (4) |
| εἰρήνη -ης ἡ | peace | (1) |
| εἰς | (+ acc) into | (1) |
| εἷς μία ἕν (ἑν-) | one | (6) |

157

| | | |
|---|---|---|
| εἰσπίπτω εἰσέπεσον | I fall into | (4) |
| ἐκ (ἐξ *before vowel*) | (+ *gen*) out of | (3) |
| ἕκαστος -η -ον | each | (5) |
| ἐκβαίνω | I go out | (4) |
| ἐκεῖ | there | (3) |
| ἐκκλησία -ας ἡ | assembly | (2) |
| ἕκτος -η -ον | sixth | (6) |
| ἐκτρέχω | I run out | (4) |
| ἔλαβον | (*aorist of* λαμβάνω) | |
| ἐλαύνω ἤλασα | I drive | (3) |
| ἐλεύθερος -α -ον | free | (3) |
| ἔλιπον | (*aorist of* λείπω) | |
| ἔμαθον | (*aorist of* μανθάνω) | |
| ἐμβάλλω ἐνέβαλον | I throw in, I thrust in | (5) |
| ἔμεινα | (*aorist of* μένω) | |
| ἐμός -ό -όν | my | (5) |
| ἐν | (+ *dat*) in | (3) |
| ἕν | one (*neuter*) | (6) |
| ἔνατος -η -ον | ninth | (6) |
| ἐνεγκ- | (*aorist stem of* φέρω) | |
| ἐνθάδε | here | (3) |
| ἐννέα | nine | (6) |
| ἕξ | six | (6) |
| ἐξάγω ἐξήγαγον | I lead out | (4) |
| ἔπαθον | (*aorist of* πάσχω) | |
| ἐπεί | when, since | (4) |
| ἔπεισα | (*aorist of* πείθω) | |
| ἔπειτα | then, next | (4) |
| ἔπεσον | (*aorist of* πίπτω) | |
| ἔπιον | (*aorist of* πίνω) | |
| ἐπιστολή -ῆς ἡ | letter | (1) |
| ἑπτά | seven | (6) |
| ἔργον -ου τό | work, deed | (2) |
| ἐσθίω ἔφαγον | I eat | (4) |
| ἑσπέρα -ας ἡ | evening | (2) |
| ἔσχον | (*aorist of* ἔχω) | |
| ἔταξα | (*aorist of* τάσσω) | |
| ἔτι | still | (5) |
| ἕτοῖμος -η -ον | ready | (5) |
| εὐθύς | immediately | (6) |
| εὑρ- | (*aorist stem of* εὑρίσκω) | |
| εὑρίσκω ηὗρον | I find | (2) |
| ἔφαγον | (*aorist of* ἐσθίω) | |
| ἔφυγον | (*aorist of* φεύγω) | |
| ἐχθρός -οῦ ὁ | (personal) enemy | (6) |
| ἐχθρός -ά -όν | hostile | (3) |

| | | |
|---|---|---|
| ἔχω ἔσχον | I have | (1) |
| | | |
| Ζεύς Διός ὁ | Zeus | (6) |
| ζῷον -ου τό | animal, creature | (4) |
| | | |
| ἤγαγον | (aorist of ἄγω) | |
| ἤγγειλα | (aorist of ἀγγέλλω) | |
| ἠθέλησα | (aorist of ἐθέλω) | |
| ἤλασα | (aorist of ἐλαύνω) | |
| ἦλθον | (irregular aorist) I came, I went | (6) |
| ἡμεῖς -ῶν | we | (6) |
| ἡμέρα -ας ἡ | day | (2) |
| ἡμέτερος -α -ον | our | (6) |
| ἤνεγκα or ἤνεγκον | (aorist of φέρω) | |
| ηὗρον | (aorist of εὑρίσκω) | |
| | | |
| θάλασσα -ης ἡ | sea | (4) |
| θάνατος -ου ὁ | death | (2) |
| θάπτω ἔθαψα | I bury | (6) |
| θαυμάζω ἐθαύμασα | I am amazed (at), I admire | (3) |
| θεά -ᾶς ἡ | goddess | (2) |
| θεός -οῦ ὁ | god | (1) |
| θύρα -ας ἡ | door | (2) |
| | | |
| ἱερόν -οῦ τό | temple | (2) |
| ἵππος -ου ὁ | horse | (1) |
| | | |
| καί | and; also | (2) |
| καίπερ | (+ participle) although, despite | (6) |
| κακός -ή -όν | bad | (3) |
| κάλλιστος -η -ον | very fine, very beautiful | (5) |
| καλός -ή -όν | fine, beautiful | (3) |
| κελεύω ἐκέλευσα | I order | (3) |
| κίνδυνος -ου ὁ | danger | (2) |
| κλέπτω ἔκλεψα | I steal | (5) |
| κόρη -ης ἡ | girl | (4) |
| κριτής -οῦ ὁ | judge | (4) |
| κύκλος -ου ὁ | circle | (5) |
| κωλύω ἐκώλυσα | I hinder, I prevent | (5) |
| κώμη -ης ἡ | village | (1) |

| | | |
|---|---|---|
| λαμβάνω ἔλαβον | I take | (2) |
| λέγω ἔλεξα *or* εἶπον | I speak, I say | (1) |
| λείπω ἔλιπον | I leave | (2) |
| λέων -οντος ὁ | lion | (5) |
| λίθος -ου ὁ | stone | (5) |
| λιμήν -ένος ὁ | harbour | (5) |
| λιπ- | (*aorist stem of* λείπω) | |
| λόγος -ου ὁ | word, reason, story | (1) |
| λύω ἔλυσα | I release | (2) |

| | | |
|---|---|---|
| μαθ- | (*aorist stem of* μανθάνω) | |
| μακρός -ά -όν | long | (4) |
| μανθάνω ἔμαθον | I learn | (2) |
| μάχη -ης ἡ | battle | (6) |
| μέγιστος -η -ον | very great | (4) |
| μειν- | (*aorist of* μένω) | |
| μέν* ... δέ* | on the one hand ... on the other | (3) |
| μέντοι* | however | (3) |
| μένω ἔμεινα | I stay, I remain; I wait for | (2) |
| μετά | (+ *acc*) after | (4) |
| | (+ *gen*) with | (5) |
| μία | one (*feminine*) | (6) |
| μικρός -ά -όν | small | (3) |
| μισθός -οῦ ὁ | payment, wages | (6) |
| μόνον | only (*adv*) | (5) |
| μόνος -η -ον | only, alone | (5) |
| μοῦσα -ης ἡ | Muse (*goddess of poetic inspiration*) | (4) |
| μῦθος -ου ὁ | story (myth, fable) | (4) |
| μῶρος -α -ον | stupid, foolish | (5) |

| | | |
|---|---|---|
| ναυμαχία -ας ἡ | sea-battle | (2) |
| ναύτης -ου ὁ | sailor | (4) |
| ναυτικόν -οῦ τό | fleet | (2) |
| νεανίας -ου ὁ | young man | (4) |
| νεκρός -οῦ ὁ | corpse, dead body | (6) |
| νέος -α -ον | new, young | (3) |
| νῆσος -ου ἡ | island | (4) |
| νίκη -ης ἡ | victory | (1) |
| νόμος -ου ὁ | law; custom | (2) |
| νόσος -ου ἡ | disease | (4) |
| νῦν | now | (3) |
| νύξ νυκτός ἡ | night | (5) |

| ξένος -ου ὁ | stranger, foreigner | (1) |
|---|---|---|

| ὁ ἡ τό | the | (1) |
|---|---|---|
| ὄγδοος -η -ον | eighth | (6) |
| ὁδός -οῦ ἡ | road, journey | (4) |
| οἰκία -ας ἡ | house | (2) |
| οἶνος -ου ὁ | wine | (5) |
| οἷός τ᾽ εἰμί | I am able | (5) |
| ὀκτώ | eight | (6) |
| ὀλίγοι -αι -α | few | (5) |
| ὀλίγος -η -ον | a little, a small amount of | (6) |
| ὄνομα -ατος τό | name | (5) |
| ὅπλα -ων τά | arms, weapons (*pl*) | (2) |
| ὀργή -ῆς ἡ | anger | (6) |
| ὄρνις -ιθος ὁ/ἡ | bird | (5) |
| οὐ (οὐκ, οὐχ) | not | (1) |
| οὐδείς οὐδεμία οὐδέν (οὐδεν-) | no-one, nothing, no (*i.e.* not any) | (6) |
| οὐκέτι | no longer | (6) |
| οὖν* | therefore | (3) |
| οὐρανός -οῦ ὁ | sky, heaven | (6) |
| ὀφθαλμός -οῦ ὁ | eye | (3) |

| παθ- | (*aorist stem of* πάσχω) | |
|---|---|---|
| παιδεύω ἐπαίδευσα | I train, I educate | (6) |
| παῖς παιδός ὁ/ἡ | boy, girl, child | (5) |
| πάλαι | long ago, in the past | (6) |
| παρασκευάζω παρεσκεύασα | I prepare | (6) |
| πάρειμι *imperfect* παρῆν | I am here, I am present | (5) |
| παρέχω παρέσχον | I produce, I provide | (3) |
| πᾶς πᾶσα πᾶν (παντ-) | all, every | (6) |
| πάσχω ἔπαθον | I suffer, I experience | (4) |
| παύω ἔπαυσα | I stop | (1) |
| πείθω ἔπεισα | I persuade | (3) |
| πέμπτος -η -ον | fifth | (6) |
| πέμπω ἔπεμψα | I send | (2) |
| πέντε | five | (2) |
| περί | (+ *gen*) about, concerning | (6) |
| πεσ- | (*aorist stem of* πίπτω) | |
| πίνω ἔπιον | I drink | (5) |
| πίπτω ἔπεσον | I fall | (4) |
| πιστεύω ἐπίστευσα | I trust, I believe (+ *dat*) | (3) |
| πλοῖον -ου τό | boat | (2) |

| | | |
|---|---|---|
| πόθεν; | where from? | (5) |
| ποιητής -οῦ ὁ | poet | (4) |
| πολέμιοι -ων οἱ | enemy (in war) | (6) |
| πόλεμος -ου ὁ | war | (2) |
| τὰ τοῦ πολέμου | the affairs of war, warfare, military matters | (6) |
| πολίτης -ου ὁ | citizen | (4) |
| πολλάκις | often | (3) |
| πολλοί -αί -ά | many | (5) |
| ποταμός -οῦ ὁ | river | (1) |
| πότε; | when? | (3) |
| ποῦ; | where? | (3) |
| πούς ποδός ὁ | foot | (5) |
| πρός | (+ acc) towards | (1) |
| προσάγω προσήγαγον | I lead to(wards) | (4) |
| προσβαίνω | I go towards | (4) |
| προσπέμπω προσέπεμψα | I send to(wards) | (4) |
| προστρέχω προσέδραμον | I run towards | (4) |
| πρότερον | previously, before | (3) |
| πρῶτον | first (adv), at first | (4) |
| πρῶτος -η -ον | first | (6) |
| πύλη -ης ἡ | gate | (1) |
| πῦρ πυρός τό | fire | (5) |
| πῶς; | how? | (3) |

| | | |
|---|---|---|
| σός σή σόν | your (of you sg) | (5) |
| σοφία -ας ἡ | wisdom | (2) |
| σοφός -ή -όν | wise, clever | (3) |
| στρατεύω ἐστράτευσα | I march, I make an expedition | (6) |
| στρατηγός -οῦ ὁ | general | (1) |
| στρατιώτης -ου ὁ | soldier | (4) |
| στρατόπεδον -ου τό | camp | (2) |
| στρατός -οῦ ὁ | army | (1) |
| σύ | you (sg) | (5) |
| συλλέγω συνέλεξα | I collect, I gather | (6) |
| σύμμαχος -ου ὁ | ally | (1) |
| σχ- | (aorist stem of ἔχω) | |
| σῶμα -ατος τό | body | (5) |

| | | |
|---|---|---|
| τάσσω ἔταξα | I draw up, I arrange | (2) |
| τε* ... καί | both ... and | (2) |
| τέλος | finally | (6) |
| τέσσαρες τέσσαρα | four | (6) |
| τέταρτος -η -ον | fourth | (6) |
| τιμή -ῆς ἡ | honour | (1) |

| | | |
|---|---|---|
| τίς; τί; (τιν-) | who? which? what? | (5) |
| τις τι (τιν-) | a certain, someone, something | (5) |
| τόξον -ου τό | bow | (2) |
| τόπος -ου ὁ | place | (6) |
| τρεῖς τρία | three | (6) |
| τρέχω ἔδραμον | I run | (1) |
| τρίτος -η -ον | third | (6) |

| | | |
|---|---|---|
| ὕδωρ -ατος τό | water | (6) |
| ὑμεῖς -ων | you (*pl*) | (6) |
| ὑμέτερος -α -ον | your (of you *pl*) | (6) |
| ὕπνος -ου ὁ | sleep | (5) |
| ὑπό | (+ *dat*) under | (6) |

| | | |
|---|---|---|
| φαγ- | (*aorist stem* ἐσθίω) | |
| φαίνω ἔφηνα | I show | (3) |
| φέρω ἤνεγκα *or* ἤνεγκον | I carry, I bring | (1) |
| φεύγω ἔφυγον | I run away | (2) |
| φίλιος -α -ον | friendly | (3) |
| φίλος -ου ὁ | friend | (2) |
| φόβος -ου ὁ | fear | (2) |
| φυγ- | (*aorist stem of* φεύγω) | |
| φύλαξ -ακος ὁ | guard | (5) |
| φυλάσσω ἐφύλαξα | I guard | (1) |
| φωνή -ῆς ἡ | voice | (1) |

| | | |
|---|---|---|
| χαλεπός -ή -όν | difficult; dangerous | (3) |
| χρήματα -ων τά | money | (6) |
| χρήσιμος -η -ον | useful | (4) |
| χρόνος -ου ὁ | time | (2) |
| χώρα -ας ἡ | country | (2) |

| | | |
|---|---|---|
| ὦ | O (*used + voc, to address someone; usually* *better omitted in English*) | (3) |
| ὥρα -ας ἡ | hour | (2) |
| ὡς | as | (4) |
| | (+ *present or aorist participle*) as, since, because, on the grounds that | (6) |
| | (+ *future participle*) in order to | (6) |

(275 words Greek-English)